D1519662

Retail Banking in the Electronic Age

Retail Banking in the Electronic Age

THE LAW AND ECONOMICS OF ELECTRONIC FUNDS TRANSFER

BY William F. Baxter
Paul H. Cootner
Kenneth E. Scott

ALLANHELD, OSMUN & CO.   Montclair

ALLANHELD, OSMUN & CO. PUBLISHERS, INC.
19 Brunswick Road, Montclair, N.J. 07042

Published in the United States of America in 1977
by Allanheld, Osmun & Co.

Second printing, 1977

Library of Congress Cataloging in Publication Data

Baxter, William F.   1929-
    Retail banking in the electronic age.

    Includes index.
    1.   Electronic funds transfers.   I.   Cootner,
Paul H., joint author.   II.   Scott, Kenneth E.,
joint author.   III.   Title.
HG1710.B39   332.1'7   76-28594
ISBN 0-916672-06-9

Printed in The United States of America

Preface

This study examines various aspects of electronic funds transfer systems and their implications for retail banking in the United States. We assume that the reader has some interest in and familiarity with these subjects, or he would not likely be perusing this volume; nevertheless we have sought to keep the presentation as non-technical as was possible. While the authors are university professors in law and economics, the presentation is designed for persons who do not necessarily have any formal training in either field.

Our objective is to provide the reader with a better understanding of the economic forces and legal constraints that have shaped our present payments mechanism, and to forecast for him the impacts on payment systems that the new electronic technology may have. We have described those probable impacts more in theoretical and institutional terms than in terms of numerical projections, although we have made some rough quantitative estimates where necessary to our analysis. Our primary endeavor has been to look ahead over the next five to ten years and examine the trends and issues that will hold the most significance for the consuming public, rather than to make a detailed empirical examination of the technology in its current state of development and deployment. It follows, in our view, that attention should be focused on EFTS as it affects transactions and linkages between banks and their customers, rather than on interbank clearing operations and institutions such as automated clearinghouses. Similarly, we believe there is greater potential impact from the use of point-of-sale (POS) terminals that are on-line to bank computer files than from automated teller machines (ATMs) or from devices in either category that are off-line. These perceptions are reflected in the allocation of discussion and emphasis in the study.

In general, the study draws on developments and information available down to the beginning of 1976. However, we were able in some instances, particularly in the areas of legislation and judicial decision, to incorporate events up to September 1976, as will be indicated in the footnotes. But such value as the study possesses should derive more from its fundamental analysis than from the currency of its reportage.

Support for our efforts came from a number of sources, to which we wish to express our appreciation. The study was originally undertaken at the instance of and with financial support from Citicorp, which wished an outside and completely independent appraisal of a field in which it was making large investments. Data were provided by a number of trade sources; we have cited the source where we had permission to do so, but some preferred to remain confidential. Some of the theoretical work was done while two of the authors (Professors Cootner and Scott) were senior research fellows in the Hoover Institution's domestic studies program. The manuscript was typed and re-typed an excessive number of times, due to our revising proclivities, by Joy St. John and Phyllis Stephens. And at times our families, colleagues and students had to put up with our preoccupation with this endeavor. To them all, we are grateful.

K.E.S.
P.H.C.
W.F.B.

Stanford, California
September 15, 1976

Contents

vii

Retail Banking
in the
Electronic Age

[1]

Technology and Monetary Instruments: An Historical View

One of the greatest dangers inherent in discussions of electronic funds transfer is the temptation to treat this new technology as an event in banking so unique that it will cause a fundamental change in the banking business and require a unique treatment of rules and regulations to bring it to fruition without wreaking damage.

As far back as 10 years ago, experts in the developing technology of electronic funds transfer systems (EFTS) were predicting that it would revolutionize the payments mechanism in our economy and making statements such as "some form of checkless or even cashless system is on the horizon."[1] A vision of future change that sweeping can be expected to arouse equally dramatic misgivings and forebodings, and they have in due course appeared. The Special Assistant to President Ford for Consumer Affairs has sounded the warning that "an electronic revolution is creeping up on the consumer," who is likely to "feel trapped by the new technology of EFTS." The solemn conclusion is that "if we go down the road to EFTS one step at a time, without ever looking ahead to see where we want to go, we are almost certain to end up someplace we don't want to be."[2]

It is the view of this study that this technological change, while important and desirable, is not likely to be revolutionary—for good *or* evil. To bring out this point, we begin by presenting a (necessarily cursory) historical review of past, similar changes in the banking industry. Our purpose is to understand why banking systems have developed and evolved as they have.

3

Lending, of course, has a long history, traceable back to the beginnings of written records. But what distinguishes banking in modern times are not its assets but its liabilities—the sources, not the uses, of funds. Any wealthy individual could make loans, and many did make loans out of their acquired wealth. Banks differ in that they are specialized institutions which invest other people's money for them. There has indeed been considerable innovation in bank lending over the centuries, including the rapid rise of credit card lending in recent years; but virtually all those innovations, including the credit card, are common to a wide range of institutional or individual lenders. What has been novel in banking through the years has been the acceptance of liabilities of indefinite term—demand deposits payable on call to the lender—often at a zero interest rate but always at a rate below that available elsewhere in the market.

EARLY MEANS OF PAYMENT

Banks have evolved in a halting, irregular, unplanned way. Traditional, if not very well-documented, history has asserted that banking arose because of the inconvenience of the preexisting transactions medium. Originally, trade took place by the very clumsy technique of barter. It required that the man with excess wheat but in need of cloth find not only a supplier of cloth but one who needed wheat. To deal with that problem, society evolved a widespread acceptance of one or a few goods as an acceptable medium of exchange: goods which were highly standardized, were not perishable and had a high ratio of value to volume so that they were convenient to use. Gold and silver are leading examples of such commodities—which came to be known as money—but not the only ones. There are some absorbing stories of prisoner-of-war camps with no metallic currency which came to use cigarettes in all the ways we associate with money.[3]

Gold and silver are, indeed, compact and relatively efficient means of storing value. Originally there were some problems in producing standardized units, but these were more or less solved early by the development of minted coins. But there were greater problems. An inventory of coins or gold was vulnerable to theft, especially when being transported in use for trade. Further, large sums were bulky, heavy and costly to transport, even with a high value-to-weight ratio. For these several reasons there were, in words of current usage, economies of scale or specialization in the storage of metallic currency. When gold was not in use, it was safer and cheaper to store it in centralized depositories; and when money was needed for trade, one could often carry a transferable deposit receipt instead of the gold itself.

It eventually became clear that the receipt itself was unnecessarily clumsy, since one did not usually wish to transfer all of his deposited wealth to any one person. In that event, each transaction required the drawing up of a new receipt, one sufficiently elaborate to guard against counterfeits. It was more convenient to have one's claims to the deposited gold in a set of standard units, which eventually came to be known as banknotes—the "notes" reflecting the recognition that this currency was no more than a liability of the bank. As in the case of metallic money, the threat of counterfeiting produced the rather elaborate pieces of paper that have represented currency over the ages.

What is lost in history is the date when it first became commonly recognized that the cost of having one's gold protected in a depository could be reduced by granting the depository the right to lend it in the interim on condition it be available when and if needed; i.e., the date at which the depository became a "bank." But whatever the date or beginning, the phenomenon was common by the Middle Ages; and, as we have seen, three major social inventions were embraced within it: the idea of a metallic standard of exchange, the development of a paper substitute and the recognition that the cost of the substitute could be reduced greatly by accepting some (hopefully) small risk in allowing the bank to put the money to use pending the depositor's call. Each of these innovations must have reduced substantially the costs of trade, perhaps to the degree that optimists assume would follow from electronic technology. Furthermore, these innovations already raised the threat of most of the problems that are perceived as potential in modern technology: (1) there were economies of scale in depositories and banks—not only the physical economies of vault size, but economies of "information;" (2) the acceptability of banknotes or receipts was limited when issued by institutions less prestigious than regional, national or worldwide banks; and (3) bankers, large or small, became more extensive repositories than had previously existed of sensitive financial information about their customers. It is not our purpose to argue that today's problems are no different from those of the past, but these analogies do suggest to us that any differences are of degree rather than of kind and that the magnitudes of those differences pose empirical questions without obvious answers.

Another principle to be drawn from this history is that, in its unplanned way, the process of innovation evolved in response to the demands of trade. Metallic coinage was sufficient unto the early times in which it thrived, with their limited volumes of trade. Depositories became necessary only as the volume of trade rose enough to create the need for substantial inventories of value, inventories large enough to warrant substantial outlays to protect them. And the relending of deposits made sense only when the accumulations became large enough to make it privately wasteful to hold the deposits in unproductive repose. Even the banker's information about his customer played an important role in the chain of credit that supported trade at a time when the lack of alternative sources of information could create considerable uncertainty as to the risk of default.

Nothing in history suggests that any of these innovations, once adopted, immediately displaced its predecessor methods. Throughout history down to the present, these technologies have coexisted; which has been employed has depended upon the scale of wealth of the individual or nation and the need for funds balanced against costs and risks.

INTRODUCTION OF CHECKS

Nor did innovation end with banknotes or intermediation. Quite early, there were traders or companies whose needs for funds were so large as to make the use of banknotes themselves clumsy and vulnerable to theft. Hence, these receipts, the innovation of a previous age, were now deposited in banks. These deposits, recorded in *nonnegotiable* statements, could be transferred through the exchange of still other negotiable instruments, called checks or drafts or bills, which could be drawn in any amount and which would be honored upon presentation to the bank.

Checks have, in fact, a very long history if one is inclined to look for the phenomenon itself rather than the scale of usage. But if one judges by scale, checks have been a relatively recent phenomenon, becoming significant in Britain around 1830 and somewhat later in the United States. Before that time, the active media of exchange were coin and banknotes. The balance sheet liabilities of commercial banks were overwhelmingly constituted of notes before the Civil War, and deposits subject to checking were much smaller. Even for the transfer of reasonably large sums, the standard technique was the withdrawal and transfer of banknotes.

But checks were rare or nonexistent prior to this period. Those bank customers who transferred large sums—businesses for the most part—used checks; and, especially in a large financial center like New York, check use was considerable, primarily for securities transactions. But check use was largely a "wholesale banking" characteristic, not typically one of retail customers. The scale and timing of the phenomenon are best revealed by the observation that New York developed its first clearinghouse for intracity checks in 1854. Moreover, even after the clearinghouse had been started, volume at first did not grow very rapidly.[4]

The development of checking in the United States did enter on a period of rapid growth after 1863, but although rapid it was hardly revolutionary. Furthermore, that growth would have been even slower if not for a set of government decrees which, in the last analysis, support our hypothesis about gradualism.

Out of a variety of motives, the most dominant of which was the desire to aid in financing the Civil War, Congress in 1863 passed what was later denominated the National Bank Act. To encourage the purchase by banks of government obligations, the act gave the newly-chartered national banks authority to issue *national* bank notes in amounts up to 90% of the par value of treasury bonds they owned. Since this was not a particularly generous provision and since a charter as a national bank imposed other onerous restrictions on its recipients, the initial growth of national banks was slow. To accelerate that growth, Congress in 1865 imposed a tax of 10% per annum on *state* banknotes, making the latter extremely unattractive. Since national banknotes were discouraged by the restrictions on their issue and state banknotes by the tax, the ultimate result of this legislation was to discourage all note issue and to favor employment of other bank liabilities.

At first, with a large issue of high yielding federal debt selling well below par, the net disincentive for national banks to issue notes was small. But after the war, interest rates began to drop rather sharply and bond prices rose correspondingly. Since notes could only be issued at a fraction of par value of the government bonds, the attractiveness of such issue was steadily reduced; the investment required in Treasury debt necessary to support a dollar of banknotes increased steadily. For example, during the Civil War, a purchase by a national bank of a $100 par Treasury bond at 80 permitted the issuance of $90 worth of banknotes; in the late seventies it might cost $110 to buy the same bond to support the same volume of notes. If the administrative costs of supporting a banknote were unchanged, the financial incentives for note issue substantially decreased.

In the existing banking literature, this discussion of banknotes versus deposits has been mired in interminable and muddled discussions of monetary policy. For our purposes, however, let us adopt the viewpoint of the issuing banks. Notes arise from the same source as demand deposits. In the one case, a customer deposits gold or silver and receives banknotes; in the other, he receives a statement of the amount owed him by the bank. To maintain the banknotes, the bank simply has to replace them as they wear out. To maintain the checking deposit, the bank has to incur the costs of processing the check. As long as there were no constraints on what could be done with the funds received, the sole determinant of the growth of checking was the willingness of the bank's customers to pay the cost of checking services. Once the National Bank Act placed limits on the kinds of assets, (i.e., Treasury debt) that could be used as collateral against banknote issue, banks had a special incentive to increase the use of checking deposits as a means of attracting funds which could be used to make more profitable loans.

We do not know just how much of a role the restriction on banknote collateral (partially offset as it was by the similarly painful capital requirements against demand deposits) played in the growth of checking deposits. On the one hand, we know it must have been important because the state banking system, which had been virtually wiped out by the 10% tax on state banknotes in 1866, actually surpassed national banks in deposits by 1874; while for the latter, deposits grew to almost $2^1/_2$ times the size of note issue by the same date.[5] On the other hand, it seems certain that increasing national wealth was making the physical transfer of notes less and less satisfactory. But the essential point is that, even with the unintended incentive of legislation, the process by which checks displaced banknotes was a gradual, if relatively rapid one. From the time checks first became commercially important to the time checking effectively won the battle, a 40-year period, from the 1830's to 1875 elapsed; and, as late as 1865, proponents of national banking institutions believed they were wiping out state banking with the 10% note tax. The battle between the two "technologies" of transferring money was a tight one, and the victory was partially won because of the incidental effects of government regulations directed to other objectives.

Thus, although today most people regard the check as an indispensable part of modern economic life, it represents a phenomenon that evolved slowly and steadily, being used first by those with the greater economic need. Even today, with the great importance of check use, between 20% and 35% of U.S. households do not choose to establish demand deposits. We will argue in this book that the problems associated with widespread use of credit and debit cards are intrinsically no different from those that surrounded the evolution of checks.

Nor does the story end with the invention and acceptance of checking accounts. Throughout the last 100 years, there has been continual evolution in transaction technologies: the clearinghouse, telephone and telegraph, airmail, check processing by machine, magnetic ink, computer batch processing and, now, on-line computer processing. Even from this skeletal history of technological change, the lesson is clear. The adoption of a technology is not caused by some exogenous, overpowering force. An idea is typically quite old before it is in wide use. Whether for checks or electronics, the technological potential exists long before it becomes standard usage. The speed of adoption is a function of the increase in costs of doing things the old way and the decrease in cost of the new technology. The technological *potential* may burst upon society through some specific breakthrough; but the critical cost relationships, nevertheless, will usually change gradually.

The increased costs of using banknotes in the 19th century and checks in the 20th are largely costs of customer inconvenience, stemming from the increasing value of time with increasing income, coupled with the increasing labor and crime costs that accompany such income. New technology, even when in its period of rapid cost decline, still tends to be adopted gradually and regularly rather than in a sudden and cataclysmic fashion.

Unlike cost relationships which change through market forces, cost relationships may change suddenly and dramatically through government regulation. Change is most likely to be extremely rapid when a new technology has the potential for evading or otherwise responding to an economically restrictive regulation. In the mid-19th century, the growth of checking was, to a considerable extent, a method for state banks to evade restrictive federal banking legislation. In the mid-20th century, we will argue, a great deal of the incentive for electronic technology stems from a combination of high market interest rates and governmental restrictions on bank entry into new markets. Future developments will also be quite sensitive to any further regulations which may arise out of current controversy over EFTS and bank industry structure.

RECENT HISTORY

If we look more closely at banking history in the last half century, there have been three salient areas that invite attention and require explanation. First, in 1933 the federal government imposed a ban on the payment of interest on demand deposits and ceilings on the rates of interest payable on time and savings deposits, restrictions which have had important and continuing consequences upon the composition of bank deposits and the way in which competition for them takes place. Second, the number of banking offices fell sharply during the 1920's and 1930's, only to start rising markedly again after 1950. Third, the rate at which customers drew on or turned over their demand deposit balances likewise initially declined, from 1920 to 1950, but has subsequently risen sharply.

It is our contention that these phenomena are interrelated, and that, when they are properly understood, they lead to a useful model of banking as a form of retailing, involving the delivery of certain goods and services to the consumer. We will begin with a consideration of the implications of deposit interest rate controls.

Even in the period before the federal prohibition of interest payments on demand deposits, there were repeated attempts to impose such limits through cartel agreements and state prohibitions, about which we have only a limited amount of information.[6] What information we do have, however, suggests that the attempts at private or public restriction were sporadic because the attempts to pay interest were sporadic. Moreover, though the attempts at private agreement usually broke down quickly, the payment of interest on demand deposits generally did not long endure, and only a few states adopted legal prohibitions. This behavior was sharply incompatible with the standard view of bankers and economists alike that, in a competitive and unregulated world, banks would pay interest on all demand deposit balances at an effective rate (adjusted for reserve requirement differentials) equal to those on competing sources of funds and would charge customers separately the full marginal cost of each item of activity. The (admittedly fragmentary) evidence we have suggests that, even prior to federal regulation, no such pattern appeared.[7]

While this 50-year-old experience may not seem relevant to the analysis of EFTS, it turns out to be our only laboratory for testing speculation about the possible pricing adjustments that might follow the de facto payment of interest on demand accounts that would occur under an on-line debit card regime. In the absence of regulation, interest has nonetheless been infrequently paid on demand balances, an historic fact that is a troublesome deviation from the standard prediction, and that will offer considerable difficulty to any analysis if unexplained. However, a fuller understanding of the bank–customer relationship, to be developed in the next chapter, yields as a byproduct a hypothesis about bank pricing that fully explains this apparently anomalous behavior. Whatever the reasons for bank pricing before the 1930's, it is clear that, since the interest rate ceilings (to be found in Regulation Q) were introduced, they have had important effects on bank competition for consumer deposits. These impacts show up both in the steady decline, in recent years, of demand deposits as a fraction of total bank funds (liabilities plus equity) and in the tremendous increase in the number of bank offices, a costly competitive method of attracting deposits made necessary by the inability of banking to compete for deposits through interest payments.

To be sure, long before the federal regulation was passed, there had been a long term upward trend in the proportion of bank liabilities derived from time deposits. The fraction of commercial bank assets in time deposits rose rather steadily from 19.3% in 1910 to 31.5% in 1930 as the Great Depression began (see Table 1). Presumably this long term uptrend reflected increasing personal wealth and obstacles to investment in alternative securities. However, just as the interest rate regulations were being discussed and established, short term interest rates were plummeting and the Great Depression was depressing per capita income, both tending to deter time deposit holdings. In 1955 time deposits were still at the same 24% level they reached in 1920, and

Table 1. Deposits as a Fraction of Commercial Bank
Liabilities

	IPC Demand	Time
1896	46.1	11.6
1900	48.0	12.0
1910	44.3	19.3
1920	45.4	23.4
1930	40.0	31.5
1940	49.6	23.0
1950	58.6	23.4
1960	51.8	27.8
1970	36.0	40.1
1975	29.0	46.7

at that time IPC[8] demand deposits were as large a fraction as they had ever been.

In most of the period prior to the imposition of the prohibition of interest rates on demand deposits in 1933, high-grade interest rates had been under 4% and were rarely higher than $4^1/_2$%. Between 1933 and 1952, interest rates remained extremely low, which limited the motivation of demand deposit holders to switch to alternative assets. In 1951, however, the Treasury and Federal Reserve Board negotiated the accord to cease pegging of the price of Treasury securities. With that agreement, interest rates began to rise, and, for the first time since 1933, the interest regulations began to bind. By the late 1950's, interest rates were steadily above 4% and were topping 5% in periods of tight money, and the commercial banks were having substantial difficulty in maintaining their old market share of liabilities held by intermediaries.[9] The commercial banks' share of the total fell from 60% in 1945 to 40% in 1962. That decline hit demand deposits a little harder than time balances because there had been some room for banks to raise rates on time deposits from wartime levels, and income was rising steadily. In 1962, the regulatory authorities raised time deposit ceilings substantially, and banks were given increased freedom to borrow in the market. By 1970, demand balances dropped to the lowest proportion of funds (36%) since the late 19th century and were, for the first time, less important than time deposits, which had soared to 40.1%. Since that time, the relative decline in demand deposits has continued at about the same pace. In mid-1976, demand balances were only 27% of total funds. Furthermore, since consumers accounted for only one-third of total IPC deposits, the consumer demand deposit market has accounted for only 9% of all bank funds.

But that is not the full value of the stakes in the consumer business, since a substantial fraction of consumer balances are held in interest earning accounts. Moreover, while time deposits have been increasing as a fraction of total funds, they too have been made less attractive to depositors by interest rate ceilings, so that some money that would have been held as time balances may have been diverted into other securities, even perhaps through long term bonds of banks.

Of total IPC balances, the fraction represented by consumer deposits has been increasing recently, apparently because consumers have found it more difficult than have business firms to fine tune balances and divert funds into securities. Commercial deposits are frequently compensated on a shadow version of the "ideal price scheme." There is a charge for each kind of activity and a credit for dollar balances—presumably a response to the ability of corporate treasurers (if not necessarily small businesses) to move excess balances easily into interest earning accounts.

To say that consumer demand deposit accounts (DDA's) offer less opportunity than commercial accounts for indirect competition circumventing interest ceilings does not mean that there are no such opportunities. Competition for consumer deposit dollars is reflected in the growth of bank offices. The proliferation of offices is a device—a very expensive device from the standpoint of the bank—to compete for consumer accounts by affording to the consumer geographic convenience and hence transactional savings. In the 1920's there was a drastic reduction in the number of bank offices, attributable largely to the spread of the automobile and the telephone into rural America,[10] a reduction which continued into the early 1930's and was accentuated by the economic decline.[11] Because new bank offices compete for consumer funds by reducing consumer time and effort, it is fully consistent that we should find that innovations which independently reduce consumer costs should compete vigorously with new bank offices as a tool for the reduction of total costs.

These technological changes and the Great Depression merely accentuate the pattern that we would expect to find as a result of interest rates. With low or declining interest rates in these years, the attractiveness of demand deposits declined, and banks had little incentive to raise costs by adding banking offices in order to seek out such deposits. If we turn from the 1920–1935 period and examine the 1935–1950 recovery period of declining interest rates, we find that bank offices hold approximately constant in the face of steadily rising population, resulting in a continuing decline in the number of offices per capita through the prewar recovery, wartime prosperity and initial postwar boom.

When interest rates started to rise to historically high levels in the late 1950's, branch offices began to rise faster than population, picking up some speed even before the appointment of Comptroller Saxon in 1961.[12] The Comptroller's freer policy of granting charters and branches produced a moderate upsurge of offices in the 1962–1966 period, a factor which disappeared by 1967.[13] Obviously, the change in regulatory policy caused an upward movement to the feasible or target level of offices; but, once the immediate adjustment was accomplished, the level of demand for new offices returned to normal.[14] Indeed, an observer who did not know about the policy change and had only the banking office data available might not even notice the policy change which attracted so much contemporary attention (see Figure 1). More offices were opened (net) in the 5 years after long-term, high-grade corporate bonds[15] first topped 7% in 1969 than had been opened in the entire period from the low point in 1933 until 1965. Interest rates, moreover, continued to rise after 1970; and, as they did, banks became even more aggressive in opening offices. New offices opened in 1970 were already above the previous peak levels of 1964; but in 1972 they were twice as high as in the earlier peak; and they more than doubled again the following year.

This brief history gives us some perspective on the issues of bank-consumer relations and their interaction with technological change in the past. We have seen that change in the banking system has been continuous, even when it has been disturbed by bank regulation; that such change has been more rapid at times in the past than anything that is likely to result from EFTS; that such change has always been gradual rather than abrupt. We have also seen that interest rate ceilings have recently produced a huge increase in numbers of bank offices, an increase which is undoubtedly inefficient and which would be sharply reversed by changes in interest rate regulation alone, independent of any change resulting from EFTS. Moreover, we have seen that a rather common assumption about the impact of Regulation Q—that its repeal would lead to the payment of market rates on demand deposits—is at least questionable. And despite the attempts of banks to substitute services for interest, they have not been completely successful; their efforts have not prevented a sharp decline in demand deposit holdings. Therefore, the interest rate regulations must have imposed substantial costs on consumers and society compared to a more efficient pattern.[16]

In the succeeding chapters we will spell out the implications of these points. In the next chapter we develop a model of bank-consumer relations. In the following one we extend the analysis to its implications for competition between debit cards, credit cards, checks and currency.

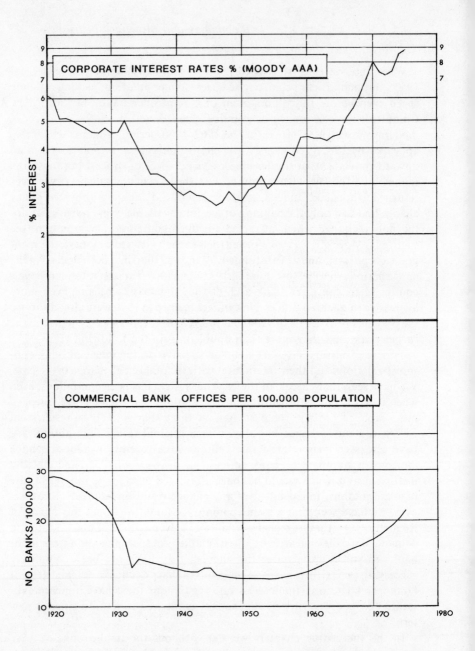

Figure 1. Relationship between density of commercial bank offices and interest rate levels.

REFERENCES

1. D. Reistad, "The Coming Cashless Society," 10 *Business Horizons,* Fall, 1967, p. 32.

2. Address by Virginia Knauer to the Texas Credit Union League, Houston, Texas, April 22, 1976.

3. R. A. Radford, "The Economic Organization of a P.O.W. Camp," *Economica,* Nov., 1945, pp. 189–201.

4. Check clearings in New York were only 20% higher in 1862 than in 1854. *(U.S. Bureau of the Census, Historical Statistics of the United States, Colonial Times to 1957,* p.640, Washington, D. C.,1960, hereinafter *Historical Statistics.* As late as 1857, total deposits (of which checking was only a small fraction) of all banks *and* savings institutions outside New York were about the same volume as banknotes. It is probable that *demand* deposits were much less than one-quarter of notes outstanding outside the financial centers of New York, Philadelphia and Boston.

5. *Idem* at pp. 627, 629.

6. Albert H. Cox, *Regulation of Interest Rates on Bank Deposits,* Mich. Bus. Studies, Vol. XVII, No. 4, pp. 1–11, Ann Arbor, Michigan (1966).

7. In the 1920's, it appears that charging for individual checks was uncommon: a strong advocate of banking service charges at that time writes as if a major step forward in his campaign was the institution of monthly fees for accounts under a prescribed level of balances. W. Gordon Jones, *The Service Charge on Demand Deposits,* The Bankers Publishing Co., New York (1930). Jones suggests that an average account drew nine checks per month, about one-half of the current level (chapter 3). It may seem anomalous that banks, prior to regulation and to significant rates of income taxation, chose to offer free services in lieu of interest or even offered, on occasion, free services plus some interest instead of charging for services and paying separately for balances. It hardly seems likely that, even in a day of pen-and-ink rather than computers, the calculation costs were excessive, at least for accounts with an average number of checks. In the next chapter we develop a model which accounts for this behavior.

8. Deposits held by individuals, partnerships and corporations; those not held by either governments or other banks.

9. The commercial banks' share of the total fell from 60% in 1945 to 40% in 1962. Federal Reserve Board, *Flow of Funds Accounts, 1945–72.*

10. Auto registrations more than doubled and miles of telephone wire tripled from 1920 to 1930. *Historical Statistics,* pp. 462, 482.

11. The suspensions, 1930–1935, show the same predominance of rural, non-member state commercial banks as in the prosperous 1920's although the incidence of urban bank failures rises substantially in the latter period. *See* D. Carson and P. H. Cootner, "The Structure of Competition in Commercial Banking in the United States," in Commission on Money and Credit, *Private Financial Institutions,* Prentice-Hall, Inc., Englewood Cliffs, N.J. (1963).

12. Bank offices rose 30.5% between 1950 and 1961, compared to about a 20% rise in population. *Historical Statistics,* pp. 7, 634; and United States Bureau of the Census, *Historical Statistics, Continuation to 1962,* pp. 1, 88, Washington, D.C. (1965).

13. New offices opened in 1967 were less than in the two pre-Saxon years. Federal Reserve Board, *Federal Reserve Bulletin,* August 1975.

14. Perhaps to less than normal to the extent that banks had anticipated a later reversal in the Comptroller's very controversial policy.

15. We use long term rates because the branching decision is a long term decision even though bank lending itself is mostly short term. We use AAA bonds to avoid confusing risk premium with interest rate considerations.

16. The social costs must be approximately equal to the interest revenues lost by consumers due to the regulations, because banks have an incentive to spend resources up to that amount in order to attract the valuable, low interest deposits to the bank.

[2]

Banks and Their Deposit Customers

In the typical discussion of the economics of manufacturing a product, it is assumed that the firm is engaged solely in production within its gates and that the consumption process occurs costlessly at the gates. There is little concern about customer relations—tailoring the product to the customer's needs, informing him about its characteristics and availability and delivering it to his door. For many purposes this abstraction is perfectly satisfactory; and, for most occasions on which it is not adequate, the economic principles yielded by the abstraction can then be applied to the more complex and realistic issues which are posed by merchandising. But while it is feasible to treat the world of merchandising in economic terms, it has rarely been done; and, without such an analysis, the broad range of activities intermediating between production and consumption cannot be fully understood.

This is notably true in the financial area. In many of its aspects the bank is a manufacturing firm: acquiring funds, processing pieces of paper, manipulating data and producing loans, investments and deposit services. But a characteristic of banks that distinguishes them from, say, auto manufacturers, is the fact that consumption of a bank's services requires inputs of the consumer's time and energy which are large relative to the bank's own costs. When the customer writes and mails a check, the banking system accepts the check from the payee, moves it through a national distribution system to the payor's bank, processes it and returns the funds to the payee and the check to its depositor. The costs to the bank of this activity are important to it, but the customer has his own costs: postage and stationery to mail the check and a variety of time costs, such as time to write the check, to do his own account-

16

ing and to reconcile balances when the check is returned. In all this, the customer's costs for a check typically exceed those of the bank. In the same way, a customer making a deposit at a bank imposes accounting and handling costs on that bank. But his own costs of going to the bank, waiting in line and returning to his normal activity add up, at reasonable opportunity costs for his time, to more than those of the bank. We will provide some estimates of these costs later. But our present point is simply that, in each of these cases, the real final activity requires inputs of both the seller and the customer.

Again, this is not a unique feature of banking. It applies in varying degrees to all shopping activity; but there is a marked difference of degree between a consumer's banking activities and his car-buying or even his food-buying activities. Typically, in his banking activities, the percentage of total inputs represented by the consumer's direct inputs is large. Accordingly, our analysis of the bank-customer relationship in this section does not depend on any qualitative differences between banking and other activities. What is argued is that the magnitude of these consumer inputs into the process is large enough that we cannot understand the economics of banking and, thus, the economics of EFTS unless we take the implications of that consumer activity into account.

For example, there are a number of specific questions answered by our analysis which cannot be understood in the conventional terms. Why, in an industry characterized by tens of thousands of banking-type firms with even more individual offices, do we tend to find firms with unexhausted economies of scale? Why do we find banks supplying widely different amounts of services per dollar of bank balances held and, in particular, handling small accounts at less than full cost? Why, even when there was no prohibition on interest payments on demand deposits, did banks in competitive markets nonetheless rarely make such payments?

THE MODEL

We propose to develop a model of the financial institution which takes into account explicitly these direct consumer costs. To make the initial presentation of the model clearer and easier to follow, we will abstract from the real world; we will initially assume that the basis of a customer's inputs is overcoming distance, i.e., he must incur transportation costs. That simplification is only for convenience and concreteness, and the argument will later be reconstructed to cover explicitly the opportunity costs of his time. Similarly, we will present some diagrams which assume that a bank's costs first decline over some range and rise thereafter. Again, that specific shape is inessential; the costs could decline first and thereafter become constant, or they could continue to fall at a declining rate. The use of specific examples does not imply that the results are only valid in the cases described.

Let us first explore a simplified abstract problem. We assume that banks supply (1) a single product, to (2) identical customers, who are (3) spread uniformly over an extended geographic area. To make the example concrete, think of the product as a custodial and accounting service for funds to be deposited and withdrawn in person. (We will later deal with complications raised by checking and depositing by mail.) Assume also that there are no restrictions on bank entry.[1]

As a first step, let us postulate that all banks have identical economies of scale so that the least-cost size of bank is one with 10,000 demand deposit accounts (DDA's). In a static world of certainty, with no transportation costs, productive efficiency will require that banks spread symmetrically across the area at discrete distances from one another such that each has a market area corresponding to 10,000 DDA's. Thus each bank will be closer to its 10,000 customers than is any other bank. Under those circumstances, if each bank charges its customers a price equal to its (minimum average) cost of a DDA, the total cost of supplying DDA's by banks will be at a minimum. If we set out to minimize the use of resources by banks in producing such accounts, we can characterize this solution as an optimal one.

Even a little thought, however, reveals some problems with such a characterization. First of all, it is wrong to ignore the costs to a customer of using the DDA. Assume for the moment that the customer can make a deposit only by walking in person to the bank. The total social costs of the DDA are not only the costs of the resources used by the bank in producing a DDA on its books, but also the cost to the customer of walking to the bank to make his deposit. The proper measure of total costs includes not only the costs of production but also the costs of consumption, i.e., those involved in making use of the product.

Diagrams will make this clearer. First, let us think of the bank only in its capacity of producing DDA's at a single location (Fig. 2). Production is subject to initial economies of scale followed by diseconomies, so that the average cost curve *(AC)* has a well-defined minimum at a scale of production Q. If we have no other variables to consider, competition will require all banks to operate at that scale.

To bring the customer into the relationship, let us first take customer location as given. While it is typical in banking for the consumer to go to the bank, a rational banker will want to consider the transportation costs of the customer, regardless of who supplies these transport services. While the existence of those costs can be thought of as reducing demand for bank

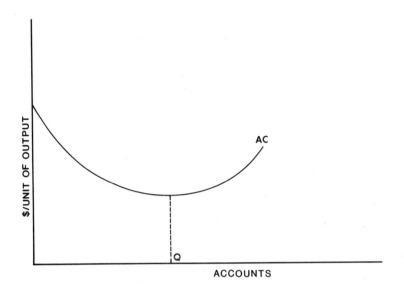

Figure 2. Average costs to the bank without reference to customer cost of access.

services, it will be simpler at the start for us to think of the bank as furnishing a delivered product and including the delivery costs in its own cost curve. If the customers are spread smoothly around the bank with uniform per mile transport costs, those unit marginal costs will look like the solid line in Figure 3. Each customer added will be farther away and will require higher outlays to reach. Hence, larger outputs will entail disproportionately greater average costs of delivery. If there is an irregular pattern of location, the curve might look more like the dashed line. Whatever the detailed shape, however, the curve will be nondecreasing.

Now, if we add these transport costs to the in-house production costs, we will get a pattern like that in Figure 4. The nondecreasing nature of the transport costs will always have effects shown. Trivially, delivered average costs *(ac)* will exceed mere production cost *(AC)*. (For simplicity the conventional cost curves [excluding delivery costs] are denoted by capital letters. Curves including delivery costs are marked with lower case letters.) More importantly, the discrepancy will increase as output increases and more distant customers are served. The "U" shaped cost curve of the bank, reflecting scale economies, dominates over the early range of outputs, imparting a similar shape to the total, or delivered, cost curve. But the positive slope of transportation costs causes the total average cost curve to turn upward at lower outputs and then to rise more steeply. As a result, the

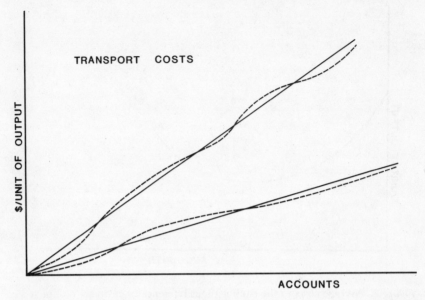

Figure 3. Average and marginal costs of transportation or "access" experienced by customers without reference to bank costs.

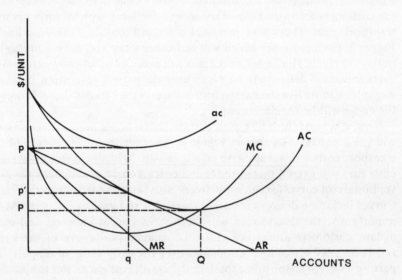

Figure 4. Average costs of deposit services including both bank costs and customer costs.

minimum point on the average cost curve for the delivered product *(ac)* will always lie to the left of the minimum point on AC. The optimal level of operations will be at an output q, less than Q, and the average "price" of the delivered product to the customers will be p, which includes average bank costs equal to p' and average customer costs of $p-p'$. We stress that we have been speaking of *average* costs to customers and to the bank, and not of the actual costs incurred by or on behalf of a particular customer. The cost of effecting delivery to each customer is different. However, the uniform delivered price, p, is the only one which will just cover costs at the socially desirable output: higher uniform prices will induce entry by others, and lower uniform prices will lead firms to leave the industry. A more difficult point to make, and which we reserve for later, is that it will not be possible to charge higher uniform (or discriminatory) *delivered* prices to customers under competitive conditions, nor will it be economic to charge less than the indicated delivered price to any customer, so long as it is possible to identify customers by their location.

The resulting equilibrium is one of zero profits in the economic sense (i.e., profits just equal to the cost of invested capital), not only for a firm that delivers to its customers but also for a firm, such as a bank, which serves customers at its own doors. This is indicated by the fact that, when the delivered price of the output to all depositors is p, the net average revenues which must be received by a bank, represented by AR, are equal to p minus the average transportation cost for delivering the various amounts of output. Recall that average delivered costs *(ac)* are equal to the bank costs *(AC)* plus transportation charges and that the full price to depositors *(p)* is equal to the average revenue received by the bank *(AR)* plus transportation charges. Therefore, if p is equal to ac at an output q, then AR must also equal AC at that point, since the last two costs both differ from the two revenues by the same amount. From the bank's point of view, it faces a declining net average revenue curve for its output; and, at the optimum output, that curve is just tangent to its average cost curve *(AC)*, and its revenue received is just equal to its costs. That these minimum profits are also the maximum attainable is marked by the intersection of marginal revenue *(MR)*, i.e., revenue received from the marginal sale, and marginal bank costs *(MC)*; i.e., the cost of the incremental unit at an ouput q. Producing any less will forego revenues in excess of the costs of the unproduced quantity, while producing more will incur costs in excess of the incremental revenue.

This equilibrium represents a social optimum with price equal to marginal cost, as reflected in the intersection of mc (not shown in Figure 4) with total price p at the minimum average cost point on ac. That is quite standard. What is superficially disturbing, however, is that the equilibrium for the bank itself has the appearance of a noncompetitive solution, with marginal cost *(MC)* less than average revenue *(AR)*. The key to this anomaly is revealed when we turn, as we now do, from focusing on average costs and prices to focusing on costs and prices to particular customers. The average revenue curve is not equal to the explicit price that, optimally, will be charged to any particular customer. Hence, *AR* is not the demand curve facing the bank in the usual sense. Each customer incurs the same delivered costs, *p*. That can only happen if the service price charged to each customer by the bank is equal to *p* minus his unique transportation costs. From Figure 3, with rising average cost of delivery, we know that customer marginal costs exceed the average. Indeed, since the difference between *p* and the *AR* curve is the average transportation cost, it follows that the difference between *p* and *MR* is the marginal delivery cost; and the bank must charge to each customer a service price which corresponds to his position on the marginal revenue curve, *MR*, in order to insure that he pays the full delivered price of *p*.

To put the issue in another perspective, the *ac* curve is the sum of two benefits: (1) the marginal value (costs) of the bank services received and (2) the marginal benefits to the customer of having the bank located more conveniently to him. The customer is buying two products, bank services and delivery (or convenience). For economic efficiency he must pay the marginal cost of producing both. If customers were buying the delivered service, each would be charged the flat price *p* even though the actual cost of delivery would differ for each customer; and the firm would locate itself among its customers so as to minimize the bank's total cost. Where, however, the customer arranges the "transportation," the price he pays must nonetheless give the firm the proper incentive to locate optimally. This is feasible only if each customer pays a price for both services he is purchasing; a price for the demand deposit itself and an appropriate reward for furnishing the amount of geographic proximity, or convenience, he desires. This is accomplished if the firm collects from each customer a price equal to the customer's position on the marginal revenue curve in Figure 4, which results in the firm receiving *AR* for producing the optimal output, an amount just equal to its average costs and enabling it to operate at the efficient level. Looked at another way, this is the result that would be obtained if each customer could costlessly bargain with a large number of competing banks on the question of bank location, with the competing banks receiving from each customer the value of the transportation savings to him of the locational decision made by the bank after the bargaining.

Hence, the optimal solution for the bank is to charge the nearby customer more than the more distant one, the difference in price being equal to the difference in transportation costs..There has been a tendency in the past to identify such pricing as price discrimination since different customers will pay different prices for the same bank output. However, if we recognize that the products, deposits in a specific location, are indeed different for each customer, the price differential reflects simply the price of propinquity or locational advantage to each customer. If the nondiscriminatory solution was required by law, those nearby customers who had been "discriminated against" would be made worse off; for fewer and larger firms would exist because propinquity could not be sold to those who valued it. And those who had not been "discriminated against" would be made better off because they did not value propinquity and would enjoy lower nominal prices. Moreover, those formerly paying the higher prices would lose more than the others would gain and would probably be willing to bribe the beneficiaries of the law to restore the old discrimination against themselves.

A more serious question is not the desirability of the solution we have outlined but its feasibility. Clearly, if the firm's cost of delivery is less than that of its customers, the firm will sell only the delivered product at a uniform price and no one will notice that the "discrimination" is taking place. But if the firm's delivery costs exceed those of its customers, the firm can only sell the product at its door. To get the optimum solution, it is necessary that the firm be able (1) to identify customers by their location and (2) to prevent those customers who are charged the low prices from reselling to those who are charged the high prices.

The reselling problem, which may be quite serious for manufacturing firms, will be more apparent than real for organizations engaged in distribution. If the store or bank has economies of scale in selling goods to customers (with the consequence that propinquity becomes a scarce and valued good), those same scale economies will prevent any of the subgroup of "low-price" customers from competitively reselling goods to the subgroup of high-price customers.

Since paying the higher price is advantageous to the customers nearer the plant as a group, one might think that the former problem—of identifying those customers—would be similarly straightforward, but in fact it is the central problem of marketing in the context being considered. This is so because what is advantageous for customers as a group is not in the interest of each as an individual. That is, while each customer would be willing to pay the appropriate price for convenience in order to get a firm to locate nearby, he has an incentive to understate his desire for propinquity because (1) he may get almost as good a location if all other customers pay and he does not or (2) his payments may be ineffective in getting a firm to locate nearby unless all other customers are also truthful.

Despite the customer's incentive to avoid paying for the benefits of con-venient location, he will not be able to do so if his own transportation costs are larger than those of the bank. In that case a policy of selling the product at a flat price and supplying "free" delivery would dominate any consumer alternative. If, on the other hand, the consumer's "pickup" costs are uniform and are less than the cost of delivery by the firm, the extraction of a price for convenience becomes more difficult for the firm. If the difference between the firm's and the customers' delivery costs is not too great, the firm may subsidize some delivery costs in order to extract some of the location benefits, but the firm's flexibility in achieving the optimal price structure is reduced.

In the case of banks and other financial intermediaries, both the firm and the customer participate in the process of delivery, but, traditionally, cus-tomer delivery has predominated. Banks often pay for costs of mail deposit, but customers make their own pickups and deliveries in most cases. There are a number of factors which account for this. Customers have an incentive and opportunity to schedule bank visits when they are in the neighborhood and their marginal costs are low, e.g., on a shopping trip to the vicinity or at an off-peak time of day such as the lunch hour. In addition, the security problems for a bank messenger are much greater than for individual pickup. Finally, and probably most important, where banks have tried deposit pickups, the pickup unit (armored car) has been legally adjudged to qualify as a branch,[2] which reduces its economic viability.

So long as customers find it cheaper to effect delivery at the firm's premises instead of purchasing a delivered product, they will make discrimination on the basis of distance more difficult. However, personal pickup results in an array of transportation costs that varies widely with the customer's oppor-tunity costs of time. We move from the customary market situation, in which everyone pays the same price for a product or service based on its competi-tively determined price, to a situation in which each person's price is deter-mined largely by the opportunity cost of his own time. In that case, as in the case of uniform per-mile transport costs, the firm's propinquity continues to be valuable to customers. The difference is that, in this second case, the locational value of the firm is not a function of distance alone, but of both distance *and* the opportunity cost of time. The addition of time costs as factors in locational convenience opens up major new opportunities for pricing methods which motivate firms to produce socially valuable con-venience.

In the first version of our model, differential pricing was made possible by access costs which differed because they involved uniform per-mile costs of spacially differentiated customers; we now turn to a more realistic version of the model. In this version, the geographic characteristics of customers are not known and need not be known to the bank; customers differ in that they have very different opportunity costs for their time and hence very different costs of providing their own pickup services.

PRICING OF BANK SERVICES

In conjunction with the present, more realistic, version of the model, we will speak more generally of access costs rather than of transportation costs. One customer's access costs differ from those of another customer primarily because of differences in their opportunity cost of time. In other senses, both the model and the underlying bank management problem remain the same: What pricing mechanism induces the bank to take properly into account not only its own costs but also the costs of its customers? What induces the bank to strive to reduce its customers' costs through the bank's locational strategies and service characteristics? How is the bank rewarded for reducing those customer costs? Clearly, transportation in the strict sense is neither essential nor even important to the validity of the model. All that is needed is that there be some problem of access to banks by customers. The problem could be ignorance, to be overcome by expenditures on education or advertising; it could be customer time requirements, which are to be costed in opportunities foregone; it could be varying packaging requirements of customers, requiring increasing outlay by banks to widen the market; or it could be licensing or regulatory costs. The phenomenon of opportunity cost of time is the problem, among those mentioned, that appears most important for our model; the pattern of personal execution by customers of banking transactions is very pervasive. The consumer buying goods on credit, writing checks, balancing his account and visiting his bank is usually unable to hire an unskilled clerk to do the job for him or to have the bank itself supply the needed service. The businessman can, indeed, hire people to perform such services; and, even when he cannot, his average transaction size is large enough to make such costs proportionately much less important. But for the personal account, such costs are both substantial and correlated strongly and positively to the customer's own wealth position.

A few examples may help develop this issue. For the average U.S. worker outside of agriculture, a minute eliminated from the work day represents a loss of 7.5¢; for a $20,000 a year executive, that minute is a loss of 18¢. On that basis, relatively small differences in customer time inputs will offset big differences in bank costs. The 25¢ to 30¢ typically estimated as the bank's cost of accepting a deposit at a teller window is small compared to the value of the average 6 minutes the customer is reputed to spend in line at that window,[3] let alone the time he spends getting to and returning from the line. If, as industry sources estimate,[4] a customer spends 5 minutes verifying a bill, writing a check and balancing the item in his checkbook, he will be more receptive to a credit card which enables him to reduce the number of checks he writes than he will be to an innovation reducing by 90% the other elements of check writing costs to him.

Even more important for our purposes is the fact that people with high opportunity costs of time earn more money and spend more money than those with low costs. With greater demand for bank funds against which to write checks and greater time costs of replenishing balances and making careful accountings, it is likely that such people will carry larger balances than those with low incomes. To the extent possible, they will try to shift the tasks to others—a secretary, an automatic payroll deposit or deduction plan, mail deposit and so on—but such devices seem unlikely to change the main result.

As the value of the customer's time falls, a closer control of balances makes more sense. It is not simply that those with low incomes have less money to put in the bank; for in theory a customer can balance income with outgo very closely with any level of deposits. It is simply that, given the lower value of time, it is more productive to visit a bank and fine tune one's balance than to economize on time. "Playing the float" and small-scale check kiting seem much more productive, and therefore "necessary," for the low-income depositor. Moreover, as income declines, spending becomes less discretionary, and the short-run variability of expenditure declines. The need for balances may be so low as to discourage bank accounts altogether, in which case paycheck cashing at supermarkets, utility bill paying at drug stores and money orders displace the bank account. Thus, as the opportunity cost of time falls, balances decline as well until the point is reached where the demand account offers no net advantage at all.

In practice, most firms in such a situation approximate the efficient solution by trying to isolate classes of customers with different "access" costs, charging different prices to different classes but charging each class a price uniform across the class, so that the total set of classes yields revenues approximately the competitive ideal. Banking offers some particularly interesting special opportunities for differential pricing which have an important impact on the bank-consumer relationship.

The key to a differential pricing scheme is to have a cheap, readily available index of consumer's demand for convenience, an index which cannot be disguised by the consumer. For banks there is such an index. As we have noted, accessing his bank account involves mostly the customer's own time. An important fraction of that time is the portion spent going to and from the bank and waiting in line while at the bank. Another important fraction is spent in monitoring his balance: entering checks in his books, doing the elementary but tedious bookkeeping, reconciling statements and planning his future cash flows. Another fraction is spent in the actual writing and mailing of checks and deposit slips. The customer obviously has an incentive to produce his utilization of bank services as efficiently as possible. One such way clearly is to utilize, at any given price for services, a bank as conveniently located as possible, since that will reduce his time inputs. Another way to reduce his time inputs is to increase his bank balance. At one extreme (with an infinite balance), he need never make deposits, he need never perform the intramonth accounting that is requisite to the equally unnecessary planning of future cash flows to avoid overdrawing, nor need he ever have to arrange a loan.

If holding bank balances involves an opportunity loss, as it does if less than market interest rates are paid on balances, the infinite bank balance solution is not an economic one. The self-interested consumer will want to hold some balances to reduce his time inputs into bank-service-consuming sector, but not by "too much." What he will optimally do is to increase balances up to the point where the opportunity cost of a further balance addition is just equal to the value of the time saved by that addition. Thus, each customer will reveal, by his own self-interested behavior, his valuation of his own access costs. As long as bank balances are underpriced (i.e., as long as the interest paid is less than the market rate for such funds), balances will become a proxy for the customer's costs of accessing bank services. The amount of underpricing will be determined by competition among banks, such as will leave none of them earning excess profits. Furthermore, this underpricing would exist, perhaps to a lesser extent, even if there were no restrictions on interest payments on deposits.

This last point may need some elaboration, since it may seem intuitively obvious that banks will compete to attract these deposits and bid up the interest rate to market levels in the absence of ceiling regulations. That certainly would be the case if the amount of deposits maintained by customers was independent of the services provided by the bank. If there were not costs of access to the funds, consumers would demand the market rate and banks would compete to pay it. Banks, of course, do compete for the valuable deposits, and some may in fact compete by paying market rates and charging marginal costs for services. But such competition is only feasible where the marginal cost price covers full costs; that is, at the bank minimum average cost point; and that implies a large scale of operation attracting only customers with very low access costs—the phenomenon of "wholesale banking". Other banks compete by foregoing some cost savings of large scale, locating closer to customers and charging higher prices for bank services but attracting customers whose own costs are reduced by greater ease of bank access.

Perhaps these relationships may be seen more readily in Figure 5, which is a simpler version of the basic model set forth in Figure 4. A bank operating at scale q, which is the minimum point on the average total curve *(atc)*, will impose an explicit charge of D (equal to its marginal cost) for its account service on all its customers. But in addition each customer seeks what is for him a cost-minimizing trade-off between devoting more time and effort to his banking transactions and increasing his level of balances; and he thus selects his own position along the marginal revenue curve *(MR)*. Customer i, for example, located on MR at point q_i, pays the bank for his transactions \$a in direct charges and \$b in foregone interest income on his balance and incurs \$c in personal access cost. In the aggregate, customers pay the bank ODEq in explicit charges and DpE in earnings on uncompensated balances; it is competition for the latter earnings in particular that leads banks, through office location and in other ways, to seek to reduce the access costs of their customers. The problem of determining customer demand for more convenient access and time saving, and of receiving payment for providing it, is solved by the automatic measuring device of the (undercompensated) balance level which each customer chooses to maintain.

IMPLICATIONS OF THE MODEL FOR BANK COSTS

This analysis has some important implications for the literature of banking costs. First, it implies that studies of individual bank costs and operations will almost always show banks as operating on the declining portion of *their* cost curves, AC, with still unutilized economies of scale; and, if not properly interpreted, this finding will lead to the erroneous implication that there are serious dangers of a shift from a competitive environment to a highly concentrated, or even a monopolistic, market structure.[5]

To make our second point, we need an intermediate argument. Envision now a whole series of banks, identical in production technology but located in a wider range of market environments characterized by different population densities (Figure 6), which for simplicity we will take to be smoothly distributed. In the most dense markets, we can satisfy any given number of customers with small transport outlays (e.g., at_1). The less populated areas imply larger costs of transportation to service that same number of customers (e.g., at_3). The implications of this optimal scale are shown in Figure 7. The less dense the market, the smaller is the optimal scale of bank operations when we consider delivery costs.

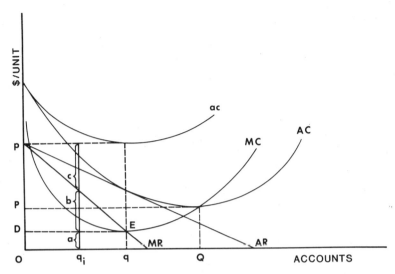

Figure 5. Average costs, bank and depositor, of deposit services and resultant direct and indirect costs to depositor.

There is nothing uneconomic about the conclusion that less dense areas will be served by smaller banks. But if empirical analyses merely refer to internal bank costs *(AC)* in relation to size, they will conclude that the smaller banks are high-cost operations that are less efficient than larger banks. That is, in effect, the verdict of many empirical studies, although even these find most of the so-called scale economies exhausted at modest sizes.[6]

THE PRICING OF BALANCES

Let us now turn to the question of the exact extent to which balances will be underpriced. To give our discussion some precision, let us assume that all customers have the same *technological* opportunities for bank access; i.e., they are all equally efficient at substituting balances for time and trips, even though they may differ in economic incentives to economize. Under that condition, balances actually held will reflect the cost of a transaction to the depositor, which will depend upon both the time a transaction consumes and his opportunity cost of time. The greater the underpricing, the more all customers will seek to restrict their balances and substitute their valuable time. On the one hand, the greater the underpricing, the more incentive banks will have to increase the number of their locations and to bid up the payment for balances in their competition for deposits. If economies of scale

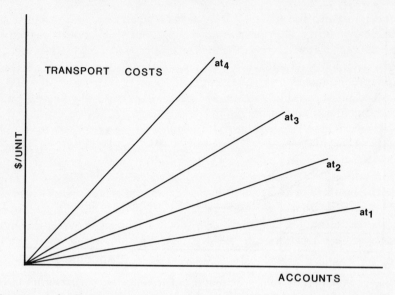

Figure 6. A family of average transportation costs functions, each function corresponding to a different population density in the geographical banking market.

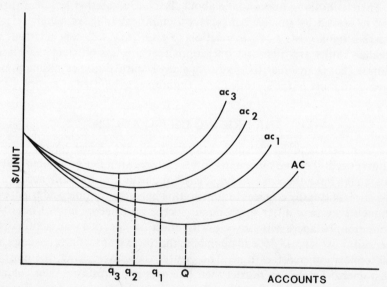

Figure 7. A family of average cost, bank and depositor, functions resulting from a single average bank cost function combined with a family of average customer cost functions.

in operating an office are very small, banks can build branches very near each consumer at little cost so that the marginal value of propinquity is very small, and deposit rates will be near market levels since banks will have no need to recover special outlays for customer convenience. On the other hand, if there are large economies of scale, the price consumers are required to pay for bank propinquity is high; and underpricing will be correspondingly large to cover the higher cost of providing convenience.

So far we have been writing as if the marginal customer pays the simple marginal cost of the bank service, needs to pay no premium for convenience and hence will keep no balances. In fact, the uncertainty of knowing when a check will clear will require even a man with very low time costs to keep positive balances in his account. Because of this fact, every check written in reality carries with it some amount of requisite balances. Since balances are, in a sense, technologically tied to check writing rather than to the convenience of bank location, any underpricing of balances, unaccompanied by below cost processing charges, will lead to excessive costs for checks. In practice, that can be and probably is corrected for by setting check processing charges below the pure accounting costs by an amount equal to the unpaid interest on technologically linked balances. To indicate the order of magnitude, we note that if checks are written for an average of $40 each, if average balances equal one-quarter of monthly dollar volume of payments and if deposit rates are 4% per annum less than market rates, then the required reduction of actual check charges below full cost per check should be 3.3¢.[7]

These comments apply to all balances, but obviously it makes economic sense to classify balances further—say, into time and demand—if there are different technological relations between balances and services. If we have a category of balances demanding very little in the way of services, so that the price of services adjusted for technologically necessary balances is always negative, we will pay positive interest rates on that category of balances; but the rates will still be below market. High time-value users will continue to pay higher implicit prices, since they will hold larger underpriced balances, and there will be an average implicit price equal to average cost for services across all customers.

Several problems arise in assessing the impact of interest rate regulation. When market rates are low, the law may have no effect; as rates rise, the law has economic consequences. Clearly, if interest rates on savings deposits are by law held below the competitive levels described in the preceding paragraph, there will be strong incentives to supply still additional services in return for such deposits (including the service of reducing distance to the nearest office). There will be, at times of high interest rates, an attempt to supply demand deposit services under the guise of a time deposit; and organizations which are restricted in their ability to offer services will find themselves less able to compete through these indirect methods. At low market rates of interest, the zero ceiling on demand deposits will probably not be meaningful, since even in an unregulated economy we should expect some underpricing. From the limited evidence we have on payment of interest on demand deposits prior to Regulation Q, the rate paid on balances should be much less than market rates. As market rates rise, however, the ceiling becomes effective. The initial impact is to reduce charges for other bank services, which tends to subsidize check writing and related services. An equally important impact, which has been generally overlooked, is the incentive to increase the construction of bank offices so as to reduce the cost of consumer inputs; when viewed in the long-term perspective of chapter 1, the behavior of bank offices does indeed seem to have been determined in greater degree by the fluctuation in long-term interest rates than by regulatory discretion or bank profitability.

Our theory, then, suggests that, even without legal interest rate ceilings, we should expect to find time deposits (which are unaccompanied by the provision of payment or other services) offered at market interest rates; saving deposits, with limited free services, offered at below market interest rates; and demand deposits, offering services priced somewhat below cost,[8] with still lower interest rates. Moreover, if regulation imposes a zero ceiling on demand deposits, we should expect that the impact of varying market rates of interest over time should show up primarily in variations in the number of bank offices per capita and in the degree by which services are underpriced. As far as we know, these observations are all consistent with the data, which is not the same as saying that the data confirm the theory.

EFTS IMPACTS

Having developed a model of bank-customer relationships, we apply it in this section to an analysis of the implications of the new EFTS technology for the deposit side of the banking business.

Many analyses of the new electronic technology have tended to emphasize the role of the innovation as a labor-saving device—the substitution of expensive capital equipment for paper handling and other labor inputs at a great net saving. It seems reasonable that, in fact, as transaction volumes increase, electronic systems can be depended upon to reduce bank check processing costs per item by a substantial percentage. Estimates of that reduction run from 5¢ to 10¢ per item on current costs of about 16¢ per check handled.[9] Such estimates look more impressive than they really are, since they emphasize gross savings without allowing for the additional capital costs of the new networks; but, for the moment, let us accept these estimates of the savings.

The main implication of our model is that these bank cost savings may be much less critical than other aspects of the new technology. Let us look at some of these other aspects. Despite the increase in capital costs in the electronic payments network, the system will make individual terminals capable of supplying most bank services desired by the customer, at far lower cost than current branches. The expected result, in the absence of restrictive federal legislation, is that the number of terminal-type substitutes for bank offices will increase dramatically; they will also be much more accessible, especially if the limitation on bank office hours is taken into account. This would represent a continuation and acceleration of the historic tendency of banking to move out toward its customers so as to reduce their access costs. Without regulatory restraint, terminals would be able to accept deposits, shift deposits within the bank, cash checks, make limited payment arrangements, access prearranged credit facilities, handle bank credit card transactions and possibly initiate more complicated transactions as well.

Such offices would be very effective in attracting customers, not because of any 5¢ or 10¢ savings on per item costs, even if these are fully passed on, but because of the much greater savings in customer time and convenience. What is often overlooked, however, is that, by lowering the costs of bank access, the new technology radically changes all the aspects of the banking relationship in which consumer input is involved. The first and most obvious of these aspects is that it will leave the industry, as presently constituted, with substantial excess capacity in the form of traditional branch offices and personnel. To be sure, the reduction in bank and consumer costs will result in increased demand for services; but, nevertheless, it will simultaneously result in an even greater reduction in demand for conventional, convenience-oriented branch capacity. In the long run, of course, this is simply a reflection of the typical reduction in social cost brought about by technological innovation; but it is also typical that there is some difficulty in achieving a desirable reduction in capacity without aggressive, privately unprofitable competition. This is because it is not easy for competitors to agree as to who should leave the industry and when, while trying to keep fixed or semifixed capacity utilized. Of course, this kind of situation often leads the industry to support legislation to achieve socially undesirable restrictions on competition.

A second, and perhaps even more important, reaction is probable. Since customers pay for the convenience they desire by holding larger balances, an exogenous increase in convenience—i.e., a reduction in the costs of bank access—will result in a sharp reduction in desired balances of all types. While all customers in the aggregate cannot reduce balances (given any specific monetary policy), a reduction in desired balances should result in a reduction in actual balances required to maintain the same level of money output. Moreover, the reduced costs should result in a major shift of balances held from demand to time deposits, resulting in a sharp rise in bank balance costs. This will be the immediate reflection of the "excess capacity" in the industry; customers, who before were willing to hold balances in low-interest or no-interest form for convenience, will now hold less and raise the cost of deposits. This change will occur fairly promptly after the new technology becomes available, and undoubtedly faster than the closure of offices that are superfluous. This is particularly so if the new technology diffuses slowly from high access-cost customers to low access-cost ones, a probable pattern; so that the closing of branches will result in the loss of those customers who are not yet using the new technology and are still dependent on the old system.

Thus, banks should experience some reduction in total balances and a sharp shift of the composition of balances toward higher yielding varieties. This pattern will be even more pronounced if, simultaneously, interest rate ceilings are eroded or eliminated, since the increase in yields would be even greater if current yields are being held down by the ceilings. In the long run, any bank with superior management or technology will benefit from change in a competitive struggle untempered by regulatory restraint, as will consumers in general. In the short run, however, with bank marginal costs less than average costs, there is the substantial possibility that the advantage may take the form of smaller losses rather than net gains.

REFERENCES

1. If we were to further assume that there were no economies of scale in banking, profit maximization would lead to the rather artificial solution of an infinite number of banks spread smoothly over the whole area. In fact, one can interpret this as implying the nonexistence of banks: each man becomes his own banker, writing his "own checks" on his "own account." In such a world there is no need for "intermediation"; we get direct production of checks as needed by the consumer.

2. *First Nat'l Bank in Plant City* v. *Dickinson,* 396 U.S. 122 (1969).

3. These numbers have been taken from proprietary studies of banking operations, and substantially identical numbers are commonly used by industry spokesmen.

4. See note 3, *supra.*

5. Notice the anomaly. If the product were sold in delivered form, the banking industry would appear to be perfectly competitive in the conventional sense, operating at minimum costs. If we ignore cost of delivery, we get a situation that looks like conventional if profitless monopoly.

6. See, for example, Paul M. Horvitz, "Economies of Scale in Banking," in *Private Financial Institutions,* Prentice-Hall, Inc., Englewood Cliffs, N.J. (1963).

7. $\$.033 = (\$40.)\,(^1/_4)\,(^{.04}/_{12})$.

8. The subsidy to check writing deserves some further scrutiny since there is considerable reason to believe it has had a major effect on check writing. Let us accept the commonly quoted estimate of bank processing costs of 16¢ per check. In addition, there are numerous estimates of the consumer's costs of check writing, including postage, envelopes and time, which have been estimated at from 27¢ up to $1.50; the higher number includes dictating and typing a letter to go with the check. We assume those costs average 32¢. At present, the depositor pays no part of the bank costs, so that if the bank were, in fact, to charge for those costs, the depositor's perceived costs would rise from 32 to 48 cents, an increase of 50%. The price elasticity of many individual food products at the retail level is around .4—implying a 4% reduction in demand for each 10% rise in price; this is somewhat understated for our purposes, since that elasticity figure, unlike our estimates of check writing costs, does not allow for the full consumer costs of shopping for the food products. If we assume that checks are no more necessary than food, then we might expect a 20% reduction in check demand with full pricing. If we assume that demand elasticity for checks is more like that for, say, copper than food, we might visualize a 67% reduction in demand in the long run if check subsidization is eliminated. To the extent these figures seem reasonable, a good part of the recent rapid growth in check writing has been produced by the progressive reduction in explicit check charges by banks as interest rates have increased.

In view of the interest in NOW accounts, it may be worthwhile to add some comments on the economics of savings account competition to the bank-customer relationship. The typical regular savings deposit at a bank is substantially (60% or more) larger than the typical personal checking account. From the 1973 *Functional Cost Analysis,* we can see that savings accounts have also been substantially less active, with about 8 transactions a year as opposed to 330 for a personal checking account. Finally, conversion of the withdrawal method from a teller-window transaction to a check processing transaction reduces costs, for the traditional window withdrawal process is substantially more expensive. For these reasons, the institutions using NOW accounts have been able to offer an attractive combination of interest rates and transaction charges. As the savings account becomes more and more like a normal checking account, with both balances and transactions moving closer to the average, the pricing of that package may have to be altered. In any event there can be little doubt that the NOW account experience, permitting checks to be drawn on savings accounts, is initially much more profitable than the converse, paying interest on demand deposits.

9. See pp. 61–62 below.

[3]

Banks and Retail Sales

We have noted that the new phenomenon of bank debit cards will offer customers greater ease of access to funds deposited at a banking institution, through serving as a means of depositing, withdrawing and transferring funds at the bank. However, there is another broad field of debit card use which has not yet been touched on—the use of the card as a substitute for a check at the retail point of sale.

As a new product, the debit card competes with a whole range of existing products. Most discussions of the debit card have centered on competition between the debit card and the ordinary bank check, from the standpoint both of costs to the bank and, to a lesser degree, of costs to the consumer of using the competing instruments at the point of sale. Another topic of considerable interest has been the cost to retailers of supplying cash or merchandise to customers through checks versus debit cards.

While our discussion also will cover this range of competition, it will extend to yet another field of competition, that between the debit card and the credit card. At the margin every credit transaction competes with the alternative of immediate payment, whether by currency, by check or now by credit card. As every merchant knows, the lines between these alternatives are not sharp; there is some risk in accepting a customer's currency, and there is a substantial element of credit risk in "cash" payment by check. And even honest customers know, and often depend on the fact, that payment by check involves a few days' extension of credit. As credit competes with checks and cash, so will the debit card compete with all of these; and, in the days of

36

electronic technology, the debit and credit cards may well be the fiercest competitors. So, in analyzing the market for debit cards, we turn first to a discussion of credit.

Bank credit cards are simply a new technological tool for competing in a market which has existed for a long time. The consumers of credit are individual customers of retail establishments. The leading competing suppliers of such credit at the point of sale are the retail establishments themselves. Consumer finance companies serve as another major supplier of consumer credit, although their loans usually are not linked to a specific purchase. In addition, many retailers, while offering credit directly, have not held the customer obligations but have passed them on promptly either to a manufacturer's credit subsidiary or to independent factoring companies. Until relatively recently, banks have been reluctant participants in direct consumer retail finance, preferring to funnel credit to others who engaged in direct dealings with the final consumer. If we adopt the reasonable presumption that banks were correct in the earlier decision not to participate directly, then the recent change to credit card competition must reflect some fundamental change in the economic environment.

From this point of view, an adequate analysis of the credit business requires, first, an understanding of why stores have offered credit to customers for some time and, second, the areas in which banks have recently found a competitive edge in supplying consumer credit.

A MODEL OF RETAILING

Before turning to the subject of retail credit, it is important to sketch out some critical features of the retailing industry, using much the same model we used in discussing the banking industry. Just as financial intermediaries operate between ultimate borrowers and lenders, retailers intermediate between manufacturers and final consumers. Both banks and retailers attempt to profit by reducing consumer inputs into the purchase of goods and services, through supplying propinquity, providing information and offering convenient packaging. Economic optimality is achieved when the marginal payments customers are willing to make for such services are just equal to the marginal costs of providing the services. As in the case of banks, the optimal pricing policy requires the store to charge to each customer the store's own internal marginal cost plus the opportunity savings to the customer of the store's superior provision of services.

As we have discussed before, optimum pricing policy is not easily achieved, because the store, once built, is open to all customers; and customers cannot easily be differentiated in terms of the value each places on the store's location or service. The bank achieves the differentiation by undercompensating balances which are associated technologically with customers' opportunity costs. Stores must try other techniques. One such technique is the holding of periodic "sales." Customers with low opportunity costs of time will make themselves aware of potential savings from sales. They will find it economically attractive to spend time traveling to the appropriate store; and, thus, over any time period they will pay a lower average price for their purchases than customers with high time costs, who will tend to economize on search and travel time and buy on impulse (i.e. when convenient) and from closer establishments.[1] Advertising serves much the same function; it is read and absorbed by those with low time costs and influences their purchases, while it appears generally excessive and wasteful to those with high time costs. Similarly, generous provision of retail clerks would attract high-opportunity-cost consumers; queuing produces both lower cost of merchandise and lower full costs of purchase to customers "with plenty of time" than to those for whom time is a relatively scarce good.

What we observe, then, is a situation in which, when prices are caused to fluctuate stochastically, customers with high time costs are led to pay higher average prices for goods than are those with lower time costs. If there are no propinquity or service benefits to customers, the stochastic fluctuation of price will be impossible to maintain, since competition will force all firms to the lowest single maintainable price. The advantages of propinquity, when paid for, however, lead firms to establish numbers of outlets such that each appears to exhibit excess capacity, operating on the declining portion of its internal cost curve.

Traditionally, these phenomena have been viewed in terms of locational monopoly, but in our terms they arise out of the competitive provision of valuable consumption services. Firms cannot survive by employing classical marginal cost pricing. If they operate at the scale and service level indicated by minimum average store costs and price at that cost, they cannot drive out their competitors because operating at that scale imposes greater transportation and shopping costs on their customers; and if they produce at a smaller scale—the optimal scale indicated by our model—marginal cost pricing will not cover total costs. But by varying prices, they can extract from the customers who value propinquity the appropriate extra charge for supplying it. Assuming that store managers have accurate information about the behavior of their competitors, they may all charge the same price for each good at each moment (corrected for quality and information differences), but stochastic variation over time of the price for any given commodity will remain. Different customers, over the course of a year, will pay different average prices for each good depending upon their shopping costs, with average prices across all customers equal to average cost.

This pattern is consistent with coexistence of stores of different scale, but we would expect the larger, low-cost stores to depend upon customers who are drawn from a larger geographic area and who respond to a widespread reputation for low prices for a given quality of merchandise and service. This tendency will be accentuated if we recognize another statistical correlation-- the high association between income and opportunity costs of time. In general, customers with high costs of search are high-income customers, so that the large stores specializing in low-cost pricing will also tend to specialize in goods most likely to be demanded by low-income customers. We distinguish sharply, however, between paying higher prices for the same quality goods and buying higher quality goods. High-income customers will tend to do both, but our analytical model depends only on the former.

THE ROLE OF CREDIT IN RETAIL COMPETITION

Now that we have, by hypothesis, made a connection between income and search costs, we can turn to the role of store credit. Remember that the typical retail outlet, to survive, must both attract some higher search cost customers and identify them for the purpose of charging them higher prices. There are, of course, incentives and methods for high-time-cost customers to avoid paying higher prices and the same skills that enable them to earn high incomes will also operate to reduce any such price discrimination as much as possible. They can reduce search costs per item by buying large quantities per trip and maintaining larger inventories at home.[2] Furthermore, they will be able to identify and patronize stores which, on average and for any given level of convenience, have lower price variability, and hence they will be able to pay the lowest prices. And stores will be even more willing to compete by all means possible because of other desirable features of the high-time-cost customer—the likelihood that he will use less clerk time per dollar of purchase because of his interest in economizing his own time and that, for the same reason, he will avoid peak hours. Retailers will compete for such customers in a variety of ways, employing each to an extent such that all are equally cost-effective at the margin. Propinquity is only one attribute desired by such customers. Another is a reduction of the time spent both in shopping and in managing their finances, including time spent going to and from the bank, time spent writing checks and time spent balancing checking accounts; a charge account consolidates all the month's purchases into a single check. An impulse buyer is quite likely to see and desire a commodity at a time when he is without sufficient funds in his checking account or indeed without knowledge of the amount in his checking account. (This would be particularly true in families where one member specializes in doing the shopping while the other maintains centralized control of the family finances.) Such impulse buying is exactly what every store would like to encourage, since it is most likely to be unmotivated by careful advance price search and hence more likely to take place at advantageous prices. Yet, other such customers will be fully cognizant of the checking balance and have sufficient funds but will find budgeting household expenditures a difficult task made easier by centralized accounting and billing. For all such customers, the convenience of a charge facility is an important one. For the retailer, it is desirable to provide these higher-price-paying customers with that convenience.

The key question is, how desirable? Is it, for example, desirable not only to offer such a charge facility, but to offer it below cost? If propinquity were the only service desired by customers, stores would compete so vigorously in that way through outlet proliferation as to eliminate any profits that might be achievable were a single store able to provide locational convenience. If credit facilities were the sole attractive service, competition would center on low priced credit, credit priced as far below the cost of providing credit as was necessary to reduce to zero total profits of attracting the marginal customer. With both characteristics being demanded, the competition will be divided among the two techniques so long as the consumer preferences for the two are not perfectly correlated.

In fact, over many decades we observe stores offering "subsidized credit" with no observable tendency to reduce or eliminate the subsidy, leading us to believe that the practice in fact reflects intelligent self-interest. Moreover, we are led even more confidently to that conclusion by looking at the structure of the "subsidy."

The leading element of subsidy is the so-called "free period": accounts are not charged interest if the account is paid within a specified time after the billing. Thus, customers who use the charge facility for only this very short term credit pay no interest, while those who desire longer credit pay interest frm the billing date or even the purchase date. Consider the interaction of this factor with other features of credit arrangements. First of all, credit facilities are extended, on the average, to a higher than average income group of customers. Moreover, it is probably true that for customers from any given income class, the subclass with credit cards is further biased toward those with higher aversion to the tasks of accounting for balances, of budgeting and of careful shopping.[3] Among customers with credit cards, it is the highest income customers who are most likely to pay off their balances during the free period, which further isolates the subsidy to those customers whose purchases are most likely to be highly profitable from a noncredit point of view. The structure of the credit subsidy is just as might be expected if it were serving the role implied by our model.

It should be noted that our explanation is perfectly consistent with a quite different line of argument which claims that there is no differential subsidy to high-income credit customers. Once a customer fails to pay during the free period, he is charged the same interest rate (usually 18%) regardless of his income or other characteristics. But some portion of the interest rate charged represents costs corresponding to the probability of default loss and differential collection costs. Both prior expectations and the available data lead one to expect that high-income credit customers are less likely to default or to pose payment problems than low-income credit customers. In fact, Shay and Dunkelberg[4] have developed data which suggest that the various income groups using credit actually use the free period to different degrees, such that the cost of credit is roughly equalized across income groups: i.e., the increased use of the free period by high-income groups reduces their average cost of credit by about the same amount as their default and collection costs fall below those of low-income groups. The advantages of the low-cost credit accrue to those who pay promptly, not simply to those with more income. Households with a given income differ in the amount of capital they possess, both in monetary terms and in specialized education; they differ in time costs and in tastes. In any income group, some pay promptly and some do not. In theory a retailer might wish to charge low-risk customers lower interest rates directly, by charging them a risk-adjusted rate on all credit extensions. The existing method of charging enables stores to approximate this result, charging less to those customers who are consistently able to furnish, on receipt of their bills, the funds required to pay for their purchases. We surmise that when high-income customers do occasionally revolve their accounts, they do so because, for the small sums and brief periods involved, the transaction costs of procuring a low-rate loan directly from the bank raises its cost to more than the 18% rate charged through the card.

The Shay-Dunkelberg proposition, that there is little or no cross-subsidization among income groups within the overall group of credit users, does not constitute an assertion that there is no subsidy to credit users as opposed to cash customers; it says only that any subsidy which may exist does not differ by income group among credit card users. Consistently with our analysis, all the data that do exist suggest that department store credit card divisions lose money when viewed as a separate organization using money valued at market rates.[5] This would suggest the existence of a subsidy in favor of credit users as a group over cash customers as a group, if one were to assume that these two groups, on average, paid the same price level for their purchases. But that assumption, we have argued, is incorrect. Card holders produce higher net revenues, they are prized by the retailer for that reason and the merely apparent subsidy reflects one aspect of the retailer's endeavor to compete selectively for their patronage.

Hence, neither the Shay-Dunkelberg argument nor our own lends any justification to the belief that credit extension involves costs in excess of the contribution of the service to total revenues and, therefore, that cash payment for merchandise is likely to justify a discount equal to the cost of "free" credit. Although this view is of very doubtful validity, it has recently secured legislative recognition in a law to prevent credit card systems from prohibiting merchants from offering such discounts,[6] and it is also prominent in the marketing plans of some debit card proponents. We do not maintain that some discounts may not occur. But we do urge that the existence of the free period is not irrational and that its persistence over time suggests that it was indeed undertaken for the kinds of reasons we have outlined.

Even the recent trend toward shortening the free period is consistent with our model, as opposed to the contrary hypothesis. The free period is a means of attracting highly profitable customers, and the extent of the correct amount of attraction is measured by balancing the amount of the profit such customers would otherwise earn for the store against the capital costs of the free period. But the value of any given free period depends on the current market interest rate. During a period of sharply rising rates, we would expect to see some pressure for shortening the free period to maintain any given amount of attraction to customers. While stores will wish to subsidize credit to attract high-income customers, they do not wish to subsidize them indefinitely. As interest rates rise, the subsidy resulting from a given free period increases beyond the optimal level to maintain the correct amount of subsidy, and the free period must be reduced. Moreover, interest rate ceilings which hold down retail credit rates charged will increase the total cost of any credit program, i.e., for unsubsidized customers as well, and will increase the incentive to substitute store location as an attraction for high time-cost customers.

Finally, we should note that the extent of economies of scale in retail stores will affect the demand for devices to discriminate among customers according to their demand for convenience. The greater the size of the optimal retail outlet, the greater is the total cost of shopping to the customer with high time costs. It therefore becomes more essential for an aggressive retail competitor to find a way to extract the locational benefits to a consumer, if the competitor is to find it economic to build smaller, convenient stores. In other words, the sharper the decline in store unit costs with increasing volume, the more important it becomes to find a device which permits customers to pay for propinquity, if the firm is to operate to the left of the minimum average cost point.

To summarize, the economics of retail credit suggests that (1) it will continue to grow as per capita income increases; (2) it will be favorably affected by anything which increases the economies of scale of retail establishments, thus making propinquity relatively more expensive and lack of propinquity less expensive; and (3) at the margin merchants have no desire to shift sales from credit to cash to avoid losses on the former.

BANK CREDIT CARDS

Our previous comments dealt with the economics of all retail credit. We now attempt to account, from the retailer's perspective, for the growth in demand for credit cards in general and in particular for bank credit cards. To begin with, some aspects of a credit sale by retailers are often overlooked. The alternative to a credit card transaction—the so-called cash sale—has its own disadvantages which can be reduced by installation of a credit system. There are two kinds of cash payments—currency and checks. Currency is relatively riskless, though counterfeiting is an ever present problem, not only because of the losses themselves but because of the costs of prevention. More important, the possession of significant amounts of cash sharply increases the risk of robbery, burglary and larceny, which accounted for over one million arrests alone in 1972.[7] Even when the risk of loss from intruders is avoided, the store faces the increased risk of loss to larcenous employees. To avoid these losses and to maintain accounting controls, the store must buy cash registers and reconcile cash balances at least daily. Moreover, it must lose the interest on initial cash balances required to support those daily transactions. We know of no figures which fully account for the costs of currency handling in retail establishments, but the amounts are not negligible.

Moving from currency payments to checks, we again find some rather imposing costs. Every merchant knows that check acceptance is itself a form of credit extension. The potential for fraud is probably fully as great in accepting a check as in accepting a card. It may be easier to steal a check or to alter or forge one than to do the same with credit cards, although the loss from a given check fraud may be less than that from a card fraud. But even the absence of fraud does not mean that a check will be honored or that, if dishonored, it will be easy to collect. Thus, the merchant accepting a check has to involve himself in a relatively time consuming and therefore costly *ad hoc* credit investigation of the customer involved, sometimes leading to rigid policies of rejecting all checks or at least some limited classes of checks.

Thus, for a number of reasons, there has been a long-run trend of growth in the provision of consumer credit, which makes bank card entry easier. That, however, is not enough to explain entry unless there is a special economic niche for this new service. To isolate that niche we note that (1) the retail establishments using bank cards are largely those at the smaller end of the distribution by firm size and (2) the larger retail establishments using bank cards are disproportionately represented among those in financial difficulties. Successful larger establishments maintaining proprietary card systems show no signs of moving to bank cards and, indeed, show some hostility to the idea.

Our conclusion is that the demand for bank credit cards on the part of these smaller or weaker retailers arises out of some diseconomies of small size in the establishment of in-house credit systems, diseconomies that have become more significant in recent years. Two such warrant consideration. One is in the provision of a system of credit investigation, evaluation and collection, especially for firms dealing with a relatively transient customer population. The second involves the acquisition of funds to support customer credit demands. Although both of these factors have existed to some degree for many years and consequently may appear inadequate to explain a current development, we will set forth hereafter the way in which their confluence with each other and with rising per capita income and higher interest rates does afford an explanation. But we start by taking up two scale factors.

It is clear that major retail chains that organize their own credit systems are generally prime or nearly-prime borrowers. The largest firms not only borrow at prime rates when necessary, but frequently, or even usually, satisfy their capital needs by direct resort to the commercial paper market at rates less than prime.[8] To some extent this is possible because the large firms are well managed and hence highly regarded by the money market, but the economics of the commercial paper market are such that it is unlikely that even the largest local department store could sell paper on prime terms. For still smaller firms of the kind that dominate the list of bank card merchants, there would be even more substantial premiums on their retail credit financing. The point is that the acquisition and maintenance by ultimate lenders of accurate credit information on smaller merchants will add a premium to their interest costs over and above the pure risk of default on their retail credit portfolio. For small merchants with relatively small credit lines, these costs loom relatively large. In addition, commercial banks which lend only in local markets are much less diversified, both geographically and in their dependence on specific industries, than are banks lending to larger organizations; and they must reflect this in their lending rates.

One need not overstate the size of these cost-of-money disadvantages to smaller establishments to make this factor important. Given the fact that in recent years the actual interest received by retailers on outstanding credit balances is around 13% and assuming that the retail establishment breaks even on its credit operation, it is clear that a prime rate of 7% to 9% alone accounts for the major share of retail credit costs. If one's competitor is paying the prime rate and breaking even, a premium of only 1% over prime implies losses equal to 7% or 8% of total credit revenues. For example, it is this aspect of the credit situation, rather than an early perception of the superior economics of bank cards, that probably accounts for the defection of W. T. Grant Company from the list of major chains not using bank credit cards just prior to its much-predicted bankruptcy.

Now let us return to the first type of scale economy in providing credit. For the smallest firms, managed largely by the proprietor, there is no room for any specialized credit personnel, either for credit evaluation or collection. Even for somewhat larger firms, credit operations are largely managed by part-time personnel, and information on credit risks and collection of bad debts are services typically purchased from outside firms. The very large retail firms perform these functions internally and with highly specialized personnel. By itself, this is only weak evidence of economies of scale, and indeed the actual argument on this point is largely inferential. What data there are do suggest that such economies exist. We draw that inference from our comparison of data, for example, on average bad check losses for the supermarket industry as a whole with the figures given by large supermarket chains and from our comparison of data on credit losses by large department stores with data in trade publications on credit losses by smaller firms.

There is further evidence of economies of scale in credit operations in the structure of merchant discounts charged by bank credit card systems. The discounts are structured so that the charge declines with volume. Whether or not these discounts reflect bank servicing costs, they would not be offered to the larger firms unless charges, in their absence, would be higher than the costs to the larger firms of maintaining their own system. The declining structure of charges does not indicate what the economies of scale actually are; it only places a lower limit on those economies. Moreover, we should note that since the largest chains do not belong to bank card systems, we must conclude from revealed preference that their own systems are cheaper.

The refusal of the largest chains to join bank card systems does not necessarily mean that there are unexhausted economies of scale in producing bank card services. It seems probable that these proprietary credit cards may, for reasons we will discuss later, constitute a different product—with different kinds of credit risks, income characteristics and credit terms. If, however, the bank cards do charge discount fees to some or all merchants in excess of the bank's costs of servicing them, the fact would be consistent with the kind of price discrimination involved in operating profitlessly on the declining portion of the bank's internal cost curves.

Let us turn now to the implications of all these factors for the bank credit card business. Over time we have had a rise in real per capita income. This has led to an increase in the value of customer time and, therefore, increased pressure for firms to supply such time-saving services as consumer credit. Smaller stores suffer relative disadvantages at supplying such services, because of diseconomies both in the cost of finance and in the cost of other credit services.

Banks have always been in the business of supplying the funds for consumer credit, but formerly they did so through the retail firms rather than directly. By setting up credit card systems, banks reduce the resources involved in credit investigation both of customers and of stores. They need not perform investigations of retail firms that no longer need to borrow since they are using bank cards to finance their sales, and even for those that continue to borrow there is presumably a reduction in the amount of credit investigation as the volume of loans shrinks relative to the firm's equity. Moreover, the cost of customer credit investigation is reduced, because there need be only one investigation per customer by each bank instead of one for each customer by each merchant serviced by that bank. Even if customers have multiple bank cards, there is still a net saving.

The advantages of bank cards have, however, existed for some time. To explain the recent rise of bank card activity requires that these different trends have reached a critical point in the last fifteen years. This seems reasonable in light of what we know about the growth of nonbank credit cards. The rise of per capita income has been going on for centuries; but, by the late 1950's (as indicated by the appearance of travel and entertainment cards, oil company cards and cards of major retailers), it appeared to have reached a point where the cost of time spent on finances began to compete seriously with propinquity as an interest of retail customers. The rise in market interest rates, giving customers a stronger incentive to economize on bank balances, was an added factor.

The growth of card demand did two things. It put increased competitive pressure on smaller establishments to extend credit; and it was not until that demand began to grow that the banks achieved a critical scale advantage in short-circuiting the retailer in the extension of consumer credit. The delayed arrival of bank cards is, by this analysis, not a sign of lack of foresight, but merely the expected timing; for the T&E and the oil company cards were associated with travel and thus nonlocal markets, for which the banks were ill-equipped to compete under existing market structure.[9] The major chains, next to enter the market in a major way, had low borrowing costs. Until it became common for a customer to have more than one card, the real advantages of bank cards could not become effective.

Nevertheless, not all the aspects of bank cards are favorable to merchants. A store credit card links the customer to that particular store. Even if the customer has a walletful of cards, he still will hold cards that represent only a small sample of all potential retail competitors. In general a customer will incur the time costs of completing an application for a proprietary card only if he is a regular customer of the issuing store. Furthermore, time costs of a transaction are not reduced and probably are increased by card use if only one transaction is executed with a card during a billing period. Thus, the fact that a customer carries and uses a proprietary card marks him as very probably a regular shopper rather than an occasional, sale shopper of the store and hence as one who frequently purchases at full retail margin. It may also be the case that, to some degree, possession of the card not only reflects the customer's shopping patterns but influences his patterns, causing him to reduce the extent of his search for low prices and to go routinely to the issuing store. But at least the first factor identifies the card holder as a profitable customer, to whom free-period benefits and promotional mailings are appropriately extended.

Use of a bank card by a customer in a store carries a somewhat similar but far weaker signal: he is likely to have a relatively high income, high time costs and those profitable shopping patterns exhibited by such customers. But the card's wide acceptability rather than any relationship to the particular retailer is the probable reason for its possession. In addition, the bank credit card is a relatively inflexible merchandising tool. Credit offerings by stores are made primarily to attract customers with relatively high search costs, but characteristics which would make a given customer relatively attractive in one retail environment will make him a relatively less desirable customer in another. For example, a firm specializing in low-priced goods marketed in a large establishment may find that, among the customers attracted to its store, the preferred customers have a lower average income than do the favored patrons of a specialty store in a small, high-income neighborhood. If income and default risk are negatively correlated, as they seem to be, and each store is committed to a single interest rate for all customers, the larger establishment will wish to accept lower quality credits and charge a higher interest rate (or follow less lenient free period policies) than will the smaller firm with the higher income clientele.[10] Furthermore, even with a given nominal interest rate there will be a range of effective rates depending on the customers' "revolving" habits, which will tend to differ with income level and with ethnic and cultural differences among neighborhoods.

With these kinds of complications, it becomes difficult for stores with specialized clientele to accept the inflexibility inherent in adopting the uniform credit standards associated with a bank card. The merchant loses the advantage of flexible credit terms in attracting his higher search cost customers. The ghetto merchant will find the bulk of his customers ineligible for bank cards at the standard bank card rates, while the storeowner in the wealthy neighborhood would be much more willing to grant longer free periods. Indeed, the Big Three department store chains have a distinctly lower income customer population than the U.S. average and respond by granting credit to many customers who would not meet ordinary bank card standards.

The existence of these disadvantages to bank credit cards means that their advantages in terms of financing cost and credit evaluation for a given merchant must be significant to induce him to switch from store credit. That the advantages are important for many merchants is evidenced by the rapid growth of the bank card systems. That is not in dispute, but hopefully this analysis of the causes of bank card success will add to our ability to project the impact of competition from the new generation of debit cards.

REFERENCES

1. This procedure will lead to some "cross-hauling"—customers traveling to more distant stores—but it would be wrong to call this suboptimal in the presence of costs of determining customer time costs.

2. Stores can and do make this more difficult by holding sales on a fraction of all items of a given type at any one time.

3. The frequency with which non-card-holding households quote a fear of slipping into wasteful shopping habits as the reason for their decision suggests that those who do have cards are those who have decided to exercise less care, for reasons which they find quite sufficient, whether it is higher income status or simply greater personal "disutility" for shopping activity.

4. William C. Dunkelberg and Robert P. Shay, *Retail Store Credit Card Use,* Columbia University Press, New York (1975) p. 51.

5. See, for example, Touche, Ross and Co., *Economic Characteristics of Department Store Credit,* National Retail Merchants Association, New York (1969). For 1973 data, see Dunkelberg and Shay, *op. cit.,* chapter 3.

6. The Fair Credit Billing Act, 15 U.S.C. sec. 1666f (Supp. IV, 1974).

7. *Information Please Almanac,* Simon & Schuster, New York (28th ed., 1974), p. 730.

8. The Citibank formula, for example, sets the prime rate each week at $1^1/_2\%$ above the average for commercial paper over the preceding 90 days.

9. In fact, one can describe American Express Company as the one U.S. "bank" then competing on a nationwide basis, and at that time only a travel card could maintain the high discount rates.

10. Note that analogous differences in policy distinguish bank cards from travel and entertainment cards; and similar differences exist in stores between credit and charge accounts.

[4]

Competition Among Means of Payment

We have no doubt that a debit card which accesses customer bank electronic terminals will be considered a desirable banking product by customers and that competition among banks will lead to its introduction. For the customer the card will reduce the cost of accessing his account, and for the bank it will be cheaper than alternative methods of providing propinquity to customers, like bricks-and-mortar branching.

These observations, however, leave open the equally important issue of whether the debit card will make important inroads on either the credit card or the check at the retail point of sale. It is at least conceivable that the debit card may substantially replace visits to bricks-and-mortar branches for depositing, for check cashing and for transfers between time and demand accounts, without substantially affecting the use of credit cards or checks for retail purchases. This latter question is the one we turn to now.

THE ELEMENTS OF COST

As in the case of demand deposit transactions with a bank, payment by check or bank credit card at a point of sale involves not only costs to the bank but additional outlays by the customer making the payment and by the merchant receiving it. It is worthwhile to characterize and catalogue these costs for each of the parties, deferring until later any discussion of changes in the pattern of charges that may result from expected innovations.

First, *for the bank,* the cost of a check transaction is the cost of receiving it as a deposit, imprinting the amount on it, transferring it through intrabank accounting and then on to the writer's bank through the clearing system and receiving the funds through the clearinghouse. At the drawee's bank, there are the additional costs of posting it to the customer's account.

If the purchase is made with a credit card, much of the process is the same, with a draft replacing the check itself. The main difference arises from granting credit to the customer instead of debiting his account. Up through the sending of the statement, the process is unchanged, but there are additional costs of (1) evaluating the credit risk of the customer and authorizing the extension of credit, (2) collecting the debt and (3) any foregone interest.

The more modern electronic debit card will supply full positive authorization[1] and eliminate most of the handling of the check, at the expense of incurring costs for a network capable of granting such authorization. But it must be assumed that any network capable of granting full positive authorization on a debit card will be capable of granting up-to-date full negative authorization[2] on a credit card at equal or lower cost. Therefore, all comparisons made hereafter are to be understood as comparisons between the present technology, involving checks and credit cards as presently used, and the future technology, involving fully on-line credit and debit cards.

Second, *for the merchant,* accepting a check involves the cost of his own method of control over check acceptance (credit authorization) plus the write-offs and collection costs of bad checks. There also may be a small delay in having funds credited to his account, compared to currency payment.

Accepting a credit card involves paying the discount charged by the bank, plus the costs of following the bank's authorization procedures, including phone calls under present standard technology or terminal authorization under the new electronic technology. It should be kept in mind that the merchant may ignore bank authorization procedures and, in effect, pay the discount plus the cost of the store's own credit authorization procedures plus any items that may be charged back as a result, if he thinks those total costs are lower.

Accepting a debit card eliminates the risk of bad check loss as long as bank authorization procedures are followed. It can also permit instantaneous crediting to the merchant's account if that is desirable (taking into account the customer's offsetting desire for float).

Third, *for the customer,* paying by check involves the bank's charge (if any) for checks; the time spent in writing the check, getting it accepted and reconciling the bank statements; and foregone interest on the balances that must be held to make sure it is honored. The latter is reduced by the extent of dependable float.

Use of credit cards under present technology involves the time the clerk takes preparing a draft, the time spent in the authorization process and the time spent in checking and paying the bill when it arrives. If the amount is not revolved, there are the advantages of a more leisurely opportunity to arrange for the transfer of funds to cover the bill[3] and, in comparison with using checks at the point-of-sale, a reduction in the number of checks to be written. Currently there is no per item charge to the customer for drafts as there may be for checks.

Electronic technology will offer substantial reductions in authorization time for both credit and debit cards and will, eventually, probably eliminate much of the actual writing of either checks or drafts. For the credit customer, other things being equal, it will shorten his free period; for the debit card customer, it will reduce the float.

The above assumes, of course, an honest customer. The fraudulent customer will, under the electronic system, shift his preference toward checks, except to the extent that the superior acceptability and greater access to funds encourages theft of cards and their use before the theft is detected.

Having sketched this outline of the cost impact of credit and debit cards and the new technology on various market participants, we now proceed to a more detailed economic analysis which will spell out the pattern of demand and probable structure of prices.

THE CONSUMER'S VIEW OF THE NEW TECHNOLOGY

We start with the outlook from the consumer's point of view, which is probably the most straightforward, and examine first the considerations determining whether payments are made by check or credit card.

THE CHOICE BETWEEN PAYMENT BY CHECK AND BY CREDIT CARD

Our outline of the different techniques of payment suggests that the customer who intended to make only a single purchase per month, who did not need credit financing and who had an account with no service charge for checks should prefer to pay by check rather than use his credit card. For, once he has paid by check, the transaction is virtually completed, requiring only a minor incremental effort in statement balancing at a later date. With standard technology, the time spent in effecting a credit purchase is approximately the same as for check writing but requires an additional and similar outlay of time when the bill is received and final payment made.[4]

But while the check dominates the credit card in these circumstances, the very restrictiveness of the assumptions suggests that check dominance will be atypical. At a minimum, of course, transactions in which credit is necessary will result in dominance of the card. Moreover, as the customer's number of transactions per month increases, the extra cost of card transactions (writing the check for payment of the credit card statement at month end) diminishes as a factor in discouraging credit card use. Furthermore, as the number of transactions increases, it becomes increasingly likely that the customer will face some cash management problems: (1) he will have to replenish the checking account from savings or from a spouse's account to cover a desired purchase or (2) he will have to defer a purchase until an already scheduled deposit is made or (3) a current transaction will increase the possibility that some future transaction will produce either of the aforementioned effects.

All these advantages of the card over check use are intensified if the transactions are occurring relatively far from the customer's bank, as on a trip. They are also intensified in family situations where two or more members are drawing on the same account or demand balances are split between multiple accounts. In the latter case, whatever the algorithm for splitting the balances, there will, for any given amount of balances, be situations where one is depleted and the other not. Whatever the level of transaction costs, maintaining optimal multiple balances requires an increase in total balances, unless some low-cost overdraft feature like a credit card is available. In addition, there will be an incentive to use the card rather than the check whenever the card can be used to simplify budgeting—to separate expenditures for tax purposes, for intrafamily purposes, or for other record-keeping purposes. As a result, we should find that, other things being equal, cards are used in place of checks to a greater degree by customers who travel, who are married, who have relatively greater expenditures on discretionary goods or a high degree of variance in expenditures and who have high opportunity costs of time.

In addition, use of the card *for credit* will be split among two quite disparate groups: those whose cash flow problems are important and those whose time costs are high. The first group will include (a) young professionals whose present income is low compared to future expectations and who wish to borrow against future opportunities, (b) persons whose income is variable and find it helpful to use credit to help smooth the fluctuations,[5] and (c) those whose purchases are lumpy relative to total consumption.[6] The second, high-time-cost, group of credit users will use credit card credit because, given the small amounts usually involved, the cost of applying for a bank loan at lower interest and waiting for its authorization is greater than the premium interest rate paid on using the more expensive card.

Finally, we should find that nonrevolvers will use credit cards in lieu of checks in almost every situation in which either is acceptable, so long as they expect to use one or the other several times a month. Revolvers will be more selective, using the card either occasionally for larger purchases or with high intensity when income is less than expected. Even if we ignore the convenience aspects of credit card use, pure interest rate considerations call for this behavior. The nonrevolver is being extended credit at a marginal cost of zero; the revolver is getting credit at 18%. With any opportunity for a positive alternative return on demand balances, nonrevolvers will avoid check writing wherever possible, while revolvers will minimize their use of credit. For nonrevolvers, the only impediment to using credit cards for all substantial transactions to free funds for investment is that the cost of managing bank balances that closely may offset any feasible interest earnings on invested balances. And as we will see, the debit card may ease this constraint.

While existing data have not been collected with our hypotheses in mind, what information we have typically supports our view. The data even suggest that the relative lack of interest by older families in credit cards may be attributable as much to smaller credit needs and more stable consumption patterns as to the usual explanation of conservatism and aversion to change. For any given income level, the older household will have more accumulated wealth, greater stability of income, a larger stock of durables and a lesser expectation of income growth, all leading to a lower degree of card use. Similarly, single persons appear to use cards to a greater degree than families with the same income, but this is fully consistent with our model because the opportunity cost of time of the single person is usually, in fact, higher than that of the family.[7]

Thus, in the absence of electronic technology, something approximating the existing balance between credit cards and checks seems likely to continue. Cards have undoubtedly replaced checks and are probably slowly continuing to gain market share, in a disequilibrium sense. That is, as marketing of credit cards and awareness of them continues to increase, we would still observe the switch to cards by people who, if fully informed, would have found it profitable to switch even earlier. If we describe as "maturity" the situation in which everyone is using cards at what would be the optimal level with full information, then even after maturity we should continue to see some switch away from checks to credit cards as per capita income grows and both the volume of transactions per household and the opportunity cost of time increase.

THE IMPACT OF THE DEBIT CARD

How will this picture change when we add the debit card with the new electronic technology to the list of choices, if at the same time we assume that technology will be applied, to the maximum extent possible, to credit cards as well? The immediate impact of the electronic terminal is to reduce the consumer time required for authorization for any card accommodated by the terminal. Let us concentrate first on what this means for the competition between debit card and check. If a debit card payment can use the terminal while the check payment cannot, the customer is faced by a trade-off between reduced time costs for debit card payment and immediate rather than deferred transfer of the funds.

If the immediate transfer and loss of float involved only the market interest rate on the funds, the comparison would be easy. A $40 payment deferred 3 days at 7% interest rates saves only 2.3 cents, considerably less than 1 minute of time at even minimum wage rates. Even without some price incentive by the merchant or bank, the majority of checks would be displaced by debit cards; and as we will see in our later discussion, there would be ample economic reason for the merchant and bank to grant such an incentive, e.g., by delaying the actual transfer of funds for 2 or 3 days or by offering the nominal discount required to offset float loss.

A more difficult analytical problem arises in those cases where the advantage of float is the opportunity to cover a check for which there were insufficient funds when it was written. Various studies of check use suggest that this is not an uncommon occurrence. Variations of this and other uses of float[8] constitute a major consumer objection to automatic bill paying. For example, while it is expensive to write a check which requires an immediate trip to the bank to cover (deposit by mail is particularly ineffective in this case), it may be still more expensive to be unable to complete the purchase at all. What seems most likely, however, is that, although a large fraction of customers may use the float this way at some time during a year, each customer does so only infrequently and in the aggregate they constitute only a small proportion of total transactions. Hence, these considerations seem unlikely to retard significantly a shift from checks to debit cards, if other factors favor the shift.

Introduction of the debit card will enable merchants to discriminate between these two kinds of checks. As the card becomes more common, it is likely that ordinary checks will increasingly be subjected to charges that reflect their status as short-term credit extensions. In a world in which every demand depositor was given a checkbook and a debit card, any store with facilities to accept both would know that customers who insisted on tendering checks were in effect demanding credit and would treat them as credit customers. Thus, it is likely that if terminals were costless to the merchant (and that is an important "if"), check transactions would be diverted either to debit cards or to some explicit form of credit, although as we will see, all of this credit might not take the form of the current credit card.

Thus, debit cards are likely to dominate checks backed by money in the bank, but they are unlikely to dominate credit cards. Creation of a debit card makes payment by check easier, but the same electronic technology also makes payment by credit card easier. If merchants have terminals accepting all cards, then any customer who is offered an opportunity to pay with his debit card will also have the opportunity to pay with his credit card. Any nonrevolvers among this group will have every incentive to use the credit card in that situation. Not every such choice by nonrevolvers will be for the credit payment. There will be some cases of aversion to credit use, some cases where credit is temporarily limited by the bank's limit on advances, some cases where the customer is not sure whether he will or will not be able to revolve and so on; but the credit card choice should predominate. Paradoxically, the existence of debit cards, by reducing the costs of fine-tuning demand deposit balances, will create some incentive to switch to credit cards from checks for high deposit balance individuals who did not feel formerly that the opportunities for increased interest earnings were large enough to outweigh the costs of funds transfers. There will be a similar incentive to shift currency transactions to credit cards as the latter become more economical of time; but, as we will see later, this shift should be much more modest than that from checks.

If we now turn to customers who have revolved their accounts in the past, we see that they will have an incentive to open two bank credit card accounts: one for charging amounts they intend to revolve and another which they will not revolve for payments they would previously have made by check. Sums corresponding to the latter account can then earn interest at the savings account rate and can be accessed and transferred by debit cards. At present any tendency to do this is reduced by the costs of shifting money among accounts; and, for relatively small interest payments, is not presently economic. A depositor paying $500 per month through his demand account for purchases which could have been charged through credit cards could earn a maximum of about $1 per month in interest by charging them. Anyone with that level of monthly check payments is earning far too much to make that practice attractive at present, if it involves one or more trips to the bank.[9] With a debit card that reduces bank access costs it will be more attractive, though it is difficult to predict the extent to which such activities will develop.

There are a few more minor effects that are likely to work in favor of credit cards. A present advantage of checks is the checkbook, with its continuing physical record of balances. It does not seem that most credit card holders keep a similar cumulative continuous record of credit card debt; instead, they concern themselves primarily with keeping the balance under the card's credit limits (or their own personal limits, if lower). Indeed, this lower degree of surveillance is one of the attractions of the credit card. With a debit card, it would appear to be more difficult to keep the same degree of control as with checks over demand deposit balances, thus increasing the risk that a proferred debit card would be rejected by the terminal, causing embarrassment. This is generally recognized, and it is commonly assumed that many debit cards would carry an overdraft provision to avoid such a situation. Overdrawing a demand account with a debit card would, however, be more costly for nonrevolvers than proferring a credit card in the first place, since under prevailing practices it would result in instantaneous interest bearing debt. Therefore, for nonrevolving customers with both cards and with any substantial uncertainty about their demand balances, there will be an incentive to use the credit card in place of the debit card; prior use of the debit card will be likely to increase uncertainty compared to prior use of checks. While this situation is almost surely going to exist to some extent, we have very little evidence on its quantitative effect.[10]

THE MERCHANT'S POINT OF VIEW

THE COSTS OF CHECK ACCEPTANCE

The merchant's situation is a little harder to evaluate, not because it is analytically more difficult but because the correct evaluation depends upon empirical magnitudes which are not known. We have already alluded to the fact that merchants incur substantial costs in accepting cash, both currency and checks, for their goods. Indeed, an average merchant who pays a marginal 2% discount on his sales by credit card can actually save money, if he does this in place of accepting checks on which he incurs 2% credit and collection loss. It is, however, virtually impossible to collect systematic data which indicate whether the appropriate number is 2% or 0.1%. Some supermarkets claim to have check losses less than 0.1%—a figure which is so low as to make it barely rational to pay (as some do) 10¢ a check for terminal-based check guarantee cards, even in the absence of charges for the terminal itself. On the other hand, many small merchants when offered the choice of a check or bank card prefer the card, which supports an estimate nearer 2%. Indeed, one can find estimates in retail trade journals as high as 5%.

It is probably true that these wide ranges reflect some economies of scale, with the largest establishments actually having costs near the 0.1% level and the smaller ranging upwards of 2%. Accounting data suggest that many other factors are very influential—that such losses vary widely among types of retailers and among regions of the country and neighborhoods within a city, in response to a broad range of economic and cultural phenomena.

It is important not to draw the wrong conclusions from this variation. If there is a higher loss rate in smaller establishments because of economies of scale, these more convenient establishments will charge higher prices for the goods sold, for any given set of locations, than they would if their costs were not so high; and they will operate at a somewhat larger scale with less convenient locations than they otherwise would. If any one of those firms could eliminate the diseconomies of smallness, it would profit; if all of them knew of the innovation, no one would profit but the consumer, but all retailers would be forced to adopt the innovation and more propinquity would be supplied.

The greatest significance of the magnitude of check losses for this study arises from its impact on the acceptability of checks versus debit cards. Again in this context, economies of scale are important. It is probable that much of the scale economy lies not in credit evaluation but in credit collection. A store of any size can ask for the same identification cards and get the same identifying data on each check cashed, which is all that most of them do. What diseconomies of smallness exist in this sphere probably turn on the fact that the proprietor-manager of a small store is required to do more of this work at a higher time-opportunity cost than in a larger establishment. So it is unlikely that the percentage of bad checks taken is much larger in small retail stores than in large ones (other than supermarkets); what really creates scale problems are costs of collection without specialized personnel.

Supermarkets are a special case, not only because of their large volume of transactions but because of the frequency of customer visits and stability of their clientele. Most large retail establishments are low-price nonconvenience stores, which draw customers at irregular intervals from a wide geographic area. Supermarkets draw customers from a smaller area, and those customers usually come to the store once a week or more. For a supermarket to require a special card for check cashing does not inconvenience customers much and does not require the maintenance of an enormously large file. This requirement of a card, or even visual recognition in many cases, probably accounts for the low supermarket loss rate; and this factor may explain why even large nonfood stores may have loss rates many times higher, as the data indicates is the case.

THE EFFECT OF DEBIT CARDS ON CHECK ACCEPTANCE

For our current purposes, let us assume that general bank card retailers, other than supermarkets, experience from 0.5% to 2% loss rates on checks. Now, assume that we arrive at a system in which all banks offer demand deposit accounts with both checks and debit cards. Consider a merchant equipped with terminals which can read all cards. He knows that his customers can pay him with either checks or cards but will lose (say) 3¢ worth of float by making a debit card payment. In general, their loss is not his gain, since his bank may well be giving him credit for the deposits before the checks actually clear. However, each customer who pays him with a debit card increases the default risk of each remaining check payer; all the outright fraud and stolen checks, plus the customers who write checks without adequate balances with the intention of covering them either before or after they bounce, will be concentrated in the check-presenting group. Since the groups are of identifiably unequal risk, the merchant will seek to encourage the less risky customers and discourage the more risky customers. The result is instability. Under the postulated conditions, the merchant may not accept checks at all or may accept them only for a significant fee.

All customers who previously offered checks who do have money in the bank will receive enough to induce them to offer debit cards instead.[11] The remainder constitute fraudulent checks, third party checks and checks offered without funds but with good intentions. In the place of forged or stolen checks offered against stolen identification, the merchant will occasionally be offered a fraudulent credit card. But for present purposes we will assume either that fraud will not be feasible or (more likely) that the bank or real card holder will bear the loss rather than the merchant. Where a customer would now write a check without funds, he will have to offer a debit card with an overdraft feature, a credit card or (if the category is important enough, which is doubtful) some special high-risk credit. Policy toward third-party checks will remain roughly unchanged; there will be no reason to look upon them with any great suspicion; but, since the average return-risk ratio of alternative means of payment will have improved, they will be relatively less attractive for payment and standards for acceptance might be raised.

These results have been arrived at under strong assumptions. First, let us weaken the assumption that all banks offer cards, but continue with the assumption that with terminals the merchant's loss rate is reduced to zero on all debit card payments. Obviously, merchants will prefer the cards of Bank A customers to the checks of Bank B customers. The consequence in practice is not clear. At a minimum there will be some increase in the care (and time) taken in check authorization. This will discourage banking at B, particularly by the more valued, high-time-cost customers, and produce a switch of high risk customers from A to B. If these switches are extensive enough, there will be no stable equilibrium that allows Bank B to remain in existence. Not much attention has been given to the minimum scale of a bank that can economically provide on-line computer access to its DDA's, but unless this is feasible at small scale, very small banks may be jeopardized. It is probable that smaller banks will have to contract out such on-line computer control to larger firms, and this might limit their flexibility.

THE ISSUE OF MULTIPLE TERMINALS

Now consider a situation in which all banks issue debit cards, but some merchants do not have terminal facilities for all cards. For cards which are accepted by the merchant's terminals, we assume that all losses are eliminated. With respect to customers holding cards not compatible with the merchant's terminals, there are two factors operating. The widespread use of cards will discourage checking account fraud since it reduces the opportunity to use the account fraudulently, i.e., only at stores without terminals. But, while there will be a reduction in the overall fraud risk of accepting a debit on any given bank, all of the remaining risk will fall on the stores which continue to accept checks and off-line debit cards. Merchants without terminal facilities for all cards will be at a disadvantage, but the situation is not necessarily unstable, as is the case for the bank without a card.

To get a clear grasp of this situation requires some discussion of the reasons why merchants might not have terminals for all cards. If terminal costs to merchants were zero, obviously all merchants could accept all cards; but zero costs imply not only that no charge is made for equipment and maintenance, but that the space used by the terminals has no alternative use. While it is conceivable that banks might assume all equipment costs, space has alternative uses, enough so that merchants have sometimes claimed that all cards must be accommodated by a single terminal. If there are numerous terminals, if they are hardwired and have printing mechanisms and particularly if they must be accessible for the customer to enter personal identification numbers, the space costs may not be negligible; but it is unlikely they will be quantitatively important, as we will show later. On the other hand, it is also not likely that terminals will be supplied free, and, given the cost of such systems, the problem of multiple terminals will be significant. We will, therefore, attempt to estimate the costs to the merchant of terminals.

THE VALUE OF A TERMINAL FOR DEBIT CARD USE

As the new systems are introduced, each one will have a certain set of initial customers. In the short run, merchants will install terminals if the costs of attracting those customers are exceeded by the benefits, regardless of any long-run, ideal situations that they may expect or prefer. Let us analyze these costs and benefits, using a cost figure per terminal of $35 per month—a figure which is lower than anything currently available, which applies to a terminal that would not include a printer but which private sources estimate to be feasible in the immediate future. Estimates of check procesing costs to banks for on-us checks vary considerably, but 16¢ seems to be a common figure. In addition, there are estimates that one-third to two-thirds of these costs can be eliminated by electronic technology. For simplicity, let us use 10¢ as the saving for each check displaced by a debit card. In addition, each merchant may save 0.5% to 2% of bad check expenses, or 12¢ to 50¢ on a $25 transaction, by using the terminal. Estimates by others, which seem reasonable to us, suggest that such a terminal might save 10 seconds per transaction. If there is never a queue at the point of sale, this will be the complete time savings; with a queue, savings will be greater. If we assume a 15-second average time saving, 8¢ per minute customer costs and 5¢ per minute clerk costs, we get roughly an additional 3¢ savings per transaction. There will, of course, be greater savings for higher income customers and for stores with longer queues. Thus total savings will come to about 25¢ to 63¢ on a $25 transaction.[12] If terminals are only used for debit transactions, it will take between 56 and 140 such transactions per terminal per month to defray the costs of the machine.

Our analysis implies that the bulk of the savings will accrue to the merchant, who should expect to bear the bulk of the costs. It also seems reasonable to assume that the merchant will be in the best position to extract a reward for the customer's time savings. If we make that assumption, the merchant should, on the average, pay somewhere between $^{15}/_{25}$ and $^{53}/_{63}$ of those monthly terminal costs, or from $21 to $30, although the actual charge is likely to be a fixed monthly fee plus a marginal charge per item.

Of course, more elaborate terminals can effect much greater savings of merchant and customer time and bank processing costs by automatically printing customer receipts and short-circuiting the flow of paper through the banking system. By one estimate, such systems can save 55 out of a currently estimated transaction time of 90 seconds for a check payment. Even without queueing, such time savings will amount to around 12¢, with concomitantly larger savings in bank and merchant processing costs. But such savings can only be achieved with more expensive terminals, and we have no current estimate of the increment in capital cost.

THE VALUE OF A TERMINAL FOR CREDIT CARD USE

If allowance is made for credit card customers using the same terminal, the required number of debit transactions is reduced and with it the fraction of costs to be borne by the store. The current marginal merchant discount on credit card purchases is around 2%. Let us assume that the current average free period across all customers is 30 days and the opportunity cost of money is 8%. Then the cost of the free period is about 0.67% of sales, leaving about 1.3% to cover bank processing costs of the merchant draft, initial cardholder accounting (i.e., not including repeated billing or collection efforts) and authorization costs. On a $23 item, this is about 30¢. If we assume that the cost of processing a credit draft is approximately the same as that for a check, about 16¢, this leaves 14¢ for statement and authorization costs. If we assume that authorization cost is reduced by an even greater proportion than check processing, we may assume that 20¢ out of the 30¢ charge can be saved on each item electronically processed. In addition, on revolved accounts, there is an average credit and collection cost of about 3% of outstandings, which is equivalent to about 1.5% on sales.[13] This represents a cost to the bank of about 35¢ per transaction. If we assume terminal authorization will reduce that cost to 10¢, we get total savings to the bank, per credit transaction through the terminal, of 45¢.

Present costs to the merchant of a credit card transaction, aside from the discount, are largely time costs: the costs of completing the draft and of following bank card authorization procedures or of accepting chargebacks, whichever is smaller. The savings in credit card transaction time are about the same as those for debit cards—around 3¢ per transaction. Savings on authorization procedures will be only a few cents per transaction. Total savings to merchants should be no more than 5¢. If that figure is correct, for credit transactions the bank will end up bearing the major fraction of the terminal cost, probably 90%.

The value of store space. In making the above analysis, we have to this point neglected the costs to the store of the space used by the machine. However, even if we assume that the terminal itself will entirely occupy a square foot of floor space (which is very large if we recognize that a foot of floor space supports several feet of display and storage space) plus several more square feet for auxiliary equipment, the opportunity cost of the space should probably be less than $15 per year or a little over $1 per month per terminal and, thus, a relatively small fraction of total terminal costs. Whatever such costs there are should be added to the cost of the capital equipment itself, and such costs will be divided, in the long run, in proportion to the benefits derived, regardless of who makes the actual installation.

It is from this point of view that one should analyze the recent suggestions by some merchants that banks should pay stores for the opportunity of installing their terminals and utilizing store personnel for executing bank–customer transactions. Just as supermarkets were not able to pass on check cashing costs to banks prior to the debit card, so retailers generally will not be able to charge banks for terminal transactions under EFTs *if* the benefit accrues to the retailer. If, however, terminal access becomes so ubiquitous that there is no competitive advantage to any retailer over supplying cash to its customers, that burden will, indeed, be shifted back to the banks.

The impact of terminals on cash sales. To have a major impact on the current volume of currency payments, a terminal transaction will have to possess some element of superiority to offset its higher time costs. Available estimates indicate that a typical cash sale saves 60 seconds as compared to either a credit or a check transaction. For the higher income customer, that time saving can range from 8¢ ($5 per hour) to more than 25¢. A terminal with printing capability might displace cash transactions by providing superior evidence of payment. At present, the biggest obstacle to cash payments by high-time-cost people is the necessity of maintaining and replenishing a large cash balance. A credit card which saves only 10 seconds per transaction will have little impact on the level of cash transactions. A debit card with the same time savings, but which also makes cash replenishment much quicker and easier, might actually encourage the use of cash relative to checks and point-of-sale-(POS)-debiting. A full, paperless EFTS service, which makes cash and debit card use equally easy, might make huge displacements, but that will call for a more expensive terminal system with a printer.

The impact of terminals on the scale of retail operations. It is difficult to predict just what level of transactions will flow through a terminal system at a given store, since it depends in part upon the ability of the machines to attract sales which are currently made for cash or off-line credit. We can, however, get some idea about likely transaction levels from existing pilot experiments with terminal authorization of credit cards. In Wilmington, Delaware, a terminal system test averaged 25 transactions per month. In a WSBA study in California, the corresponding average was 65 transactions per month per terminal.[14] Since the distribution of sales is usually highly skewed, these averages suggest that as many as half the merchants were not producing a volume at which it would have been profitable to use the terminals. Even if we assume that adding debit card capability will double these averages, a substantial fraction of the merchant population will not be able to cover the costs of the single terminal unless inelasticity of demand for convenience permits a rise in store prices sufficient to cover some of the costs.

Presumably, with a single terminal capable of handling all cards there will be a greater volume of transactions per store and, therefore, more stores will be able to justify their installation. However, in any event the installation of terminals will increase the economies of scale in retail establishments, and, if single terminals will not accept all cards, the increase will be even greater. This need not reduce the number of stores in direct proportion to the increase in the size of the minimum cost store, since customers' demand for propinquity may be quite inelastic; but it will make some stores superfluous.

Even if one ignores the impact of multiple terminals on the ability to attract customers, we can see from the cost figures that larger stores could easily afford to have multiple machines. Furthermore, some small stores which can not justify multiple machines based solely on savings in costs may be able to justify more than one machine because of customers' willingness to pay an incremental price for the convenience. In still smaller outlets, it may be possible to charge prices which permit installation of one machine and check acceptance from other customers. But it seems inevitable that the widespread adoption of debit cards will increase the optimal scale of retail outlets, and in the short run this will produce pressure on profits. It is this prospect that produces the insistence of merchants that all debit cards be accepted by a single terminal.

THE BANK'S POINT OF VIEW

Our previous discussion has already defined the advantages and cost savings that EFTS technology holds for banks in the process of payment transfer and credit extension. We now consider the implications for the structure of bank competition and profitability.

Notwithstanding the restrictions imposed by the regulatory authorities, banking is essentially a competitive industry furnishing a wide variety of financial products jointly with services designed to facilitate customers' use of those products. The branches, the number of bank officers and teller windows, the after-hours facilities and so on are not supplied out of any philanthropic urge but because the force of competition requires that they be provided, if the bank hopes to attract customers in the marketplace. To be sure, interest rate ceilings or restrictions on branching may mean that the services produced are not precisely the ones that the consumer would prefer in an unrestricted environment; but, given the hobbles placed on competition by the law, the consumer services provided are the ones the customer demands with his pocketbook and patronage. Furthermore, the same force of competition implies that the provision of these services, while competitively necessary, leads only to ordinary profits in the long run. The incentive for seeking innovation stems from a desire to do better than one's competitors in the interval between first adoption of the innovation and the time when all competitors have had time to adjust. This superior performance may, with good fortune, result in additional income earned in the process of introducing a new product much desired by customers. Alternatively, it may merely enable the innovating bank to avoid even greater losses during the period of adjustment. These two kinds of situations will produce different degrees of cheer in the company boardroom, but either may be an inevitable result of technological advance so long as the industry cannot appeal to government to forestall the competitive process. If the new product is desirable in the eyes of consumers, someone will produce it unless restrained by extramarket forces. The best that any competitor can do is to adjust either more quickly or in the most profitable (or least unprofitable) sector of the industry, regardless of whether the result is to enhance profits or to cut losses.

From our analysis in the preceding pages, we conclude that the introduction of electronic technology will be unequivocally advantageous to consumers in terms of time and money. (For a discussion of other issues, such as privacy, see chapter 9.) Managing one's financial affairs is an activity which typically involves more inputs from the consumer than from the bank, and the consumer's time will be economized by EFTS even more than by resource inputs by the bank. Similarly, merchants as a group will find the fully electronic debit card very attractive in savings on check losses and increasingly attractive in savings of time as the technology advances. In the case of the credit card, the initial benefits of the new technology will be felt mostly by the bank, so that demand for the innovation will grow only as the benefits arc passed on through competition to merchants and consumers. Hence, there is no question that EFTS services are socially desirable and, legal barriers aside, that they will be introduced as rapidly as competition demands.

On the other hand, the role that the debit card is likely to play in breaking down interest rate ceilings, plus the independent role it would play in creating excess branching capacity in the banking industry even if ceilings did not exist, suggests that, for those banks which already have substantial investments in a branching network, the addition of an electronic network will not necessarily be profitable. Therefore, any individual bank will find it most profitable to apply the new technology in market areas where it does not already have a system of branches and in functions where, as in the credit card system, the immediate benefit falls on the bank itself. Similarly, since the advantages of the electronic network results in greater economies of scale for some activities than for others, some banking and retail credit markets will be more profitable than others. In the following pages, we address these issues in more detail.

ELECTRONICS, EXCESS CAPACITY AND MARKET AREAS

For both banks and customers, access to bank services through cards and electronic terminals is more efficient than access through conventional branches, at least for those services that can be performed by terminals at merchant locations. Even if all existing banks, knowing they will be disadvantaged by unrestrained competition, were to agree to restrict utilization of the new technology, new organizations unconstrained by an existing branch network will have every incentive to enter the market. Thus, savings institutions have been among the most aggressive entrants into debit card activities precisely because the gains they envision in their business are least likely to displace existing savings and loan business: to a considerable extent, S & Ls attract funds that were formerly in demand deposit accounts, new business not previously served by now obsolete S & L branches. Since they never have had zero interest demand deposits to spur branch construction, they will suffer no loss from paying interest on such new funds as they attract.[15] And although debit cards will probably force removal of demand deposit rate ceilings, that innovation, by itself, does not put much pressure on the ceilings on savings deposits.

But even within the commercial banking system itself, the same reduction in transaction costs that renders current branches obsolete also makes it technologically feasible to expand into market areas in which the bank has no branch network to serve as a hostage against change. In a minor way, we have already seen this in the credit card arena. The advent of cards, even in the nonelectronic technology context, has substantially increased intermarket bank competition. Already the geographic mobility of the U.S. population has produced substantial numbers of bank credit card holders using their cards with merchants far from the market area of the bank that issued the card.

Viewed in conventional bank lending terms, this means that individual customers are regularly receiving installment credit extensions in transactions thousands of miles removed from the bank office. Meanwhile small business enterprises, executing a much larger volume of business, are restricted by the costs of access to dealing with banks much closer to home. A sharp reduction in the transactions cost of making the loans to card holders has produced this rather anomolous result: the consumer gets his credit through a merchant thousands of miles away from the bank merely by presenting a card, while the businessman still has to deal directly with the local bank. This overstates the case a bit, since a businessman who established a line of credit with his bank could presumably draw on it anywhere in the country. The difference is important, however, since the card-holding customer who has moved to a new city can now compare credit terms and conditions for the card with those offered by banks in his new location. For that customer, there is direct competition between widely separated banks.

With the new electronic technology, the opportunities for widening market areas are even greater. Were it not for regulatory restrictions, it might already be feasible for a bank to operate an electronically based consumer business across the country at a cost which, while large, would be substantially less than would be required by conventional means. In those circumstances, the branch obsolescence that would occur would be that of some other bank. To be sure those other banks would have the same incentive to invade the territory of the first bank; but, for the innovating bank with some technological advantage and a small "home territory" relative to the total market area feasible under the new technology, expansion outside of its existing market has economic advantages. Such behavior is not predatory; indeed it would result in a more rapid rate of technological implementation and greater consumer benefits than would be feasible if each bank were confined to its own initial market.

But, since placement of terminals is restricted with reference to geographic area and other conditions pursuant to present regulatory structures, this analysis suggests that there may be a substantially slower rate of change, since a bank with an advantage in technology should introduce EFTS no sooner than the time at which its competitor achieves an equal technological status, *unless* the deposit accounts gained by moving more rapidly (1) are large relative to existing accounts and (2) once gained, would stay with the bank, even at some premium in price. The first condition would be most true for smaller banks (and nonbank savings institutions). The second condition, which is perhaps true under present-day banking, will be harder to meet once the relatively location–free electronic technology is installed. Under present conditions, a depositor may not be willing to transact with a bank several extra miles distant merely for a small advantage in banking services. With card-based accounts, customers will be much less "loyal."

It is worthwhile to stress that these future impacts of EFTS will be quite different from the prior experience with credit cards. To be sure, bank card credit business has not all been a net gain in bank business. Much of the credit business attracted to bank cards would have come to the bank, or at least a bank, through credit extensions to merchants, which would, in turn, have been passed on to the merchants' customers. An additional chunk of the business has been a substitute for individually negotiated personal loans. But there have been no huge fixed costs in the old lending system which could not be converted to the new method of extending credit; and indeed the effects of the new business on the level of bank personnel were positive, because the bank was taking over tasks formerly performed within stores. Since those tasks could be handled more cheaply by the banks, credit personnel requirements for the economy as a whole have probably been reduced, but the excess labor was outside the banks (except perhaps to a minor extent in the section of the bank lending to retail merchants). Moreover, to the extent that bank cards reduce the full cost of credit to consumers, there has been an increase in the total business to be shared.

One other point about competitive advantage may be worth making. The elements of noncompetitive behavior that can be detected in the U.S. banking system are more apparent in one bank towns, where incumbents are protected by either regulation, transportation costs or scale economies, than in urban areas containing large banks. These one bank towns may prove to offer highly profitable opportunities for extending the new technology. Although an electronic network shows even greater scale economies than a unit bank, it may well be true that marginally extending a leased wire into such an area along with the attendant equipment will produce service at less cost than a new or existing bank, to the substantial advantage of small town residents. It still seems likely however, that the ultimate obstacle to such entry (aside from legal barriers) will be the cost of marketing in such a town.

IN SUMMARY: CUSTOMERS FOR THE NEW TECHNOLOGY

If electronic terminals are unhampered by regulation, they will be much more common than bank branches are now, but they will be not nearly so common as are current credit card outlets. The electronic units are much more costly than mechanical card imprinters, and this will have a significant impact on retail outlets accustomed to offering credit facilities and accepting checks. Although the cost of such terminals will restrict the potential market for the installation of terminals at POS locations, these costs will be more than offset by the conversion of cash and check transactions to the new technology at relatively high volume locations; and at such points the terminals will be installed.

At the outset and with a nonprinting terminal, it seems likely that relatively few cash transactions will be converted to either debit or credit cards. Indeed cash transactions may well increase as a result of easier access to cash through the new technology. We also predict that presently nonrevolving users of credit cards will generally prefer to continue to use such cards to the exclusion of debit cards, whenever the choice is available. Credit card users who actually revolve their accounts will continue to use credit; they do not, in general, have the practicable alternative of a debit card because of the lack of funds. Such customers will have a preference for using a debit card over current use of checks, but they will also have a still better alternative—opening a second, nonrevolving credit card account—as long as the amount of use is enough to warrant the (small) extra bother. Thus, present credit card users should continue to use such cards with the new technology, even perhaps switching some current checking transactions to credit cards.

Electronic debiting will dominate check writing in most places where debit cards are available. Checks should ultimately be restricted to transactions which cannot be effected on a terminal: payments sent by mail and purchases made at smaller establishments. The total volume of debiting will be increased by the greater ease of debit card acceptance relative to present checking technology, and debiting will be retarded only to the (probably small) extent that customers use checks for short-term credit extension.

All this suggests that a very large market for the new technology will develop very quickly, given the substantial savings in costs; and there will be rather more use of the technology employing credit cards than is commonly supposed, compared to the more novel debit card. Over the longer run, as the electronic network begins to provide both truly paperless transactions and adequate evidence of payment, there will be increasing competition for the large segment of POS payments currently being made in cash. As electronic payment approaches that of cash in speed, the former should increasingly dominate the latter, slowed only by the increase in costs of electronic transactions as the technology becomes more complex and expensive in order to achieve the elimination of paper. With increases in speed, a substantial fraction of the larger cash transactions will convert to electronic credit, reflecting erosion of the superiority of currency for customers with high time costs. This tendency should be reflected primarily in an increase in nonrevolving credit rather than in debit card use, because the value of time will continue its historic rise and debiting requires closer attention to balances.

We have also spelled out some of the economic problems for banks attempting to introduce electronic technology. For the most part, these center around the role of the new technology in intensifying competition between terminals and branches, as well as between savings and demand deposits, and in eroding bank "loyalty." The debit card poses problems because most of the savings accrue to nonbank activities: the customer's time savings and the merchant's savings on bad check losses are larger than even the important savings to the bank on check processing.

That is not true in the credit card sphere; here, the savings are in credit, collection and fraud losses, costs all currently borne by the bank. Even the large capital costs of a network may improve the relative position of the bank in retail credit granting by increasing the bank's advantage over those merchants not participating in bank card programs. For an innovator in this field, the initial impact on profits of electronic authorization of credit card transactions is uniformly positive, limited only by the fact that most smaller merchants will not be able to justify the terminals, because of high terminal costs, if they can only be used for credit card transactions. To the extent that banks are in a position to initiate the marketing of the new technology, instead of responding to competitive forces, the credit card arena is likely to offer the greatest potential for profit. As competition enters the field, those profits will be eroded, as should be expected, but at least it will be profits rather than losses that will be getting smaller as the industry returns to equilibrium.

REFERENCES

1. Full positive authorization means assurance that the customer has sufficient funds in his account at that moment to make the payment.
2. Full negative authorization means assurance that the card has not to that moment been withdrawn or reported lost or stolen.
3. The customer's opportunity for lengthening the time duration of the credit period by revolving involves a separate decision that he will not select unless it is separately advantageous.
4. We assume that a single purchase would not require a special replenishment of the bank account.
5. This latter population includes both low-income blue-collar workers and high-income salesmen and entrepreneurs. Low income by itself is not an important factor in credit extensions, since a steady low income does not make supplying credit attractive, no matter what it does for demand.
6. This is, of course, outstandingly true for such nonretail trade items as houses but it is also true, to a lesser degree, for other consumer durables. It is not true, however, that durables, per se are natural items for credit. For a well-to-do family, kitchen appliances and cars may be bought for cash; while, for a low-income family, even clothes will be treated as durables and purchased on credit.
7. To be sure, the family income is frequently understated because an "unemployed" housewife is usually producing valuable, though unpriced, goods; but it is usually true that the family member taking care of the home has a lower opportunity cost of time. Also, at any given income level, the single person is likely to be younger and thus to have greater future income potential.
8. One advantage of float is the opportunity it gives for reconsidering a purchase and stopping payment of a check to create leverage for recession. This is, however, a relatively costly procedure that is only rarely used.
9. Since a large volume of monthly payments is made by mail, at establishments not accepting credits or in amounts too small to warrant the customer's trouble, $500 worth of *shiftable* monthly outlays probably corresponds to an annual pre-tax income exceeding $20,000.
10. To the extent that debit cards offer overdraft facilities they are, of course, indistinguishable from credit cards for customers who normally revolve. Thus, in the United Kingdom, where such overdraft facilities are normally available to customers, demand for the U.S. type bank credit card is sharply reduced. The credit card in the United Kingdom becomes, then, a tool for offering the optional free period to higher income customers, and marketing of the card is aimed at a higher income group and emphasizes, much more than in the United States, the no-interest feature.
11. This may not be completely accurate, as noted later in this chapter.
12. In addition, if debit cards displace cash transactions, they might also reduce robbery losses, but we neglect this.
13. For bank credit card operations, outstandings have averaged about 50% of monthly sales on credit.
14. Payment Systems Research Program, *Report V: EFTS Value Analysis,* New York. The cited source actually shows two values; 65 and 130 transactions per month, but the 65 figure has been verified as correct.
15. Of course, S & L's have had an independent incentive to engage in competitive branching because of the interest rate ceilings on time deposits, and those branches will also be made superfluous by EFTS; but attracting commercial bank demand deposits can only help.

[5]

Antitrust Considerations: The Balance Between Competition and Cooperation

Up to this point, we have been exploring the implications of the new EFTS technology as if the outcomes will be determined solely by considerations of economic gain for customers and users. But the economic forces do not have free play; legal rules enter in, limiting alternatives and changing costs. In subsequent chapters we will discuss those bodies of law explicitly addressed to the conduct of financial institutions—in particular, our elaborate system of bank regulation and supervision. In this chapter, we take up the body of rules and policy embraced under the heading of antitrust law.

Antitrust law can be divided, albeit crudely, into two major subdivisions. The first of these, which is intended to deter unilateral efforts of single business enterprises to achieve unduly large market share, does not appear to pose any unfamiliar or uniquely important problems in the area under examination. The second major area of antitrust concern is that which imposes limitations on the extent of cooperation between two or more business entities, and it is this body of doctrine which will bear importantly on EFTS.

Even under the most favorable circumstances imaginable, the activity of banking would have to be concerned with the tangled thicket of antitrust proscriptions. So long as there are at least two banks in existence, occasions will arise when a customer of the first will wish to cause a transfer of funds to a customer of the second, and some minimal degree of cooperation between the banks will be necessary to achieve that objective. Complete independence is impossible. The question to be addressed in this part is not whether the payment systems of the future will be characterized by competition or by cooperation, but, more realistically, how much of each there will be and in what subparts of the payment mechanisms will one or the other be predominant.

THE DEVELOPMENT OF ANTITRUST DOCTRINE

A rather abstract statement of antitrust principles may be a useful prelude to examining the particular financial and technological contexts in which antitrust problems may be posed for EFTS. As previously indicated, the great preponderance of the issues that will be raised in the EFTS context will involve the permissible type and degree of cooperation among separate banking entities. The statutory language predominately involved will be that which appears in section 1 of the Sherman Act: "Every contract (and) combination. . .in restraint of trade or commerce. . .is hereby declared to be illegal."[1] Although one can imagine contexts in which either section 3[2] or section 7[3] of the Clayton Act might also come to bear, each of those sections substantially overlaps Sherman Act section 1, and the foreseeable problems would arise within the area of overlap. Thus, at least for the present introductory purpose, it is sufficient to think of section 1 as the statute in question.

As will be evident from the sweeping and yet obscure phrases which comprise section 1, the statute, on its face, constitutes little more than a broad delegation of power from the Congress to the federal judiciary to formulate, in a case by case fashion, a body of law regarding competitive and cooperative behavior. Such a process of judicial formulation has now been underway for nearly a century.

In the course of this judicial experience, the courts have attempted to stake out certain areas where they deem it both possible and desirable to lay down fairly precise rules of behavior. The primary example of such rules is that "price fixing is illegal per se."[4] That is, an agreement between competing firms that neither will sell an identified product or service at a price less than the agreed-upon price constitutes of itself a violation of the act; the courts will not entertain proof intended to show that the behavior was reasonable or socially desirable given the particular circumstances of the market involved. Similarly, several other types of agreements between present horizontal competitors which have the effect of eliminating all, or particularly important, parameters of competition between them—for example, agreements to allocate geographic areas, product markets or customers between the agreeing firms—are said to be illegal per se.[5]

Certainly one can imagine circumstances in which two or more banks might enter agreements which would run afoul of one or more of these per se rules. Nevertheless, it is not these per se subparts of section 1 that are of interest in the present context. For, although it is true that it would be possible for a combination of banks to violate them, the critical fact is that it will not be very difficult for the banking community to function in the EFTS environment without violating them.

In short, the body of section 1 jurisprudence that is of importance to the banking community with reference to the EFTS environment is precisely that subpart as to which no clear rules have been laid down, that subpart which is said to be governed by "the rule of reason."

Doctrinally, the rule of reason is said to have had its genesis in the *Standard Oil*[6] and the *American Tobacco*[7] cases decided by the Supreme Court in 1911. Prior to those cases the federal judiciary had struggled, without success, to reach sensible results in the cases that came before it by a textual interpretation of the actual words which appear in section 1 of the Sherman Act. But the language posed great interpretive difficulties. It extended to "every combination," so the courts found it very difficult to exclude cooperative behavior thought to be socially desirable on the ground that it did not involve a combination. And given a combination, the only question which seemed to remain open under the statutory language was whether the combination was "in restraint of trade." The pattern of decisions prior to 1911 was to review the facts of the case, decide implicitly that the behavior was or was not socially desirable and then to announce in a totally question-begging manner that trade had or had not been restrained by the behavior. Thus, the "findings" in these early cases, that there was or was not a "restraint," had no factual content but represented only an awkward judicial technique for stating a conclusion reached on the basis of considerations that remained undisclosed.

The change that occurred with the Supreme Court's decisions in 1911 consisted primarily of a more honest recognition and acceptance of what the courts had been doing theretofore. The issue posed by section 1 cases could not honestly be dealt with as one of whether or not the contract or combination exerted some "restraint" on the behavior of one of the parties; for it is always true as a factual matter that an agreement, if complied with, restrains in some way the behavior of the parties to it. The issue was frankly recognized to be whether such restraint as existed was "reasonable" or "unreasonable." And, thus, the rule of reason was not so much a coherent rule as it was a candid recognition that the courts were empowered, and indeed required, by section 1 to wander through the whole of the social and economic calculus, in an effort to say whether a given instance of cooperation between separate entities was likely to yield more by way of social benefits than was lost by the resulting diminution of competitive rivalry.

The evolution of section 1 jurisprudence since 1911 does not permit one to say much more on this topic. In major part, the efforts of the federal courts have been directed at the articulation and refinement of per se rules with reference to conduct widely thought to be socially undesirable. In areas where per se rules are acknowledged to be inapplicable, the passage of time and decisions has done little to narrow the framework of the analysis resorted to, to improve the predictability of outcomes or to give much assurance that justice, in any· of its many meanings, is being served.

Such improvement in rule of reason cases as there has been has resulted from the contemporaneous development of microeconomics as a fairly rigorous and useful predictive social science. But, for the most part, neither the judiciary nor the antitrust bar has any significant formal training in microeconomics, and no statutes or authoritative decisions unambiguously announce that the microeconomists' criterion of allocative efficiency (or even that criterion tempered by some consideration of egalitarian income distribution) is to be the social objective sought under the rule of reason rubric. Nevertheless, the allocative efficiency criterion of microeconomics is probably the best single predictor of outcomes in this antitrust area, and it is probably the most widely accepted analytic framework both for the trial and argument of such cases and for the professional criticism of judicial decisions. In this study, except where some other criterion is particularly identified, it will be assumed that allocative efficiency is the guiding criterion in the rule of reason area.

Although there are many possible formulations, fundamentally the efficiency criterion is that every resource available to a society ought to be deployed so as to maximize the present value of the stream of goods, services and satisfactions those resources are capable of yielding. Both in making comparative evaluations between present satisfactions and in comparing present with future possibilities, the criterion accepts each individual's registered preferences as equally valid and equally weighty. In this calculus, individuals register preferences by commiting to each preference, either through direct production or through market place trades, some portion of the resources which they own. The criterion says nothing regarding the optimum pattern of resource ownership or income distribution; rather, it takes any such distribution as given and recognizes that a different resource allocation will be optimum given one pattern of resource ownership than will be optimum given another, at least if the preferences of the first group of resource owners differ from those of the second group.

Even if the criterion of allocative efficiency were authoritatively enthroned as supreme, it would not, in and of itself, shed any light on the issue of competition versus cooperation. In theory at least, a single, totally pervasive entity, whether a private organization or a government agency, could gather all appropriate information unto itself and then issue orders to all of its subparts to behave in those ways which would yield the maximum attainable quantity and quality of goods, services and human satisfactions to all members of the population. But in the antitrust context, when the choice is between atomistic units and centralized privately administered units, the premise of the law is unambiguously clear: atomistic private units are presumed to be more conducive to optimum allocation.

When the choice is between atomistic private units and centralized public units, the legal choice is far less clear; but, under our pattern of government, this choice is not generally left to the courts to be decided in the antitrust context. The choice of centralized governmental dictation is almost invariably made by legislators; and, when that choice is made, the legislative choice has the consequence of removing the activity in question from the operation of the antitrust laws.

Analysis of the issue of competition versus cooperation by financial institutions in the EFTS environment is particularly difficult precisely because it involves the melding of a variety of activities, some of which have historically been left to the competitive marketplace but others of which have historically been subjected to extensive government regulation at both the state and federal levels; and much of that regulation has been anticompetitive both in its purposes and in its effects. It would be naive to suppose that the federal judiciary, in deciding antitrust cases in the banking area, will not be significantly influenced by the general ambience of this anticompetitive regulatory history, as well as by those explicit statutory provisions that may bear on aspects of any particular problem. The effects of this anticompetitive cultural environment on the courts' decisionmaking will be elaborated at a later point in this presentation. However, at this point it seems useful to make a somewhat more detailed analysis of the implication of antitrust laws for EFTS, as if the problem were not complicated by the complex history of government regulation of financial institutions.

EFTS AND ANTITRUST RESTRICTIONS ON JOINT VENTURES

At bottom EFTS is a communications system, a system for transmitting and recording the occurrence of consentually achieved changes in the asset positions of members of our society. In its fullest development, the payments system must be capable of achieving and recording reciprocal changes in asset positions between any two individuals or entities in the population. In that fullest culmination, everyone must be connected with everyone else, in one way or another. Hence there is a sense in which EFTS is part of a single system that will require an enormous amount of cooperation; and the question arises whether competition can be preserved in any meaningful sense.

To state the conclusion of our analysis at the outset, we believe that it can be and that it should be. Certainly this is true over the very substantial number of years which will intervene before there is in place a pervasive national electronic network that actually connects everybody with everybody else, if indeed that is ever achieved. We believe it would be true even in such a final configuration; for even the ultimate configuration would require merely that everyone be connectable to everyone else by at least one combination of wires and switches, not by *only* one.

But to start at the beginning rather than at the end, the predominant issue of competition and cooperation will arise as financial institutions and, indeed, nonfinancial institutions continue the process, already well started, of building pieces of that communications network designed to satisfy their own commercial needs. In our thinking about this problem, we have found it analytically useful to make a conceptual separation between networks which connect one bank to another (clearing networks) and networks which connect one or more banks to their customers, both individuals and retail merchants (customer networks).

INTERBANK CLEARING

Those segments of the network which connect banks with one another will be roughly analogous in their function to familiar clearinghouse systems. They will differ even from the most modern automated clearing house (ACH), however, in at least two respects. First, the ACH uses batch processing, whereas the electronic funds clearance mechanism or clearing network will have to be on-line if it is to achieve such fundamental objectives as ascertaining the adequacy of the deposit balance of a second bank's customer who is attempting to execute a POS debit transaction with a merchant-customer of the first bank. Second, the clearing network will have to be designed to accommodate a much wider variety of information than is true of the ACH, since the former, unlike the latter, will not be confined to communicating the facts of closed transactions but will be communicating other types of messages such as balance inquiries.

We expect that on-line clearance networks will emerge very gradually and in response to the needs of customer networks. It is of importance, as a policy matter, that entry into the activity of providing such clearance services be kept free of artificial barriers. But even in the absence of such barriers, rivalry in on-line clearance will not be a problem of the immediate future; and antitrust law, being a policy response to private restraints, will not have a significant role to play for some years.

Moreover, the very concept of clearance involves extensive interentity cooperation, and the antitrust problems,when they do arise, will be difficult. Until the demands generated by customer nets become clearer, generalization regarding the permissible limits of cooperation is certainly difficult, perhaps impossible. For the present the most important policy objective, in our view, is to assure that no governmental barriers to private entry and experimentation are created. In this regard, the most threatening prospect is that of government provision of on-line clearance services unaccompanied by charges which reflect the full costs of such services.[8]

This is not to say that classical antitrust problems could not arise in the realm of clearing networks. For example, once several such networks are in place, an attempt to merge by two networks which overlapped in whole or in part might well be attacked under either Sherman Act section 1 or Clayton section 7. And, as a further example, if the preponderance of depository institutions in a geographic area established a clearing network interconnecting one another, the refusal by the group to permit a nonmember financial institution to join the net might, under some circumstances, be attacked as an illegal boycott agreement under section 1. But even the second of these problems, and most certainly the first, is not likely to arise soon.

CUSTOMER NETWORKS

The subpart of EFTS activity in which antitrust has its greatest potential impact is that portion of the network which lies between the bank and the automatic teller machine (ATM) or the POS device. For convenience, we will refer to this portion of the network as the customer network or customer net.

One imaginable configuration of EFTS would involve ownership and use by each individual bank, however small, of its own customer network. Such a configuration would have clear social advantages. Each bank would have strong incentives to discover and adopt technologies which were superior, both in terms of minimum cost and in terms of maximum quality. The speed, the accuracy, the reliability in terms of minimum downtime and the richness in the set of services which could be delivered over the net would all represent choices of competitive strategies for each individual bank. These arguments, of course, are the traditional arguments in favor of atomistic competition, and, at least in a superficial sense, this is the configuration most compatible with the obvious implications of the antitrust laws.

It is almost certainly true, however, that the configuration just described would have disadvantages that would make it unworkable. Economies of scale undoubtedly exist. Given the present state of the technology and the fragmentary quality of the evidence regarding costs that is available to us, it is difficult to say with precision exactly how far these economies extend or even to identify with certainty the scale variable to which costs are most sensitive. We will set forth in Chapter 6 of this paper such conclusions as we have been able to reach on this scale question. It is clear, however, that the average cost per transaction executed over the customer network can be described as a function of the number of transactions executed per unit of time. Average cost per transaction will fall very sharply for a while, as the number of transactions executed increases from zero, and then continue to fall, but at an ever slower rate, until some quite large number of transactions is attained. The critical question is: at what transactions volume does the average cost curve cease to exhibit a significant negative slope?[9]

The measurement of scale economies. Although it will not be possible for the courts to bypass all the difficult factual questions when antitrust cases actually arise, for present purposes we can do so and deal conceptually with the points to be made. Consider the average cost curve illustrated in Figure 8. The units of measurement on that graph have been labeled with sufficient generality so that the curve can be thought of as representing any state of facts that may realistically be found to exist. We wish to focus on three particular points along the length of that curve. The point labeled M may be thought of as the point corresponding to the number of transactions sufficiently large that no further increase in the number of transactions will yield a measurable reduction in average cost. M represents the minimum point on the curve.

We think of the point labeled C as representing a critical point for policy purposes, for reasons to be developed. At this point, the great preponderance of savings in average cost that are attainable in a given state of technology have been achieved, although the slope of the curve here is still measurably negative, i.e., downward to the right. Point C is selected by reference to the mathematical elasticity or steepness of the curve at each point over its decreasing range. The precise value of elasticity that is selected for the purpose of identifying C can be thought of as a policy matter, an act of faith or an educated guess as to the relationship between two different kinds of social gains, the nature of which will be discussed shortly. For present purposes let us simply assume that the elasticity selected as being critical is −0.05 and that C represents that point.

We can convey some intuitive feeling for the meaning of an elasticity of −0.05 in the following way. Consider the percentage decrease in average costs that is attained by an increase of 100% in the number of transactions conducted. The percentage decrease in costs that results will vary over the length of the curve. If we focus on the increase that occurs between 100 transactions and 200 transactions, for example, the decrease in average cost

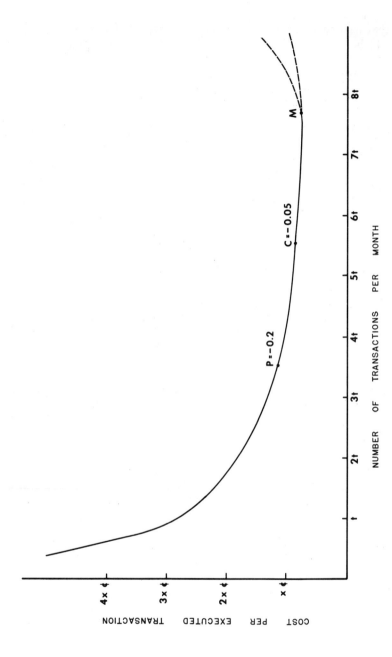

Figure 8. Long run average cost function of EFTS nets over a range of transactional volumes.

over that particular range will be very substantial. Let us assume that it is 40%. Mathematically the elasticity of the curve in this range is equal to −0.4; that is, the value obtained when a 40% cost decrease is divided by the associated 100% transaction increase. Further out to the right on the curve, a doubling of the number of transactions, let us say from 50,000 to 100,000 per week, would lead to a smaller percentage reduction in average costs. Perhaps a doubling in that range would yield a 20% reduction in average cost, and the slope of the curve in that range would be −0.2. For present purposes we define C as representing that portion of the curve over which a doubling of the number of transactions would yield only a 5% reduction in average cost; or, since we wish to think of C as being a point rather than a range, we will define it as that point at which a 1% increase in the number of transactions yields only 0.05% reduction in average cost. Point P is an analogously defined point at which the slope is −0.2.

Note that we might have defined points P and C as bearing some percentage relationship to point M—for example, that the height of the curve at P is equal to 1.2 times the height of the curve at M, and height at C equals 1.05 height at M. In theory one might argue that the type of decision under consideration could better be made with reference to these latter definitions. We would know, for example, that a firm operating at point C is at a 5% cost disadvantage relative to a firm at point M. In practice the value of the curve at M will not be known, and hence points P and C will not be known if so defined. Slope is more readily determinable empirically, and the two approaches yield very similar results. That is, the height of the curve at point C, where elasticity is −0.05, is almost exactly 5% greater than the height at M; and this relationship holds over the range discussed in the text.[10]

The trade-off with competition. With this analytical apparatus in hand, let us turn to a specific hypothetical example of the type of antitrust problem that will be raised in the context of customer networks. We assume that in a particular large but isolated city there are five banks of roughly equal size. The banks are connected to one another by a traditional clearinghouse arrangement, the characteristics of which are not now in question. Each bank is about to install its own customer network. Market studies by each indicate that the number of transactions that will occur over each of the independent networks is sufficiently large that each bank, using the most advanced systems then available, will be operating at point M on the average cost curve. But before any bank makes its individual investment, it is proposed that all five banks join together and install a single system. It can be assumed that the number of transactions that will occur over the jointly owned and operated network will be roughly five times as large as the number of transactions that would have occurred over any single network.

Given these facts, it can be asserted confidently that the proposed joint undertaking violates section 1 of the Sherman Act. Rivalry among the five banks in customer activities will be greatly reduced; and although transaction volume over the network will have been increased fivefold, by hypothesis no further reduction in average cost per transaction will be achieved; the banks can point to no gain in the efficiency of resource use which offsets the social loss resulting from the attenuation in competitive behavior.

The answer is clear, however, only because we have started with the easiest possible case. But even this easiest of cases enables us to identify some doctrinal features of the problems that will arise in the customer network area. Doctrinally, the federal courts will identify problems such as the one just stated as involving "joint ventures." That characterization will lead the court to regard as controlling a particular set of legal precedents. Factually, those precedents involve as a common theme situations in which two or more entities, which are potential competitors in a new area of activity, join forces to undertake that new activity collectively and cooperatively rather than engaging in it independently and rivalrously. In some cases falling within this doctrinal category, the individual participants, prior to the collective endeavor, were not actual competitors in any single product or geographic market (for example, Pan American Airlines and the Grace Steamship Company).[11] In other cases within the category, the individual participants were, before and after the cooperative endeavor, direct competitors in some economic activity distinguishable from the economic activity undertaken jointly (for example, the individual newspaper publishers who were members of the Associated Press).[12] But the critical question in these cases is not whether the parties were actual competitors in some other market prior to the joint undertaking; rather, it is whether the individual parties were potential competitors (that is, potentially individual and independent participants) in the activity for whose conduct the joint venture was formed.

As previously indicated, the question of whether or not a joint venture is lawful under section 1 is a question said to be governed by the rule of reason, and there is little by way of doctrine that will structure the court's inquiry; much will depend on the factual contentions the rival attorneys choose to present and the skill with which they present them. Subject to that influence, the court will conduct an inquiry at large into the general welfare of the community affected.

If the court regards its ultimate criterion as being efficient resource allocation, as most of the legal precedents seem (though not unambiguously) to suggest that it should, then the structure which the court's inquiry ought to take can be stated with somewhat greater precision. In general, the court should be seeking to ascertain whether the resource savings that will result from permitting the cooperative mode of behavior to go forward will be greater or less than the resource losses that will occur from the attenuation of competitive rivalry.[13]

Let us assume that the federal judiciary will in fact behave in EFTS antitrust cases in accordance with this approach. Even so, outcomes in antitrust cases become doubtful as we move away from the particular fact situation set forth in our first hypothetical case. Most cases that will arise will be more difficult than our first hypothetical case in two quite different respects. First, by changing the facts about the number of potentially competing banks, the presence of potential competitors other than banks and the points along the average cost curve at which operations will occur with and without the competitive venture, the "right" outcome becomes far less certain even if all facts in each individual case were known with precision and certainty; second, the facts will not be known with either certainty or any high degree of precision.

In the series of hypothetical cases that follow, we will emphasize changes in the facts and their doctrinal significance. But we will continue to set forth each of those states of fact as if it were confidently and precisely known. In actuality, real world antitrust cases of the kind under consideration, involving, as they do, future developments, almost invariably will leave a conscientious trial judge awash in uncertainty about what the present probabilities really are. Indeed, the litigants and their lawyers, caught in a moment of candor, would admit that they too have only a hesitant perception of what the facts are likely to turn out to be.

Our first hypothetical consortium is easily characterized as involving a section 1 violation because it represents a polar case: a significant lessening of competitive rivalry and no offsetting cost savings as a result of scale economies. The opposite case, which clearly would present no section 1 difficulties, is equally easy to identify. The case might arise in a large metropolitan area in a unit banking state, for example, Chicago. Let us assume that the market structure of depository institutions in such a city is as follows: there are 10 large banks, each of which holds about 5% of the market, and also about 50 smaller banks, each of which holds about 1%. One of the large banks proposes to enter a consortium with five of the smaller banks to form a customer network. Were the large bank to attempt individually to establish a network, the anticipated number of transactions would be sufficiently small that it would be operating at point P on the cost curve where slope is −0.2. By joining with the five smaller banks, the large bank will find transaction volume doubled and the average cost curve slope reduced to −0.1 or −0.05.

Plainly this joint venture should be permitted. The remaining institutions in the metropolitan area are sufficient in number and appropriate in size distribution to permit the formation of nine more joint ventures comparable to this one first proposed. The presence in a market of ten competing nets will be a sufficient number to assure effective rivalry. Significant cost savings will be achieved under these circumstances without significant attenuation of competitive pressures.

Hypothetical cases involving polar situations are helpful to achieve conceptual clarity, but they do not represent the interesting or difficult cases. The entire spectrum of consumer network consortia can be represented, with only a modest degree of oversimplification, as falling in one or another of the nine cells illustrated in Figure 9. In the horizontal dimension, the

ELASTICITY OF AVERAGE COST CURVE

	Large e>0.2	Moderate 0.2>e>.05	Trivial e<.05
M.S.<100% M.S.>50%	1 No Violation pp. 86, 88–90	2 ? pp. 86, 90–91	3 Violation pp. 80–81, 84
M.S.<50% M.S.>10%	4 No Violation pp. 86, 88–90	5 ? pp. 86, 90–91	6 Violation pp. 84
M.S.<10% M.S.>0%	7 No Violation pp. 82–83, 84 88–90	8 No Violation p. 84	9 No Violation p. 84

MARKET SHARE OF JOINT VENTURE

Figure 9. Matrix representation of antitrust outcomes resulting from relationship between joint venture market share and economies of scale. The page numbers in each cell refer to the pages in the text at which discussion appears of the fact situation represented by that cell.

consortia are classified by the extent to which they will achieve scale economies and thus reduce average costs per transaction, in comparison to the
alternative, less inclusive enterprise. Each hypothetical joint venture is assumed to achieve the elasticity shown in its column heading whereas the less
inclusive alternative is assumed to exhibit the elasticity one cell width to the
left. A joint venture in the second column, for example, achieves an elasticity
in the range −0.2 to −0.05; whereas, if the venture is prohibited, the less
inclusive enterprise will confront an elasticity greater than −0.2.

In the vertical dimension, consortia are classified by the extent to which
they create concentration in market share of EFTS services in comparison to
the alternative, less inclusive enterprise. Each joint venture is assumed to
achieve the market share shown in its row heading whereas the less inclusive
alternative is assumed to result in the market share shown one cell height
below. A joint venture in the second row, for example, achieves a market
share in the range 10% to 50%, whereas, if the venture is blocked, the less
inclusive enterprise will have a market share less than 10%.

The two polar cases we have examined so far are those which lie in the
upper right-hand corner (cell three) and the lower left-hand corner (cell
seven). It is relatively easy to say what the antitrust result should be, and
probably would be, in five out of the nine resulting boxes. In the three cells
(seven to nine) across the bottom row, the consortia should be permitted—
they involve no significant penalty in the attenuation of competition. In the
top two cells (three, six) of the right-hand column, the transactions should be
prohibited. They involve at least a moderate degree of anticompetitive loss
and afford no justifying returns to scale. The difficult and more interesting
cases are those represented by the four cells in the upper left-hand corner.
What should be the antitrust outcomes if consortia answering those descrip-
tions are challenged under section 1?

On a very abstract level, one can say that these cases should be approached
and decided by balancing the gains from cost savings against the losses from
attenuation of competition. But that pious generalization is decidedly un-
helpful unless one can go on to say more about how the balancing process
should be approached. To say more about the approach to these cases, it is
necessary to move to a much greater level of particularization in examining
the character and the magnitude of the gains and losses involved.

Types of losses from decreased competition. There are two types of losses
that are likely to result to some degree from a diminution in the number of
competitive networks. The first of these is the familiar phenomenon of
resource misallocation caused by departures from marginal cost pricing in
markets where there is only one or a small number of sellers. Each seller
perceives that he may charge a price somewhat above the cost of servicing his

marginal customer without losing all of his customers. The prevailing market price of customer network services is set somewhat above marginal costs, with the result that consumers cut back on their utilization of these services and resort instead to the most nearly satisfactory substitutes. For example, consumers substitute the use of cash for the use of EFTS services in a context in which the real costs of using cash are actually higher than the real costs of using EFTS, notwithstanding the fact that the perceived costs of using cash are less because of the artificially high price that has been imposed on EFTS services.

This type of social loss is referred to by economists as the dead-weight loss of monopoly, and it is the type of loss at which the antitrust laws are classically thought to be aimed. This type of loss also has the characteristic of being static, in the sense that it can be observed and measured at any particular moment in time; one need not refer to changes over a period of time in order to observe or measure it. We will refer to this type of loss as the "static" loss from attenuated competition, because we wish to contrast it with a second type of loss which may be even more important in the present context.

The second type of loss which should be taken into account relates to the pace, over time, at which the technology of EFTS is advanced. EFTS technology, both its hardware and its software, is in its infancy. One can be sure that the hardware and software systems in use 25 years from now will be different and superior. Whether technological advances occur rapidly or only relatively slowly will depend in significant part upon the intensity of rivalry that prevails among suppliers of EFTS services. If, to take an extreme example, EFTS took the form of a single, nationwide, totally standardized activity, administered by the Federal Reserve System for example, it seems highly probable that the rate of technological change would be relatively slow. New technology could be introduced only if all, or at least a majority, of the institutions providing the service were to adopt it. One of the major incentives for investment in the discovery of new technologies, namely the opportunity for the innovative depository institution to capture additional market share, would be eliminated.

Previously (in Figure 8) we presented the concepts of average cost per customer network transaction as a two-dimensional concept; at any particular moment in time, it was suggested, the average cost per transaction resulting from the use of a particular network was lower if the number of transactions executed on the network was higher. We have no doubt that concept has validity, but it is a static concept and perverse social results will flow if policymakers focus on it to the exclusion of all else. Probably 10 years from now and almost certainly 20 years from now, the cost of executing the typical EFTS transaction will have been influenced far more by the rate of technological change over the intervening period than by the static phenomenon of scale economies. Accordingly it could be an error of great magnitude to make substantial sacrifices today in the intensity of competitive market structure in pursuit of the fullest realization of presently available scale economies; the result will quite likely be a significant reduction in the rate at which costs fall as a function of time and changing technology, with the ultimate consequence that future costs will be higher at every level of scale utilization than need have been the case.

Striking a balance. We have identified three factors which should guide the courts in determining the legality of customer network consortia: the resource loss that stems from failure to achieve scale economies given existent technology, the static loss that stems from noncompetitive pricing and the resource loss over time that stems from the failure to preserve rivalry incentives to technological advance. In those antitrust cases that involve trade-offs between the former and the two latter of these considerations—namely those four categories of cases represented in the upper left-hand portion of Figure 9—what approach should courts take toward the balancing process?

Whether technological change should be regarded as being fully as important as the other two factors or as being substantially less important depends upon the geographic configurations that come to characterize customer nets.[14] If it proves to be the case that customer nets typically are nationwide, following the pattern of the two national bank cards, so that the question becomes one of whether we are to have two such nets or four or seven, then the technological change factor should be given equal weight with the other factors. Although two or three such national nets may come into existence, it seems to us unlikely that this will be the entire pattern. We think it more probable that a substantial number of local and regional customer nets will come into existence in addition to the several probable national nets. Some of these local nets, perhaps most of them with the passage of time, will be linked together into national systems via clearing nets, but the linkages will be looser than those that characterize the national bank credit cards and will permit substantial technological independence. If our expectation is correct, a great deal of opportunity and incentive for technological change will be present, independently of whether there are competing customer nets in the majority of local banking markets. Competing suppliers of equipment and software to these multiple buyers will innovate. Hence the technological advance consideration should play a relatively smaller role than the other two factors.

In any event, we expect these antitrust cases to be decided primarily with reference to the question of how much concentration of market structure should be permitted for the sake of achieving scale economies. The technological advance objective probably will operate only by tipping the balance in favor of competition in what would otherwise be very close cases.

Balancing the competitive pricing objectives and scale objectives would be quite simple if there existed some more or less continuous function which informed us how much above marginal cost prices would be set, given different degrees of concentration in market structure. To illustrate the mythical function to which we refer, one can imagine a precise rule of industrial organization which predicted that, if four or fewer firms enjoyed 100% of the market, they would set prices 100% above marginal cost; if the four–firm concentration ratio was 75% of the market, they would set prices 75% above marginal cost and so forth.

Unfortunately, no such orderly rule of economic behavior is tenable in light of the existing economic evidence. About the strongest statements any responsible economist would be willing to make would be along the following lines: Until four-firm concentration ratios reach a level of about 50% of the market, no significant divergence between price and marginal cost is likely to be encountered. Where four–firm concentration ratios exceed 65% or 70% of the market, an excess of price over marginal cost is quite likely to be observed; but, even at these high concentration ratios, little generalization is permissible about the percentage by which price is likely to exceed marginal cost. As market concentration ratios vary between the 50% level and the 70% level, the probability that we will be able to observe some divergence increases; but again there is no permissible generalization to the effect that the percentage of divergence is a positive function of concentration.

We emphasize that the foregoing assertions, weak and tentative as they are, command widespread acceptance only because they are worded in terms of statistical association and not in terms of causation. If the statements were changed so as to assert that it is the high levels of concentration that cause the marginal cost-price divergences, the assertions would lose the support of a substantial minority of economists, who argue that the concentration does not cause the divergences but rather that both are caused by some alternative phenomenon.[15] But this dispute between segments of the economic profession need not be pursued further, for it is indisputable that present antitrust policy embodies the assumption that concentration actually does cause marginal cost-price divergences.

Although it is not possible to make any precise statements about the magnitude of price-cost ratios as a function of market concentration, it is possible, as a practical matter, to state some outer bounds. Even in industries which exhibit high levels of concentration, it is quite unusual to find price–cost ratios which exceed 1.2 for any significant period of time. That is, even where the seller of a given product or service has a significant degree of monopoly power with respect to that particular product or service, the ability of consumers to turn to the best available substitute products or services is such that sellers maximize their profits by charging price premiums which do not exceed 20%.[16] Since customers will retain the option of using cash or checks, there is no reason to think the provision of EFTS services will be an exception.

Accordingly, a sensible decision rule in antitrust cases regarding customer network consortia would run along the following lines. A consortium including all firms in a local market must, as a practical matter, be permitted if the conclusion is reached that a consortium among firms which represent more than 55% or 60% of the market would be cost-justified; for competitive operation on the part of the remaining 40% to 45% of possible participants, if they are excluded, would not be economically viable. That is, if the market involved is so small that a consortium which included only 50% of the market (and thus left open the prospect of a rival consortium with roughly equivalent transaction volume) would experience costs more than 20% above those attainable by full realization of scale economies, then the proposed consortium should be permitted and provision made for entry into the consortium, upon application, by the remaining firms in the local market. The provision of EFTS services in such markets would properly be regarded as a local natural monopoly.

In such a market, two considerations would counsel against an attempt to use the antitrust laws to attain a rivalrous structure. First, the excessive costs imposed upon the industry and, therefore, the excessive prices imposed upon consumers, would in all probability exceed the monopoly price imposed upon consumers by a private, unregulated, profit maximizing monopoly. Second, in the long run the rivalrous structure would probably prove to be unstable in any event. Each of three alternative outcomes is more likely than is long-term stability under the circumstances described. First, each consortium would have a strong incentive to price below cost temporarily in order to capture a larger market share, gain a cost advantage through attaining the additional scale economies and thereafter exert its cost advantage to push its competitor out of the market. Second, even if neither network ever priced below cost, one or the other of them is likely at some time, perhaps for fairly trivial reasons of customer favor, to achieve a gain in market share at the expense of the other; and it would thereby gain an advantage in cost which would enable it to push its rival out of the market. Third, consciousness on the part of the consortia managers that both the first and second developments are likely to occur would generate enormous pressures for collusion between the two consortia. The results of collusion in this circumstance represent the worst of all possible worlds: monopolistic pricing by both consortia, which takes as its starting point an unnecessarily high level of costs.

Once having recognized the possibility of instability and "destructive competition" between firms of insufficient size to have realized technologically available scale economies, one must ask whether the argument does not run a good deal further than we have taken it to this point. The preceding paragraph recognizes the possibility of instability for firms in which costs are 120% or more of attainable cost levels. But the 120% cut-off point was selected, not because of its relationship to the likelihood of destructive competition, but because imposition of cost inefficiency to that or any greater degree by blocking combination would be a "cure" worse than the disease of monopoly pricing.

Is "destructive competition" likely in the case of two firms each having costs of 102% of the lowest technologically attainable level? It is likely in theory, and it might occur in practice, if the industry were selling a wholly undifferentiated product as to which price competition was the only kind of competition imaginable. But EFTS services do not represent an undifferentiated product, and competition between several such services along a variety of parameters in addition to that of price is not only possible but highly probable. In such a context, the fact that some or all rivals have failed to realize the last few percentage points of technologically attainable scale economies has no inevitable significance for the stability of a competitively structured market. With respect to a service that is susceptible to as much product differentiation as the provision of EFTS services is, we are confident that realization of the last five percentage points of scale economies is irrelevant to the viability of competitive markets.

Accordingly, if a market is sufficiently large to enable two consortia to obtain cost levels that do not exceed by more than 5% the maximum obtainable scale economies, a consortium which represents significantly more than 50% of the market should be prohibited and a rivalrous market structure should be required. At what point above 105% the natural monopoly argument loses its validity in light of the possibilities for product differentiation, we have no confident opinion. That is an empirical question as to which we do not have even suggestive evidence. But, as previously indicated, at some higher level such as 120% we would accept the natural monopoly argument, not so much because we are confident that the argument has attained validity even at that point as because of the improbability that monopolistic pricing would impose greater social losses on the community than the scale inefficiencies of separate firms. Where the cost penalty of blocking consortia is less than 20%, we would limit consortia formation in the hope of attaining stable competition. If the natural monopoly argument has validity at a lower point, say at 15%, it will prove itself in the marketplace through sustained single firm dominance.

Where the cost penalty is greater than 20% for a consortium limited to half the firms in the market, we would permit an all-encompassing consortium even though the consequence is very likely to be public regulation along public utility lines, with all the inefficiency such regulation inevitably involves. But even if such a consortium is permitted and even if public utility regulation is then imposed, entry into the market by a competitor should never be blocked by law. There is no assurance that stable competition is not possible at penalties above 20%, and the fact that a private firm is ready to bet its own capital on the proposition that it can survive is strong evidence either that the natural monopoly argument is no longer valid or that it was never valid.

To recapitulate the argument and to place it in the context of the set of nine cells depicted in Figure 9, the most recent paragraphs argue that no violation should or probably would be found in cell number one. It follows, *a fortiori*, that no violation should be found in cells four or seven, where equally large scale economies are being realized at even lower levels of market concentration. Cell number seven, of course, corresponds to our hypothetical case number two described earlier (see page 82). In cells eight and nine, as in cell seven, no violation is found for the alternative reason that the proposed consortium poses no threat of market concentration. It is true in cell nine that the *affirmative* argument against finding of violation is quite weak, for the scale economies which will be achieved appear to be trivial; but the outcome here is dictated by the salutory principle that arrangements by private parties which are satisfactory to them can be halted under the antitrust laws only upon an affirmative showing that the arrangement threatens harms to the community.

The consortium proposed which corresponds to cell number three was found to constitute a violation; the circumstances correspond to our hypothetical number one set forth earlier (page 80). And we believe that the same result should and would be reached in the circumstances of cell six where less substantial, but nevertheless significant, degrees of concentration would be brought about. In closer cases of this type, the social objective of dynamic technological advance might well come into play to tip the balance.

The most difficult cases to resolve are those depicted in cells two and five. In these two situations the magnitude of the scale economies that would be attained are not trivial, yet they are small enough to suggest that the effects of the resulting concentration on prices to consumers may fully offset the potential cost savings. This latter argument is particularly likely to be persuasive in the situation represented by cell number two, where a single, community-wide consortium is proposed.

On the other hand, as to cell number two, the set of arguments which fall under the heading of "natural monopoly" would push in favor of allowing the consortium. It is not clear, particularly in cases near the upper end of the scale economy range embraced by cell two, whether a rivalrous market structure would prove to be stable even if it were to be ordained by a ruling which blocks the formation of the consortium. If a series of antitrust cases were tried in which the facts corresponded to the range of situations contemplated by cell number two, probably the only safe prediction would be that outcomes would be mixed, a violation being more likely to be found where the cost curve elasticity approached the—0.05 level and less likely to be found where it approached the—0.20 level.

In cases represented by cell number five, a diversity of results is also probable, although the character of the arguments will differ somewhat. By definition, the consortia under consideration here are those which propose to embrace at most 50% of the market and at least 10%. Thus all contemplate some rivalry, and the proponents of the consortia will be unable to bring the set of natural monopoly arguments to bear effectively. In these cases the consortia proponents will be arguing that a less extensive consortium than the one proposed would forsake scale economies to such a large degree that consumers would be worse off, notwithstanding the fact that in the short run there would be more rivalrous units. Opponents will be arguing that a consortium as extensive as that proposed cannot be justified—that the social gains that will flow from having one more rivalrous unit exceed the sacrifices in scale economies that would be entailed. There will be no strong empiric basis for either one of these lines of argument, for the reasons previously set forth. The probabilities that the court will find the proposed consortium violates the antitrust laws probably will increase roughly proportionately to the market share the consortium would embrace.

The distinction between resource waste and income transfer. There is one final argument that might be brought to bear in the cases depicted by cells two, five and, conceivably, six. It involves a distinction that is well developed in the economic literature but, so far as we are aware, has never been urged, much less accepted, in an antitrust case. To explain the distinction, we must develop with somewhat greater precision the nature of the social loss that flows from monopolistic pricing and the nature of the social loss that flows from a failure to attain scale economies.

In Figure 10, the line labeled DD' represents the demand curve for EFTS services in a given geographic market. The line labeled AC-1 represents the average cost curve that will obtain if the supplying industry is organized into a small number of firms each of which is able to realize all attainable scale economies. The line AC-2 represents the average cost per transaction that will obtain if the industry is organized into a larger number of competitive firms, each of which has higher costs because none is realizing all attainable scale economies.

It is quite possible, as we will explain, that the same price would be charged and the same level of output would be obtained as a consequence under each of these alternative arrangements; and the diagram has been constructed on the assumption that that is the case. In that event, under either market structure the price per transaction would be equal to the dimension OP, and the number of transactions that occur would be equal to the dimension OQ_m. Thus, Figure 10 is designed to illustrate precisely the concept previously discussed of a trade-off between the attainment of scale economies and the charging of premium prices as a consequence of market concentration.

Although the same price, OP, is charged under both market structures, the reason that price results is quite different in the two circumstances. In the rivalrous market structure, competitive pressures force price down to a level (OP) which just covers costs, including a normal return to the fixed capital involved in the enterprise. In the case of the concentrated market structure, OP is a price that exceeds costs (again including a normal return) by a monopolistic premium equal to the dimension *ad*.

In the earlier discussion, these two situations have been treated as if choice between them were a matter of indifference to consumers; either way they lost equal sums. But the two situations are quite different. Let us consider first the gains to the *community as a whole* as a consequence of having EFTS services available. In the market configuration in which scale economies have been fully realized, the total cost to the community of producing the service is represented by the area of the rectangle $OdcQ_m$, which is the product of the number of units of the service supplied times the average cost per unit of supplying it. The value to the community as a whole of having the service available is represented by the trapezoid $OIbQ_m$, for this represents the amount that someone in the community would be willing to pay for each unit of the service, summed across the number of units provided. Hence, in the concentrated market configuration, the net gain to the community of having the service available (the amount by which value exceeds cost of production) is the smaller trapezoid dIbc.

Compare this to the situation of the more competitive market structure which fails to obtain scale economies. The costs to the community are now represented by the rectangle $OabQ_m$; the gross value of the activity to the community is the same as before, $OIbQ_m$; and the net value of the activity to the community is now a triangle aIb. The net gain to the community of having the concentrated albeit noncompetitive configuration, rather than

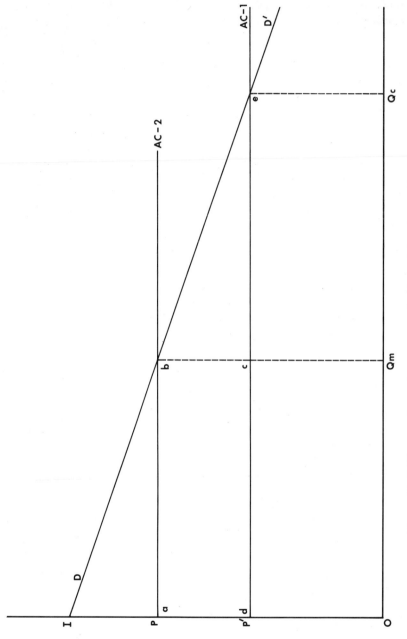

Figure 10. Different price and average cost levels, and associated different output levels, resulting from competition and monopoly in an EFTS market.

the competitive but cost-inefficient configuration, is equal to the rectangle abcd.

The implications of this may be clearer if we engage in one further comparison. Let us suppose it were possible to realize the scale economies through concentration and yet induce the several suppliers to charge a price no higher than that necessary to cover all costs including their costs of capital. Under these circumstances, a price P′ would be charged and Q_c units of services would be supplied. The gross value to the community of the activity would then be the trapezoid $OIeQ_c$; its costs would be $OdeQ_c$; and its net value to the community would be dIe. When the concentrated suppliers cease charging the competitive price of P′ and impose a monopolistic premium bringing the price up to P, two separate consequences can be identified. First, the number of units purchased falls back from Q_c to Q_m. The individuals who heretofore have engaged in those particular transactions which represent the segment of the demand curve lying between b and e now choose to resort to the next best alternative, perhaps the use of currency and checks. Assuming, as is traditional, that this next best alternative, whatever it may be, is a service that is being supplied at its actual cost in terms of the scarce resources preempted, we note that the alternative service being substituted for the EFTS services is actually more costly to the community than the EFTS services foregone—plainly a waste of resources. The area of the triangle bce corresponds to this resource waste; and it is this area that is generally referred to by economists as the static "dead-weight loss" of monopoly pricing.

But, assuming production costs stay the same notwithstanding the change in prices, the area of the rectangle abcd does not represent a cost to the community. It merely represents a redistribution of the gains yielded by the EFTS activity from consumers to suppliers of the services.

Thus, initially, when the concentrated suppliers were charging price P′, the concentrated producers were just barely earning a competitive rate of return on their invested capital and covering their other costs; they were realizing no particular gain from EFTS activities. Consumers were realizing the gain dIe. After prices were raised to P, due to monopoly or oligopoly pricing, the triangle bce disappeared and represented a true resource waste; the rectangle abcd was a wealth shift now captured by the suppliers; and the gain to consumers was reduced by these two consequences to the triangle aIb.

On the basis of the preceding observations, one can argue that, as a society, we should by no means be indifferent to a choice between (1) the situation in which price is forced above the lowest attainable average cost as a consequence of sacrificing scale economies and (2) the situation in which price is forced to that same higher level as a consequence of monopolistic price premiums. While it is true that consumers, narrowly defined, are indifferent between those situations, the community as a whole is not. In the first of the situations, the entire trapezoid abecd is dissipated in the form of waste of scarce resources. In the second situation, only the small triangle bce is thus dissipated; the much larger rectangular area abcd is captured in the form of income by the suppliers of the service but does not represent resources consumed in production. The saved resources are, of course, available for other uses, to society's gain.

The categories of consumers and suppliers are not completely distinct subsets; some nontrivial fraction of consumers will have ownership interests in EFT suppliers. Even those who are not owners will gain something by way of benefit from the fact that those incremental profits will be subject to taxation; the resources corresponding to rectangle abcd will be diverted to the production of other goods and services, reducing their prices; perhaps a small portion will take the form of gifts to charitable activities; etc. But even if the subsets were discrete, and even if none of the indirect transfer by way of taxation or charitable gifts occurred, it would be difficult not to prefer the monopolistic situation to the inefficient situation. The community can be indifferent only if it is content to see some members of the community, the suppliers, made worse off notwithstanding the fact that no one else in the community gains as a consequence of their loss.[17]

This argument, that the community should prefer a price of P which is brought about through noncompetitive pricing to a price of P which is brought about from failure to attain scale economies, we characterized at the outset of its exposition as a "plausible" argument. Our judgment is that it is not only plausible but, by a small margin, persuasive. We think the margin is small, because the argument is open to yet another counterargument about to be set forth. It should be said at the outset that the quantitative significance of this counterargument represents an empirical question, as to which the data in the literature are exceedingly sparse. Whether the preceding argument is eroded to the extent of 5% of its validity or to the extent of 99% of its validity, we do not know.

However, for what it is worth, the counterargument is as follows. Assume that a consortium of all banks in the community is formed to deliver EFTS services; hence, all scale economies are realized and average costs are reduced to the level AC-1 as depicted in Figure 10. The members of the consortium, through either tacit or explicit collusion, all set a price of P for such service, and consequently transactions in the quantity Q_m are purchased by customers. Initially the members of the consortium collectively earn monopoly profits in the amount of the rectangle abcd, and the dead-weight inefficiency loss occurs in the amount of the triangle bce.

In this situation, however, each member of the consortium has a very strong incentive to attract additional customers, for the cost of serving another customer is less than the price which will be charged to him by the amount bc. But there is no possibility (it will be assumed) of appealing to additional customers by cheating on the consortium agreement and reducing price below P. The price being charged is a relatively objective phenomenon, and, if any bank were to cheat as to price, that fact would quickly be discovered by other consortium members.

There are, however, a variety of other ways in which any particular bank may attempt to appeal to marginal customers and steal away customers from its fellow consortium members. One bank starts giving away electric blankets to anyone who opens a new debit card transaction account; the second retaliates by distributing one place setting of china for every thousand transactions one of its cardholders executes; a third gives its cardholders free safe deposit boxes; and so forth. The consequence of this form of rivalry is to force upward the level of average costs. The incentives for this form of behavior continue until AC-1 is raised so as to be coincident with AC-2, at which point all potential monopoly profits of the consortium have been dissipated in various forms of service luxuriation.

The suggestion that AC-1 may actually approach or equal AC-2 as a consequence of this sort of rivalry is by no means fanciful; that appears to be a fairly accurate description of some portions of the airline industry, for example.[18]

In one sense it can be said that the situation, when costs have been pushed to AC-2, is every bit as unsatisfactory as the situation would have been had the consortium never been formed and each individual bank faced an average cost level of AC-2 as a consequence of failure to achieve scale economies. It is just as bad in the sense that just as many scarce resources are being preempted in order to supply EFTS services under the one situation as under the other.

But that statement casts an intraconsortium rivalry situation in too adverse a light. It ignores the fact that what consumers are getting is not the same EFTS service under the two situations. In the latter situation they are receiving for their price, P, a greatly luxuriated service; and one can be sure that the frills are of some value to them. The frills would not have been adopted as techniques of rivalry unless they had the capacity to attract additional customers; and they are capable of attracting additional customers only if they are of some value to the customer. On the other hand there can be no assurance that the frills have a value to customers as great as the costs of the frills to the rivalrous consortium members. A frill which costs the bank $5 may have a value of only 50¢ to a particular customer and yet be sufficient to induce him to shift his patronage in the face of equal explicit prices from all suppliers for the basic underlying service which he desires.

What can accurately be said is as follows: resources which have a cost equal to the rectangle abcd are being wasted to the extent that those costs exceed the value of the frills to the customers. The situation may be as bad as a complete failure to achieve scale economies, but it is in reality probably somewhat less bad.

Conclusion. It seems appropriate once again to recapitulate the argument to the present point. In deciding EFTS customer network consortia cases, the courts will have to strike a balance between pursuit of the competitive objective and permitting attainment of scale economies. This process is at its most difficult in the types of cases represented by cells two and five in Figure 9. With reference to Figure 8, where the downward slope of the average cost curve of a consortium exceeds −0.2, the scale economies argument should prevail. Where the downward slope of the cost curve is less than −0.05, competitive considerations should prevail. In the difficult range between these two points, the court should block the formation of any consortium which threatens to reduce the number of rivals in the market under consideration further than is absolutely necessary to permit operations to occur along that portion of the cost curve where the slope is about −0.10 to −0.15.

In general, this will be tantamount to seeking out the market structure which will yield the lowest price per transaction to consumers. Although sophisticated arguments can be made to the effect that the failure to achieve scale economies is more socially harmful than that degree of monopoly pricing which yields an equal price, there are persuasive counterarguments. In view of the fact that neither the courts nor the parties will ever be completely certain of the precise slope of the average cost curve involved in a particular case, the attempt to take these very sophisticated arguments into account involves a self-delusive attempt at precision. Therefore, when scale economies seem to have become relatively slight, they are likely to be altogether disregarded.

REFERENCES

1. Sherman Act, 15 U.S.C. sec. 1 (1973).
2. Clayton Act, sec. 3, 15 U.S.C. sec, 14 (1973).
3. Clayton Act, sec. 7, 15 U.S.C. sec. 18 (1973).
4. See, for example, *United States v. Socony-Vacuum Oil Co.*, 310 U.S. 150, 223 (1940).
5. See, for example, *United States v. Topco Associates*, 405 U.S. 596, 608 (1972).
6. *Standard Oil Co. v. United States*, 221 U.S. 1 (1911).
7. *United States v. American Tobacco Co.*, 221 U.S. 106 (1911).
8. In this regard, see the critical comments of the Department of Justice on the proposals of the Federal Reserve Board to provide ACH services for member banks. Comments of Department of Justice in response to F.R.B. requests for comments on the F.R.B. proposed amendments to Regulation J, available by request from the Federal Reserve Board, Washington, D.C.
9. One may also ask an additional question: does the average cost per transaction shortly reach a minimum and then remain constant beyond this point over a very wide range, or does it start to rise relatively soon after the minimum point is reached? This latter question is one to which no answer can be given at this time; fortunately it has no critical policy implications for our purposes.
10. For cost functions of the type involved, the elasticity of the average cost curve bears a close relationship to the degree to which the average curve lies above the minimum point on the average curve. That is, at the output, q, at which elasticity is $-.05$, the ratio of the average cost to minimum average cost is almost exactly 1.05. And this close approximation between elasticity values and unexhausted scale economies holds roughly true over the range discussed in the text $(0.2 > e > .05)$.

We illustrate the point rigorously for one particular cost function of the general type that characterizes EFT systems. This function assumes that the system has a fixed annual capital cost of \$k which is independent of the number of terminals installed, and that it also has a variable cost of \$a associated with the attachment and maintenance of each terminal. Total annual costs for a system with q terminals are then:

$$TC = k + aq. \tag{1}$$

And average costs per terminal are therefore:

$$AC \equiv \bar{c} = \frac{k}{q} + a. \tag{2}$$

And the derivative of $\bar{c}$ with respect to q is:

$$d\bar{c}/dq = -k/q^2. \tag{3}$$

The elasticity of the average cost curve is:

$$e = \frac{\frac{\Delta\bar{c}}{\bar{c}}}{\frac{\Delta q}{q}} = \frac{\Delta\bar{c}}{\Delta q} \cdot \frac{q}{\bar{c}} = \frac{d\bar{c}}{dq} \cdot \frac{q}{\bar{c}}. \tag{4}$$

Substituting the value of the derivative from (3) into (4), we obtain:

$$e = -\left(\frac{k}{q^2}\right) \cdot \frac{q}{\bar{c}};$$

and substituting for $\bar{c}$ from (2), we obtain:

$$e = -\left(\frac{k}{q^2}\right)\left(\frac{q}{k/q + a}\right) = -\left(\frac{k}{k + aq}\right). \tag{5}$$

The degree to which scale economies are left unexhausted at any value of q is given by the ratio between $\bar{c}$ at that value of q and the lowest theoretical value of $\bar{c}$, namely, a. Thus, substituting for $\bar{c}$ from (2) we obtain:

$$\frac{\bar{c}}{a} = \frac{k/q + a}{a} = \frac{k}{aq} + 1. \tag{6}$$

Since all variables in (6) are always positive, the value of this ratio is always greater than one by some amount which we define as s. Hence we set:

$$\frac{\bar{c}}{a} = 1 + s = 1 + \frac{k}{aq}.$$

And solving for q:

$$q = {}^k/_{as}. \tag{7}$$

We wish to show that elasticity, e, at any large value of q corresponds in the manner stated above to the value of 1+s at that same value of q. More precisely, we wish to show that one plus the absolute value of e equals one plus s. Hence we set:

$$e = -.05$$

and solve for q, using equation (5):

$$-.05 = -\frac{k}{k + aq};$$

$$k = .05k + .05aq;$$

$$q = \frac{.95k}{.05a}. \tag{8}$$

At that value of q, we solve for the ratio ${}^{\bar{c}}/_a$ by substituting (8) into (6):

$$\frac{\bar{c}}{a} = \frac{k}{aq} + 1 = 1 + \frac{k}{a}\left(\frac{1}{.95k/.05a}\right)$$

$$= 1 + \frac{k}{a}\left(\frac{.05a}{.95k}\right)$$

$$= 1 + (.0526)$$

$$= 1.0526.$$

And more generally, from (5) we can write:

$$|e| \equiv e' = \frac{k}{k + aq};$$

$$k + aq = \frac{k}{e'};$$

$$aq = \frac{k}{e'} - k = \frac{k(1 - e')}{e'}$$

$$q = \frac{k(1 - e')}{ae'}. \tag{9}$$

And substituting (9) into (6) we obtain:

$$\frac{\bar{c}}{a} = \frac{k}{aq} + 1 = 1 + \frac{k}{a\left[\frac{k(1 - e')}{ae'}\right]}$$

$$= 1 + \frac{k}{a} \cdot \frac{ae'}{k(1 - e')}$$

$$= 1 + \frac{e'}{(1 - e')} = \frac{1}{(1 - e')}. \tag{10}$$

From equation (10) the following table of equivalent values is readily obtained:

e'	$\bar{c}/a$
.01	.0101 + 1
.02	.0204 + 1
.03	.0309 + 1
.04	.0417 + 1
.05	.0526 + 1
.07	.0753 + 1
.09	.0989 + 1
.11	.1236 + 1
.13	.1494 + 1
.15	.1765 + 1
.17	.2048 + 1
.19	.2346 + 1
.21	.2658 + 1

11. *Pan American World Airways, Inc. v. United States,* 371 U.S. 296 (1963).

12. *Associated Press v. United States,* 326 U.S. 1 (1945).

13. These questions about gains and losses must be asked with reference to some specific period of time. In theory they should be asked with respect to all of future time, each future year's gains and losses being discounted to present value. As a practical matter the courts have not tried to deal with such extensive time horizons, and given the difficulties probably they should not. The question of time horizons is almost never dealt with explicitly; implicitly the courts reach a fairly sensible position by focusing on the next 10 or 15 years and treating gains and losses in the last of those years as having essentially the same present values as gains in the first of those years.

14. See chapter 6.

15. See, for example, H. Demsetz, "Two Systems of Belief about Monopoly," in H. J. Gold-schmid, H. M. Mann, J. F. Weston, eds., *Industrial Concentration: The New Learning,* Little, Brown, Boston (1974).

16. See, for example, F. M. Scherer, *Industrial Market Structure and Economic Performance,* 405, Rand McNally, Chicago (1970).

17. In the United States, the traditional solution, in situations posing this dilemma, has been public utility type rate regulation. Regulation represents an attempt to avoid both types of loss and to achieve a solution of output equal to Q_c at mandated price equal to P'. In practice, regulation causes a different set of inefficiencies and results in a solution approximating output Q_m at mandated price P.

18. See, for example, George C. Eads, "Competition in the Domestic Trunk Airline Industry: Too Much or Too Little?" in A. Phillips, ed., *Promoting Competition in Regulated Markets,* Brookings Institute., Washington, D.C. (1975), pp. 13–46.

[6]

The Possibilities for Network Competition

We have discussed, in abstract, the interaction between declining costs and the antitrust limits on joint ventures. Our general conclusion was that antitrust principles require rivalrous solutions if, in any given geographic market, demand is adequate to support at least two nets of sufficiently large size to permit each to realize substantially all economies of scale. The best measure of whether economies have been realized to such a degree is the elasticity of the cost curve of a net: the percentage by which average costs are reduced by a 1% increase in output, evaluated at any given output level. All conceivable scale economies will have been realized when the percentage change in costs becomes 0% or positive. But total exhaustion of economies is not essential in the case of a differentiated product, that is, a product regarding which rivalry can and will occur with respect to differences other than price. As to such goods and services—and certainly EFTS falls in that class—minor cost differences will not lead inexorably to the disappearance of all firms save that one which enjoys an advantage in size. Elasticities of cost in the range −.05 to −.10 are not destabilizing in the case of other differentiable products and services, and in our judgment will not be in the case of EFTS. Very likely elasticities in the −.15 range will prove to be stable; but we will err in the direction hostile to our thesis that competition will be stable, and we will assume that the range −.05 to −.10 represents the limit.

The most careful cost studies we have been able to find of an EFT net, which is among the most advanced and complex and should therefore exhibit significant economies over a wider scale range than most, show that cost elasticities in the −.05 to −.10 range are reached in a net comprising about 50,000 terminals. But of course this datum does not end our inquiry, for we must ascertain the geographic demand characteristics of our economy. For example, will one net of 50K terminals satisfy demand throughout the United States?

RETAIL SALES AND TERMINAL DEMAND

To answer questions of this type, it is necessary to obtain some measure of the quantum of economic activity which will create demand for a terminal. Demand will derive from both banking activity and retail sales activity; but, because the best data available to us relate to retail activity, we will here ignore that portion of demand which will derive directly from banking activity. We assume that the network must be supported entirely by POS applications; and we note that this assumption, too, is hostile to our thesis, in that it leads to a decided underestimation of the number of nets sustainable by any given geographic area.

Several different approaches may be taken to ascertain the retail sales volume which will support one terminal. The annual cost per terminal (without printer) in a 50K terminal net we estimate to be reducible to less than $500. One may estimate the minimum retail establishment size at which a retailer will find it worthwhile to install a single terminal by inquiring into the annual retail sales volume at which savings of $500 or more will be yielded by use of a terminal. Savings to the bank, the merchant and the consumer may be aggregated for this purpose; for, if savings occur to anyone in the chain, there exists some set of contractual arrangements which will induce installation of the terminal.

Estimates of cost savings per transaction range from 25¢ to 65¢, depending primarily upon whether the transaction being replaced is a credit card or a checking transaction and secondarily upon other assumptions.[1] We will assume, in this context, that the smallest of those savings figures, 25¢, applies to all displaced transactions. It follows that 2,000 transactions per year are needed to support a terminal. The average ticket-size of present day card transactions is about $20; this size should decrease with terminal technology, since its lower costs will justify use on small transactions. Similarly, the fact that terminal technology involves higher fixed capital costs and much lower time and labor costs will induce use of the technology with smaller transactions. Nevertheless, continuing to err in directions hostile to our thesis, we assume that average size per transaction of terminal transactions will be $20. It follows, then, that the minimum annual sales volume through a terminal must be about $40,000 ($20 per transaction multiplied by 2000 transactions).

A more difficult and uncertain aspect of our prediction centers on the question, what aggregate sales volume must a typical retailer experience in order to achieve $40K in terminal transactions? National Retail Merchants Association data indicate that the size of the average sales transaction is about $15. We may proceed by inquiring how many sales transactions, in addition to 2000 transactions of average size $20, a retailer might have of smaller average size such that his *overall* average size transaction is $15; and what total annual sales volume does that imply? The problem is solved in general form[2] but on an intuitive level we note the following relationships. To bring average overall transaction size down from $20 to $15, given that there are 2,000 of the larger transactions and hence a volume of $40,000 per year, an additional 667 transactions will be necessary, even if the average size of these additional transactions is $0.00. As the average size of the additional transactions grows larger and approaches $15, a larger number of them must occur if the overall average is to be reduced to $15; and, therefore, larger increases in total annual sales are implied. The relationship is illustrated in Figure 11 (see note 2). Beyond the range of 4,000 "smaller" transactions, average smaller transaction size increases very slowly. At 4,000, the average size is $12.50. Since there will be some dispersion of these smaller transactions about that mean, the larger transactions within this smaller category will be of a size appropriate for terminal processing. This suggests that retailers with annual volumes in the range of 6,000 (2,000 large and 4,000 small) transactions will find the installation of a terminal profitable. That transaction volume corresponds to a sales volume of $90,000 per year.

The foregoing approach to the question of how much sales volume a typical retailer must have before terminal installation becomes profitable is rather speculative. Hence, we have checked its results against a wholly different approach. The large chain stores presently use terminals extensively in nets restricted to their enterprise but servicing many individual outlets and supported by leased telephone lines and central computers. These nets are quite similar to EFTS in technology, in function and in cost; and we therefore believe that the extent of deployment of terminals by such enterprises should provide an indication of independent retailer employment of EFTS terminals. In keeping with our use of figures hostile to our thesis, we will regard the number as an upper bound on independent retailer deployment. Access has been given to the authors to proprietary data of that kind, and we are able to represent that, in such enterprises, the ratio of terminals deployed is about one terminal per $180,000 of sales.

These two numbers are entirely consistent with one another. Consider a retailer whose business is growing rapidly. He installs a terminal at some level of sales, say $90,000, at which it first becomes profitable to do so. But the terminal will not be utilized to capacity at that sales level; and he will not install a second terminal until a queue begins to form at the first terminal or the physical separation of cash register locations within his establishment dictates installation of a second terminal. Hence, the average rate of sales per terminal installation will exceed the level of sales at the threshold of profitability. These numbers suggest the retailer will install a first terminal when sales reach $90,000 and will install a second when sales reach about $400,000. To give an intuitive feel for how large a store is involved, we note that retail sales volume per square foot of selling space in general merchandise establishments is about $100 per foot. Hence, installation might first occur in a store 30 feet by 30 feet in size; and a second terminal might be installed when the store has expanded to 63 feet by 63 feet.

Our threshold number of $90,000 might be challenged. It does assume that all of the larger transactions are being processed on the terminal (or, more realistically, that most larger transactions are being processed along with some small fraction of the bigger transactions from the smaller class). To err again in the direction hostile to our thesis, let us assume instead that only half of these potential terminal transactions are, in fact, processed over the terminal. (In support of this 50% figure, we note that even at present more than half of the retail transactions which are for amounts in excess of $2 are executed either by credit cards or checks.[3]) Our threshold size then becomes $180,000, which is equivalent to the average rate of installation.

As a final measure of conservatism, to simplify calculations and because it fits available data better, we choose to assume that both the threshold number and the average number are $200,000 of sales per year rather than $180,000; i.e., no terminals will be used by retailers with annual sales volumes below $200,000 per year, and retailers with larger volumes will employ one terminal for each multiple of $200,000 of annual sales.

The census data for 1967 reveal that retail establishments with annual sales volumes less than $200,000 account for 15% of national annual retail sales; 85% is accounted for by larger retailers.[4] This percentage is surprisingly constant across the country and holds within several percentage points in all states. We assume, again conservatively with respect to our thesis, that small retail establishments have continued and will continue in the future to account for that percentage and will use no EFTS terminals.

We then apply this 15% exclusion to the total level of retail sales within each state in 1974, to obtain current sales by large establishments.[5] We divide each such remaining sales figure by $200,000, to obtain an estimated number of POS terminals that will be installed in each state. The results are given in Table 2.

A RANGE OF NETWORK ESTIMATES

To move from the number of terminals to the number of EFTS nets each state will support, we can then divide by 50,000. But once again to be certain we do not overestimate the number of nets that might emerge, we assume that 60,000 terminals are necessary to achieve scale economies and divide by that number instead. The results appear in Table 2 and represent our low estimate of the number of probable nets. Hereafter, we will alter some of the conservative assumptions we have made and estimate a number of nets which is deliberately biased on the high side.

As the figures in Table 2 reveal, even on very conservative assumptions there is sufficient commercial activity so that demand based on POS retail sales transactions alone will support about a half dozen competing nets in six out of seven major geographical regions of the continental United States and almost four nets in the seventh. Nationwide, there could be as many as 40 nets.

In arriving at the foregoing low estimate, a number of variables have been employed, such as savings-per-transaction and retailer sales volume necessary to support a POS terminal. In the case of each variable, uncertainty exists as to the proper value to be assigned; it would not have been unreasonable to select any value which falls within the uncertainty range associated with each variable. Our purpose in making this first estimate is to determine whether, *at a minimum,* demand is sufficient to support a large number of efficient nets; our conclusion[6] is that EFTS systems are not "natural monopolies" which, arguably, must be regulated, but rather are capable of existing in sufficient number in different regions to constitute a stable, effectively competitive industry not requiring pervasive regulation.

Consistent with that purpose, we have first selected, with respect to each variable, a value either at the low end or at the high end of the range of uncertainty, whichever is biased in the direction of predicting the emergence of a small number of nets. For example, we assume that an efficient scale of net operation will require not 50,000 but 60,000 terminals. Because we consistently employ such a bias, which we will refer to as a "low bias," we are reasonably confident that the predicted number of nets is, in actuality, unrealistically small. Hence, viewed either nationally or regionally, there is even more potential for competitive industry structure than our low-range prediction of 40 nets would suggest.

In our high estimates, we are exploring a different point: the consequence of confining EFTS net operations to a single state. Although it may be true on a regional or national basis that there is ample potential for competitive structure, if nets are prohibited legally from operating on an interstate basis,

Table 2. EFTS Demand at POS by State and Geographical Region—Low Estimate

States	Nets	Terminals (in thousands of units)
North Atlantic		
Connecticut	.6	37.7
Maine	.2	11.7
Massachusetts	1.1	68.3
New Hampshire	.2	10.7
New Jersey	1.4	85.0
New York	3.3	196.8
Rhode Island	.2	10.1
Vermont	.1	5.8
Subtotal	7.1	426.1
East North Central		
Indiana	1.0	61.6
Michigan	1.8	104.7
Ohio	2.0	118.3
Pennsylvania	2.2	131.6
Subtotal	7.0	416.2
West North Central		
Illinois	2.2	134.0
Iowa	.5	29.2
Minnesota	.7	43.0
Missouri	.9	53.7
Nebraska	.3	16.3
North Dakota	.1	6.4
South Dakota	.1	6.5
Wisconsin	.8	50.6
Subtotal	5.6	339.7
South Atlantic		
Delaware	.1	8.0
D.C.	.1	8.2
Maryland	.8	48.5
North Carolina	.9	55.2
South Carolina	.5	27.7
Virginia	.9	54.0
West Virginia	.3	17.3
Subtotal	3.6	218.9
East South Central		
Alabama	.6	36.0
Florida	1.9	116.1
Georgia	1.0	56.8
Kentucky	.6	33.1
Mississippi	.4	22.2
Tennessee	.8	47.0
Subtotal	5.3	311.2

*Table 2—*Continued

States	Nets	Terminals (in thousands of units)
West South Central		
Arkansas	.4	21.8
Colorado	.5	32.0
Kansas	.4	25.2
Louisiana	.6	38.1
New Mexico	.2	12.1
Oklahoma	.5	30.2
Texas	2.6	146.9
Subtotal	5.2	306.4
Pacific		
Arizona	.5	28.0
California	4.3	258.2
Idaho	.2	8.6
Montana	.1	8.5
Nevada	.1	8.5
Oregon	.5	26.7
Utah	.2	13.2
Washington	.7	40.5
Wyoming	.1	4.4
Subtotal	6.7	396.6
National Total	40.5	2,415.1

will there be a substantial number of individual states in which the volume of commerce (and hence demand) is inadequate to support a sufficient number of nets to achieve an effectively competitive market structure? In short, will it be possible to achieve a competitive EFTS industry in all states and, thus, to avoid stultifying public-utility-type regulation, only if interstate operation is permitted?

If we look to the figures in Table 2 for enlightenment on this point, we conclude, for example, that only six or seven states even arguably have sufficient commercial activity to support two or more nets; EFTS appears to exhibit natural monopoly characteristics in the great preponderance of states. But such a conclusion if based merely on those numbers would not be sound; for, as has been explained, those numbers are deliberately biased toward smallness. To test the soundness of that conclusion, we will adopt the opposite bias—a high bias. By so doing, we conclude that, even if the number of nets that emerges is at the high end of the plausibility range, interstate operation will be a prerequisite to achieving competitive market structure in many states.

Although each of the variables previously employed has an uncertainty range, the significance of the range of some, in terms of how much it will influence the ultimate number of nets estimated, is great; the significance of others is very minor. To avoid tedious reconsideration of every variable, we discuss and alter estimates only of those to which the outcome is sensitive.

Previously, we have assumed that the total cost savings per POS transaction will be 25¢, the figure at the bottom of the 25¢ to 63¢ range estimated earlier for different types of transactions. We now make the assumption that the saving will be 50¢. Accordingly, the $500 annual terminal cost will be covered by a mere 1,000 terminal transactions, yielding a terminal sales volume of $20,000 at an average transaction size of $20. Using the technique described previously, this corresponds to a total sales volume threshold of only $45,000 per year. We again assume that, most assuredly, the *average* sales volume per terminal will exceed the volume threshold at which the first terminal will be installed, but we now select a lower assumed average. The actual operating data available to us suggests an average volume figure of $180,000, twice the low-biased threshold figure of $90,000. In the face of that data, we continue to assume that the 2 to 1 ratio between the threshold and average volumes will hold true, and we adopt an average volume of $90,000. From census data we observe that 90% of all retail sales are made by establishments with annual sales of at least $90,000.[7] Hence, on a state-by-state basis, we multiply retail sales by 0.9 and divide by $90,000 to obtain terminal numbers per state.

To obtain net numbers, we again adopt a "high-bias" approach; we now assume that cost curve elasticities in the range −0.15 are consistent with stable, competitive operation and hence that nets of 40,000 terminals each will adequately exhaust scale economies. Hence, state-by-state we divide terminal numbers by 40,000 to obtain net numbers. The numbers of nets and of terminals that would be sustained by retail POS demand thus computed appear in Table 3.

We emphasize that the net projections so far made from both a low bias and a high bias viewpoint have been based on demand derived from cost savings potential in retail sales of merchandise and nonbanking services. Additional demand for terminals will derive from cost savings potential in conducting financial transactions that currently are conducted in financial institutions—namely, deposits and withdrawals, including "withdrawals" via check cashing. Some fraction of the terminals that appear in response to this financial transaction demand may be freestanding ATM's; and since such devices are more expensive than POS terminals, their number will be fewer. But we next assume that all such demand will be satisfied with a still larger number of POS-type terminals.

In this context too, data that would permit confident prediction are unavailable. We attempt to couple available data with plausible assumptions. Data are available which group banks into categories of different sizes and reveal the number of deposits and of withdrawals executed per year through teller transactions in the average bank within each size category. The averages, including both deposits and withdrawals to time and demand deposits, are 456,000 for banks with less than $50 million in deposits, 1.3 million for banks in the $50–$200 million deposit range, and 7.16 million for banks with deposits exceeding $200 million in deposits.[8] The approximate number of banks and of S & L's in each of those size classes is also known: 15,996; 2,434; and 648, respectively.[9] Although S & Ls almost certainly have fewer transactions per dollar of deposits than banks, we assume they are alike in this respect, consistently with our high-bias approach. Multiplying the average transaction numbers by the institution numbers and summing the products, we obtain a total annual number of 15.1 billion such transactions nationally.

The cost to a financial institution of processing a teller transaction is estimated to be 25¢ to 30¢.[10] It is estimated that customers, on average, spend six minutes in line to execute each such transaction,[11] time to which we now assign a cost of 25¢. Conceivably each of these cost elements may be reduced by one-third to one-half; so we assume that the total cost saving per transaction will be 25¢.

Of the 15.1 billion transactions which now occur at tellers' windows, we assume that as many as half may eventually occur via terminal. Hence a total cost saving of $1.9 billion may constitute derived demand by financial institutions for terminals. (Obviously, it is not our expectation that these terminals will all be located in financial institutions; rather, we expect most will be located in other retail establishments.) Again, we assume a terminal cost of $500 per annum, and we assume that scale economies of nets are sufficiently exhausted at 40,000 terminals per net. On these assumptions, 2,000 transactions at 25¢ each will justify the cost of a terminal; and the maximum number of terminals that might be employed nationally to satisfy that demand is 3.8 million.

We have derived a national number because data on numbers of deposits and withdrawals are available on a national rather than state-by-state basis. If we assume that the volume of such financial transactions in any state bears the same ratio to national volume as the ratio of retail sales in that state bears to national retail sales, we can distribute those 3.8 million terminals over the states on that basis and then divide each figure by 40,000 to obtain nets per state justified by financial institution demand. The resulting numbers appear in the first two columns of Table 4. In the final column in that table, we have

Table 3. EFTS Demand at POS by State and Geographical Region—High Estimate

States	Nets	Terminals (in thousands of units)
North Atlantic		
Connecticut	2.2	86.8
Maine	.7	27.0
Massachusetts	3.9	157.2
New Hampshire	.6	24.6
New Jersey	4.9	195.5
New York	11.3	452.7
Rhode Island	.6	23.2
Vermont	.3	13.4
Subtotal	24.5	980.4
East North Central		
Indiana	3.5	141.7
Michigan	6.0	240.8
Ohio	6.8	272.2
Pennsylvania	7.6	302.7
Subtotal	23.9	957.4
West North Central		
Illinois	7.7	308.2
Iowa	1.7	67.1
Minnesota	2.5	98.9
Missouri	3.1	123.5
Nebraska	.9	37.5
North Dakota	.4	14.8
South Dakota	.4	15.0
Wisconsin	2.9	116.3
Subtotal	19.6	781.3
South Atlantic		
Delaware	.5	18.4
D.C.	.5	18.9
Maryland	2.8	111.6
North Carolina	3.2	127.0
South Carolina	1.6	63.7
Virginia	3.1	124.1
West Virginia	1.0	39.8
Subtotal	12.7	503.5
East South Central		
Alabama	2.1	82.7
Florida	6.7	267.1
Georgia	3.3	130.6
Kentucky	1.9	76.2
Mississippi	1.3	51.1
Tennessee	2.7	108.0
Subtotal	18.0	715.7

Table 3—Continued

States	Nets	Terminals (in thousands of units)
West South Central		
Arkansas	1.3	50.1
Colorado	1.8	73.6
Kansas	1.5	57.9
Louisiana	2.2	87.6
New Mexico	.7	28.0
Oklahoma	1.7	69.5
Texas	8.5	338.0
Subtotal	17.7	704.7
Pacific		
Arizona	1.6	64.4
California	14.9	593.9
Idaho	.5	19.8
Montana	.5	19.6
Nevada	.5	19.6
Oregon	1.5	61.5
Utah	.8	30.3
Washington	2.3	93.1
Wyoming	.3	10.1
Subtotal	22.9	912.3
National Total	139.3	5,555.3

combined the net numbers justified by retail POS demand (from Table 3) with those in the second column, to obtain an overall upper bound total on a state-by-state basis.

As this ultimate high bias estimate reveals, scale economies in EFTS nets are sufficiently extensive so that in only a small fraction of states will really competitive operation be feasible if operation of a net must be confined within the borders of a state. The results are portrayed in more accessible form in the two tables that follow. In the first we show the number of states that will support various numbers of nets:

Net Numbers	<1	1–1.9	2–2.9	3–5.9	6–9.9	>10
Number of States[12]	10	6	7	16	2	8

In the second table we show the numbers of states which will be unable to support as many nets as the number listed in the top row:

Net Numbers	<1	<2	<3	<6	<10	<25
Number of States[13]	10	16	23	39	41	49

Table 4. EFTS Demand for both POS and Financial Transactions by State and Geographic Region

States	Terminals (financial only; in thousands)	Nets (financial only)	Nets (financial and POS)
North Atlantic			
Connecticut	58.8	1.5	3.6
Maine	18.4	.5	1.1
Massachusetts	106.0	2.7	6.6
New Hampshire	16.4	.4	1.0
New Jersey	132.4	3.3	8.2
New York	306.4	7.7	19.0
Rhode Island	15.6	.4	1.0
Vermont	8.8	.2	.6
Subtotal	662.8	16.7	41.1
East North Central			
Indiana	96.0	2.4	5.9
Michigan	162.8	4.1	10.1
Ohio	184.0	4.6	11.4
Pennsylvania	204.8	5.1	12.7
Subtotal	647.6	16.2	40.1
West North Central			
Illinois	208.0	5.2	12.9
Iowa	45.6	1.1	2.8
Minnesota	66.8	1.7	4.1
Missouri	83.6	2.1	5.2
Nebraska	25.6	.6	1.6
North Dakota	10.0	.3	.6
South Dakota	10.0	.3	.6
Wisconsin	78.8	2.0	4.9
Subtotal	528.4	13.3	32.7
South Atlantic			
Delaware	12.4	.3	.8
D.C.	12.8	.3	.8
Maryland	75.6	1.9	4.7
North Carolina	86.0	2.2	5.3
South Carolina	43.2	1.1	2.7
Virginia	84.0	2.1	5.2
West Virginia	27.2	.7	1.7
Subtotal	341.2	8.5	21.2
East South Central			
Alabama	56.0	1.4	3.5
Florida	180.8	4.5	11.2
Georgia	88.4	2.2	5.5
Kentucky	51.6	1.3	3.2
Mississippi	34.8	.9	2.2
Tennessee	73.2	1.8	4.5
Subtotal	484.8	12.1	30.1

Table 4—Continued

States	Terminals (financial only; in thousands)	Nets (financial only)	Nets (financial and POS)
West South Central			
Arkansas	34.0	.9	2.1
Colorado	49.6	1.2	3.1
Kansas	39.2	1.0	2.4
Louisiana	59.2	1.5	3.7
New Mexico	18.8	.5	1.2
Oklahoma	46.8	1.2	2.9
Texas	228.8	5.7	14.2
Subtotal	476.4	12.0	29.6
Pacific			
Arizona	43.6	1.1	2.7
California	402.0	10.1	24.9
Idaho	13.6	.3	.8
Montana	13.2	.3	.8
Nevada	13.2	.3	.8
Oregon	41.6	1.0	2.6
Utah	20.4	.5	1.3
Washington	63.2	1.6	3.9
Wyoming	6.8	.2	.4
Subtotal	617.6	15.4	38.2
National Total	3,758.8	94.2	233.0

There would be fewer than six competing firms in half the states, a state of affairs that would not be very satisfactory from a competitive standpoint. Economists are not of one mind on the number of rivalrous firms that must exist in order to have effective competition. But almost all would agree that, on a state-by-state basis, effective competition is impossible in at least 23 of the 49, and many would say effective competition is possible in only about 10.

This general result seems inescapable to us. If, for example, one were to argue that even our high bias estimate is too low and, on some basis or other, were to double each of the net numbers which appears in the last column of Table 4 and then were to recalculate the last table presented above, the results would be the following:

Net Numbers	<1	<2	<3	<6	<11
Number of States[14]	1	10	14	24	34

Unless present legal barriers to multistate operation are removed and future barriers avoided, EFTS development will be artificially bent in a noncompetitive direction and political pressure to impose public utility type regulation upon EFTS will be likely, in at least a majority of states, to be very intense.

GEOGRAPHIC SCALE OF NETWORK OPERATION

A further point remains to be developed. We have argued that the interaction of national demand with scale economies present in EFTS nets makes at least 40, and perhaps as many as 230, nets economically feasible; and on this basis we have asserted that competitive market structures are possible. An objection to the analysis may be raised. If there are significant costs to wide geographic coverage by a net—that is, if it is significantly more expensive to install and operate a terminal several hundred miles distant from the network hub than it is to locate and operate one only 50 or 100 miles from the hub—then it is possible, first, that as few as 40 or 50 nets might come into existence, in accord with our low bias prediction, and, second, that each one will service only a local area—perhaps an urban area and its immediate suburbs. As a result, each of the 40 or 50 nets will constitute a monopoly within its own service area. A public utility approach might then be unavoidable as a political matter, notwithstanding the existence nationally of 40 or 50 nets.

Whether this pattern of local monopolies is likely depends upon two factors: first, upon the cost of extending a net geographically, relative to the cost of local operation; and second, upon the existence of user demand for geographically extensive on-line services. Turning first to the demand factor, we conclude that there will be significant demand for geographically extended service and that the level of this demand will increase over the coming years, as the population continues to exhibit greater mobility. It will undoubtedly continue to be true for the foreseeable future that the great preponderance of transactions will be executed within a relatively compact geographic area. But our population already includes a substantial number of peripatetic individuals, and these individuals constitute a market for geographically dispersed transactions services which is far more significant in economic terms than is suggested by the number of individuals in that group. These individuals are not only mobile but they are also in high income brackets and have high time costs. Their time costs are specially high when they are away from home in unfamiliar surroundings and, typically, have little leisure time in their schedule. And, as a group, they account for a disproportionately large fraction of transactions suitable for EFT processing. These characteristics, from the standpoint of the network operator, make this group a very attractive customer set. The same characteristics, from the standpoint of members of the group, make geographic flexibility a highly desirable feature of any credit or debit card which they employ. Existing patterns of credit card use suggest that 15%–20% of use occurs at a substantial distance from the residence of the card holder.[15] There is no doubt, then, that EFTS nets will have strong incentives to achieve extensive geographic coverage in order to satisfy this demand for cards with geographic flexibility.

Turning from the question of demand to that of supply, or the cost of achieving wide geographic coverage, we observe, on the basis of engineering studies employing proprietary data, that costs do increase with distance but only to a modest degree. There is no simple formulation that conveys with precision the relationship we have found between costs and geographic dispersion. In general it can be said that average cost per distant terminal is an increasing function of distance and, holding distance constant, is a decreasing function of the number of terminals to be installed at the distant location.

To be more specific, we must turn to an illustrative example. Let us suppose that a network operator has established a network of 20,000 POS type terminals in an east coast metropolitan area. Such a net does not fully exhaust scale economies, and the annual average cost per terminal will continue to drop from approximately $500 to about $450 per terminal as the net adds additional terminals in its original metropolitan area. Now let us assume that, rather than adding more local terminals, the net expands by adding 100 terminals in another city 100 miles away. The average cost per terminal for those distant terminals will be about $580 per terminal, a cost penalty of about 17%. If the remote city is more distant, the cost penalty for 100 terminals is higher; if the number of terminals to be added in a city at any given distance is more than 100, the cost penalty is lower. Table 5 suggests the critical relationships, showing in each cell of the matrix the percentage cost penalty.

Table 5. Percentage Cost Penalty of Remote Terminals in Various Satellite Areas.

Distance from Established Net in Miles	Number of Distant Terminals			
	100	200	400	800
100	17%	17%	16%	14%
200	21%	21%	21%	16%
400	30%	29%	28%	17%
800	46%	46%	32%	18%

Since geographic coverage will be an aspect of EFT service desired by users, cost penalties in the 14%–18% range will be sustainable, even in competition with localized systems of comparable size; very likely even larger percentage differences will be sustainable in many demographic and commercial contexts.

But only in very limited circumstances will competitive disadvantages of that magnitude have to be sustained. Recall that Table 5 embodies the tacit premise that there exists at the remote city an EFT net comparable in size to the net establishing the distant terminals. Often there will be no such localized net.

Our previous calculations have indicated that the nation in its entirety will support 2.5 to 5.5 million terminals, or 1.25 to 2.75 terminals per hundred population. Proportionately, then, 100 terminals will be supported by a community in the population range 3,600 to 8,000; and 800 terminals, by a community of 29,000 to 64,000. Such communities will not support localized nets approaching efficient size; so that competition in such areas will occur between net operators each of whom is extending terminals from a distant hub. The competitive handicap will be far smaller or nonexistent. Only when remote terminals are located in densely populated areas will the handicap approach the full cost penalty shown above.

Hence, taking the view of these figures most pessimistic from the standpoint of effective competition, a net should find it feasible to reach out 800 miles from its hub to serve a community of about 50,000 or to capture a 25% market share of a community of 200,000 people. Nets with hubs, respectively, in New York, Chicago, Miami and Dallas will be effective potential competitors in Chattanooga; and nets in Los Angeles, Dallas, Salt Lake and Denver will be such competitors in Albuquerque. Even the northeast corner of Montana is within 800 miles of several major metropolitan SMSAs, including Minneapolis-St. Paul, Denver, Salt Lake and Seattle. We are reinforced in our conclusion that EFTS will develop in a noncompetitive, public utility mode only if perverse legislative responses force the industry into that mode.

Barring the passage of such legislation, it seems likely to us that the industry pattern 10 years hence might be in a configuration such as the following. BankAmericard and Interbank Card Association (Mastercharge) will have nationwide, on-line systems which center on switches located in the midwest and which employ about a half-dozen regional hubs. Two additional proprietary systems servicing all major cities will have been deployed, each by a large bank or perhaps by joint-ventures of two or three large banks headquartered in different regions. Several nonfinancial enterprises, for example, TRW, IBM and Sears, will each have established a series of regional nets which will offer access on a competitive basis to savings and loan associations, smaller banks and, of course, retailers, within each of their regions of coverage. In some large cities there will be one or two nets of local coverage established by joint ventures, among for instance a computer time-sharing enterprise, a large local financial institution and several large local retailers, including a regional grocery chain.

Thus, in some large cities, the number of service alternatives available to retailers and to consumers will be as many as seven or eight. In such cities, some large retailers will subscribe to a half-dozen systems, though perhaps the terminals of ony two or three will be represented at each point-of-sale, terminals of the rest being located in a "financial convenience booth" for customer use in executing financial transactions only. Some consumers will carry the cards of a half-dozen systems, just as many now carry six or ten or more credit cards, although such consumers may have positive-balance accounts with only one or two financial institution net members and hence would be able to use only one or two of the cards as debit cards.

In small communities, not surprisingly, the number of options will be fewer. In communities which are both very small and geographically isolated, there will be no on-line facilities at all. Even in the latter, of course, commercial life will go on; transactions will be conducted using currency, checks, off-line credit cards and check guarantee cards subject to floor limits. For the same reasons that life will go on in small, isolated communities, no significant degree of monopoly power will exist in that stratum of communities serviced by only one on-line system; the preexisting technology will constrain pricing freedom and service quality.

Moreover, in one-net communities the threat of entry by nets operating in the general region will be a second and perhaps more severe restraint, although in this context, too, ill-advised economic policies may significantly weaken competitive pressures. If the potential entrant is legally free to effect entry by quietly signing exclusive dealing contracts of reasonable duration, for example, two to four years, with the larger financial and retail enterprises in a community, then potential entry into a small market is a credible threat and is likely to force limit pricing approaching competitive price levels even if such entry rarely occurs in fact. But unfortunately, there are some extreme applications of the Sherman Act and Section 3 of the Clayton Act which attach serious antitrust risk to such competitive behavior;[16] it may be hoped they will not prevail.

REFERENCES

1. See pages 60–62.
2. Let V = volume in dollars of annual sales
   At = average size of all transactions
   As = average size of "small" transactions
   Al = average size of "large" transactions
   tl = number of "large" transactions
   ts = number of "small" transactions
   By definition:

   $$V = tl\,(Al) + ts\,(As); \tag{1}$$

   and:

   $$At = V \div (tl + ts). \tag{2}$$

   We know from available data and from the constraints we
   have imposed that:

   $$V = 2000\,(\$20) + ts\,(As) \tag{1'}$$

   and:

   $$At = \$15 = V \div (2000 + ts). \tag{2'}$$

   Substituting (1') into (2') we obtain:

   $$\$15 = (\$40,000 + Asts)\,/\,(2000 + ts). \tag{3}$$

   Solving for As we obtain from (3):

   $$As = \$15 - \$10,000/ts. \tag{4}$$

   Solving for Asts we obtain from (3):

   $$\$15\,(2000 + ts) = \$40,000 + Asts;$$
   $$Asts = \$15ts - \$10,000; \tag{5}$$

   And substituting (5) into (1') we obtain:

   $$V = \$40,000 + 15ts - \$10,000;$$
   $$= \$15ts + \$30,000. \tag{6}$$

   We graph equations (4) and (6) in Figure 11. The graphs show first that V is a linear function of the number of smaller transactions; second, that As is a hyperbolic function of the number of smaller transactions, increasing rapidly in the range of 700 to 4000 and increasing slowly thereafter as it approaches an asymptote of \$15 as ts grows without limit. The intuitive interpretation of the graphs appears in the text.

3. See, for example, A. D. Little, Inc., *The Consequences of Electronic Funds Transfer—A Technology Assessment of Movement Towards A Less Cash/ Less Check Society,* Report to the National Science Foundation, Government Printing Office, Washington, D.C. (June 1975), p. 43.

4. United States Bureau of the Census, *1967 Census of Business,* Vol. 1, Table J, p. xvii. The figures were adjusted for inflation; see 61 Federal Reserve Bulletin No. 6, June 1975, p. A. 53.

5. "Survey of Buying Power," *Sales and Marketing Magazine,* July 21, 1975, p. B-5.

6. We note that one step in the necessary proof has not yet been addressed, namely the size of the geographic area over which a net might be expected to operate. This issue is discussed *infra,* at pp. 114–16.

7. United States Bureau of the Census, *1967 Census of Business,* Vol. 1, Table J, p. xvii. The figures were adjusted for inflation; see 61 Federal Reserve Bulletin No. 6, June 1975, p. A53.

8. Federal Reserve Board, "Functional Cost Analysis, 1974 Average Banks," pp. 7.1, 8.1.

9. Federal Deposit Insurance Corp., *1973 Bank Operating Statistics,* Table B; U.S. League of Savings Associations, *Savings and Loan Fact Book,* 1975, p. 97, Table 42.

10. See p. 25 *supra.*

11. See p. 26 *supra.*

12. Including District of Columbia but excluding Alaska and Hawaii.

13. *Ibid.*

14. *Ibid.*

RIGHT   VERTICAL   AXIS:
AVERAGE SIZE OF "SMALLER" TRANSACTIONS IN DOLLARS (DASHED LINE)

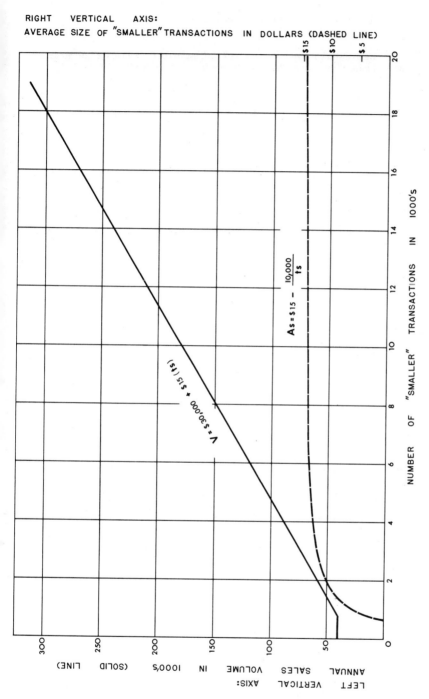

Figure 11. Relationship between retail sales volumes expressed in aggregate dollars of sales and expressed in numbers of transactions.

15. For the state of California, good data on bank card use out of the area of the card holder's residence were obtained from Bank of America. In the first half of calendar 1976, BankAmericard sales volumes processed through Bank of America in California were $811.7 million (net of charge slips deposited by multistate merchants which could not be traced further). Of that dollar volume, 9.7% was attributable to charges by Southern California residents in Northern California or the converse; 16.2% was attributable to charges by California residents in states other than California; and 1.7% was attributable to charges by California residents in foreign countries. A total of 27.6% thus was attributable to use at substantial distances from the card holder's residence. Charges by nonCalifornians in California bore a close correspondence, representing 16% of charges by Californians.

On a national basis, data that would permit quantification of demand proved surprisingly difficult to acquire. Inquiries of various credit card issuing institutions revealed none that have done any "out-of-area-use" type studies.

The two national bank card organizations did have data on the percentage of charge slips which originated with merchants who were customers of banks other than the card-issuing bank. These percentages were in the 40%–45% range in recent years and rising secularly. But only a fraction of these "interchange" items indicated out-of-area-use, and hence these data cannot be applied directly to our issue. An interchange item may arise from use within the card holder's home area (1) if, within that area, there are merchant-banks other than the card-issuing bank, or (2) if a geographically dispersed retail enterprise (an airline or an oil company, for example) processes charge slips from all areas of its operations with a single merchant bank, from which the slips are then returned through interchange to the issuing bank located in the area of actual use, or (3) if the card holder has moved his residence out of the area served by the issuing bank without changing his card. No data were available to correct for the third of these interchange sources. If it had been possible to strip with precision these types of interchange items from the total of interchange slips, present national out-of-area bank credit card usage could have been determined; but that could not be done for this study without incurring prohibitive costs.

In an imprecise way it was possible to make a judgmental correction of the total interchange figures so as to eliminate the influence of the two other types of interchange items just described. Total charge slips attributable to geographically dispersed retailers were known and could be subtracted. The difference between the percentage of interchange items in areas where there were several merchant banks and the nationwide percentage suggested the extent of the second distorting factor. On the basis of these imprecise techniques, it appeared to us that present day out-of-area use by bank card holders generates about 15%–20% of charge slips.

On intuitive grounds we expected that the percentage of dollar volume represented would be greater than 15%–20%; hence these data are generally consistent with the California data presented above. One would also have expected that percentages both of slips and of volumes would be higher for T&E cards and perhaps for proprietary oil company cards than for bank cards.

These credit card data corresponded reasonably well with studies of check usage which had indicated that about 15% of checks were initially deposited at banks over 200 miles from the drawee bank and an additional 30% were deposited 25–200 miles distant. See, for example, *Check Collection System: A Quantitative Description,* by L. M. Fenner and R. H. Long, Bank Administration Institute, Park Ridge, Ill. (1970); prepared for Interbank Payment Communications Steering Committee.

16. *Cass Student Advertising* v. *National Educational Advertising Service, Inc.*, 516 F. 2d 1092 (7th Circ. 1976); *Union Leader Corp.* v. *Newspapers of New England, Inc.*, 180 F. Supp. 125 (S.D. Mass 1959).

[7]

The Legal and Regulatory Setting of Banking

The manner in which the economic dynamics of EFTS will develop is affected, of course, by more than the general constraints imposed by anti-trust law. There is also an extensive and complicated structure of specialized law and regulation governing banking, into which this new development will be fitted. We will begin by describing the salient elements of that regulatory structure and then consider how the course of EFTS evolution is likely to be shaped.

Because, under the dual banking system, the regulatory structure is not uniform but different for national as compared to state banks and further differentiated by individual state and by the choice of a state bank to become a Federal Reserve System member or not, we shall have to select a particular perspective, in part simply for clarity of exposition. The perspective selected, that of a national bank, is not merely a simplifying choice, however; it reflects the status of most of the large, urban banks, which are thus far the leaders in making substantial investigations of the EFTS potential, and it has the broadest applicability of any single category.

THE BRANCH ISSUE

At this point, much of the controversy about the deployment of various forms of EFTS terminals has taken the form of a dispute over whether they constitute "branches" of the bank whose customer files they access or service.

In his initial ruling of December 12, 1974,[1] on customer-bank communication terminals (CBCTs), the Comptroller of the Currency determined that their off-premises establishment would not constitute the operation of a branch. In several court tests of that ruling, however, five district courts have held that some or all functions performed by an automatic teller machine do amount to branch banking[2] and four courts of appeals have ruled in sweeping terms that CBCTs are branches.[3] As a consequence of the litigation, the Comptroller formally rescinded his rule,[4] while fundamentally adhering to his view and seeking (so far unsuccessfully) to vindicate it in the Supreme Court.[5]

If an activity does constitute the operation of a branch, then it is subject to the limitations imposed by 12 U.S.C. section 36. Section 36 (c) permits a national bank to establish "inside" branches (located in the same community as the head office) and "outside" branches (located elsewhere in the same state) only if a state statute *expressly* authorizes such branches for state banks. Authorization for state bank branching by means of administrative ruling or judicial interpretation of an inexplicit statute will not suffice. In addition, the establishment of outside branches is subject to any geographical restrictions or capital requirements to be found in state law. And quite apart from state law, section 36 (d) requires a national bank to have the same aggregate capital as would be necessary if each branch were a separate national bank.[6]

The statute defines a branch as including "any branch bank, branch office, branch agency, additional office, or any branch place of business . . . at which deposits are received, or checks paid, or money lent."[7] The definition thus appears to require the combination of a physical and a functional element: (1) an office or place of business (2) at which at least one of the listed transactions takes place. In the opinion accompanying his initial ruling, the Comptroller has contended that CBCTs qualify on neither ground; they lack the physical and personnel attributes of an office or place of business, and the functions they handle either fall outside those listed in the definition or are consummated at the bank rather than at the terminal.[8]

The statutory definition has been construed by the Supreme Court on one occasion, in *First National Bank in Plant City* v. *Dickinson*,[9] but in a manner not too helpful to the Comptroller's position. *Plant City* involved the question of whether (1) an unmanned deposit receptacle located in a shopping center a mile from the bank and (2) an armored car that made customer pickups and deliveries were branches of the bank that operated them. In giving an affirmative answer, the Court effectively eliminated the "place of business" requirement from the statute by reducing the physical element to merely a "place" at which the function is performed,[10] thereby leaving only the second element as a subject for inquiry. The Court then found that both the receptacle and the armored car "received" deposits,[11] brushing aside all distinctions based on the law of agency or the time when a bank liability arose as a matter of contract law. This constructional treatment was warranted, the Court said, because "the definition of 'branch' in section 36 (f) must not be given a restrictive meaning which would frustrate the congressional intent this Court found to be plain in *Walker Bank*"[12]—namely, a policy of fostering "competitive equality" between state and national banks in the same area, so that neither system would have advantages over the other in the use of branch banking.[13]

The notion that a congressional intent to achieve pervasive competitive equality underlies the provisions of section 36 is an overbroad rationalization which bears only modest resemblance to the actual legislative purpose. The authorization for inside branches was enacted as part of the McFadden Act of 1927;[14] it limited the number of inside branches in terms of the size of head office city and barred all other branches to national banks, regardless of whether the state law was more generous with state banks.[15] When the Banking Act of 1933[16] allowed outside branches as well, it added rather severe capitalization requirements without reference to whether there was a state counterpart.[17] Part of the capital formula was dropped in 1952[18] and replaced by an incorporation of minimum capital requirements under state law, but the most onerous part of the 1933 requirement was retained: a national bank must have the capital that would be required under federal law[19] to establish each branch as a separate national bank,[20] regardless of whether state law imposes such a condition. Furthermore, national banks are allowed branches, not wherever state banks may in fact have them (under local administrative or judicial interpretation of state law), but only where the state law authorization is clear and express.[21] In each of these respects, competitive *inequality* was unambiguously mandated.

If the intent of these statutes was to achieve competitive equality in branching, the draftsmanship is faltering and inept in the extreme. A more accurate statement is that they reflect the outcome of a continuing struggle in Congress between national and state banks as to who shall hold the advantage.[22] The result cannot be fairly described in terms of pure principle, and such a principle offers a most unreliable guide to construction. Instead, the statute embodies a series of limited and partial incorporations of state law restrictions upon branching by national banks.

Even more fundamentally, the branching section does not represent an application, albeit flawed, of some basic and unifying theme in our regulation of state and federal banks. There is no general policy of competitive equality under our dual banking system; indeed, its preeminent virtue in the eyes of its proponents is that it permits or even encourages innovation and experimentation in the different regulatory sectors, which of necessity means, at least for a time, competitive inequality. The concept of competitive equality does not rule all the structure of banking law but affects at most a few areas, such as usury ceilings or branch location, and those only in part. Hence, even if the concept is accepted as a limited interpretive guide in resolving subordinate issues, such as the permissible mode of acquisition of establishments which are indisputably branches, competitive equality is an inappropriate touchstone for determining what constitutes a branch.[23] Rather, it is more appropriate to examine the section closely for indications of precisely what sort of banking operations have been singled out for special treatment and special requirements.

Essentially, the concept of a branch which was dominant in the United States throughout the 19th century and into the 20th century was that it was a semi-autonomous unit, operated in many respects as a separate bank would operate.[24] This of course reflected managerial reality in a time when transportation was arduous and communication was slow. Thus, the branches of both the first and second Bank of the United States had their own boards of directors and presidents, issued and redeemed their own notes and were assigned a specific amount of the bank's total capital.[25]

In ruling, prior to the McFadden Act, that, while a national bank could establish an "agency" to transact a particular class of business incident to banking, it could not establish a branch, the Attorney General described a branch as follows: "A branch bank requires, in effect, a division of the capital, the working force is organized, and the business conducted as if it were a separate organization, and it competes in all branches of the banking business with other banks in that locality the same as if it were an independent institution."[26] When the Supreme Court reached the same conclusion, it seemed to rest on a similar idea of what constituted a branch: "If it had been intended to allow the establishment by an association of not one bank only but, in addition, as many branch banks as it saw fit, it is remarkable, to say the least, that there should have been no provision for adjusting the capital to the latter contingency or for determining how or under what circumstances such branch banks might be established or for regulating them."[27]

It was against this background that Congress changed the law in 1927 and 1933 to give limited authorization for branches, and the new statute utilized the same conception of a branch. The McFadden Act viewed an inside branch as completely unwarranted for a bank in a community of less than 25,000 population and provided that, even in a city of 100,000 population, a national bank should have no more than two branches.[28] Similarly, the Banking Act of 1933 took the position, which is still the law, that the capital requirement for a branch should be the same as for the establishment of a separate national bank in the same location.[29]

In short, the concept of a branch embodied in the National Bank Act is that of a manned banking office carrying on a general banking business with the public, and the statutory requirements have been chosen for their suitability for such an operation. To apply them instead to an electronic terminal sitting on a department store counter will merely produce absurdities. A single department store in a shopping center, for example, might have as many POS terminals as it now has cash registers, perhaps 25 to 50; if the store were in a community with a population over 50,000, a bank installing the terminals would thereby acquire an additional capital requirement of from $5 million to $10 million![30] The same observations, it should be noted, apply to deposit receptacles (and armored cars), though perhaps in less dramatic fashion.

Thus, the Supreme Court in *Plant City* ignored the history of branching and the consequences of its interpretation in order to define the reach of section 36 and the concept of a branch in the light of an assumed Congressional objective of competitive equality—an objective of limited validity when employed within the scope of section 36 and of total inappropriateness when employed to ascertain the section's boundaries.

A decision of this sort—unsound in some fundamental respects but nonetheless authoritative—creates a dilemma for lower courts. They can faithfully carry out and extend the reasoning and premises of the Supreme Court's opinion. Or, as its shortcomings become apparent, they can strive to limit its reach as much as possible. The first two district court tests of the Comptroller's ruling have exemplified these contrasting choices.

In the *Fort Collins* decision,[31] the district court followed the latter or narrowing approach. The case involved an automatic teller machine (ATM), off-line and unmanned, in which customers could leave cash or checks for deposit or instructions for transfers between checking and savings accounts and from which they could obtain a $25 or $50 money packet, to be charged against a savings or checking account or Master Charge account or other line of credit. Because the court could see no functional difference between the ATM and *Plant City*'s receptacle box when it came to dropping in cash and checks for deposit, it was "compelled to conclude" that the machine was receiving deposits and hence was a branch under section 36 (f). But the court went on to distinguish all the other functions—the cash withdrawals were not the payment of a check or the lending of money, and the account transfers were not deposits. Thus by having the deposit slit sealed shut, the ATM would no longer be a branch.[32]

If the false touchstone of competitive equality had been relied on, the result would have been different. Instead, the district court read the Supreme Court decisions as directing it to proceed under section 36 "by applying the literal meaning of its language to the functions of this machine."[33] That is probably about the best that can be achieved under *Plant City,* but potentially it is quite a bit. Terminals do not receive deposits or pay checks or lend money; they transmit information back and forth, on the basis of which someone at the bank or in the store makes a decision. Through a literal reading of the function language in section 36 (f), in other words, a court can repair much of the damage done by the Supreme Court's suppression of the "office" element of the original definition.

The contrasting approach would be to carry out to the hilt the implications of *Plant City,* reading the section 36 (f) functions as encompassing within the definition of a "branch" any competitive activities that could substitute for the three named traditional banking operations and thus disturb "competitive equality." That was the view adopted by the district court and affirmed by the court of appeals in *Independent Bankers Association of America* v. *Smith,*[34] an action for a declaratory judgment and injunction against the Comptroller's ruling. The case represented judicial review at its most abstract, divorced from any actual fact setting. The court of appeals in particular saw itself as settling all possible issues for the entire banking system in one fell swoop. The exact form of CBCT—manned or unmanned, on-line or off-line, POS terminal or automatic teller machine, and so on—did not matter; neither did any close analysis or legal distinctions regarding the exact functions the CBCT might be performing. Following the banner of competitive equality, the court saw the only question as whether through the CBCT "the bank is providing a customer convenience and is thereby gaining a competitive advantage over banks that do not furnish this service."[35] Since, as we have discussed at length, the answer to that question is an emphatic yes, the CBCT must be a branch. All else was reduced to issues of "form," which of course should not prevail over "substance."

The conflict between these two approaches is likely to persist in the courts until settled by the Supreme Court, and the Supreme Court so far has shown no awareness that competitive equality may not be the clear and simple guidepost to questions of statutory interpretation in the banking field. Should it ultimately uphold the position taken by the lower courts in the *IBA* case, the consequences for EFTS development by banks under existing law are disastrous. If a terminal is a branch, the pattern of terminal networks within a state is confined in whatever way a state confines bank branches, e.g., in some states a bank could not place a single terminal in the entire city or county which contained another bank's head office, while in others a bank could not place a terminal beyond its home county. Without regard for the content of state law, there will be no possibility of a national bank establishing a terminal network across state lines,[36] even in metropolitan areas like New York or Washington or St. Louis, which happen to encompass several jurisdictions. Furthermore, each terminal will carry the capital requirements of a branch, which will prove completely crippling for national banks and for state banks as well in some states, if they adopt the federal characterization.

It is not surprising, therefore, that a number of states have given specific legislative recognition to EFTS facilities and, in doing so, have afforded them treatment different from real branches. By September 1976 some 25 states[37] had passed legislation to govern off-premises facilities such as ATMs and POS terminals.[38] Twenty-one of the twenty-five states did not categorize such facilities as branches, not even as a new subspecies;[39] most specifically stated that they were not branches. The new legislation did not impose capital requirements based upon the number of such facilities, and in many instances did not limit them as to number or location. In short, the dominant trend in the state legislation has been to recognize that branch treatment was inappropriate for these new terminal facilities.

At the same time, the state legislation represents something less than a new wave of ardor for unfettered competition. A distinctive feature in a majority (16) of the state statutes[40] is a provision for mandatory sharing of such facilities with other banks or financial institutions, at least under certain conditions. And to the extent recognition is given to the possibility of competition from out-of-state banks, it is strongly disfavored; 13 states[41] would peremptorily ban it, as compared to four[42] willing to give it conditional consideration.

By determining that CBCTs were not branches, the Comptroller in his December 12, 1974, ruling had opened up the prospect of just such broader competition across the banking market boundaries artificially established by branching limitations and state lines. But faced with state bank opposition to his original ruling, the Comptroller modified it on May 8, 1975,[43] to limit CBCTs to within 50 miles of the bank's office or a branch, thereby excluding anything like a national or even regional network, unless the CBCT was made available for sharing with other financial institutions. In effect, this reduced the amount of competition that a bank in a locally protected market area might face from more distant banks. At the same time, the Comptroller excluded from the requirements and limitations of his ruling a terminal performing only debit card and credit verification functions and not involved in cash withdrawals or deposits.[44] Thus, an ATM or manned-teller-station type of CBCT would be subject to the notification and mileage limitation requirements of the Comptroller's ruling, while a suitably limited debit card terminal, presumably at a retailer's POS, would not.

The amended ruling also raised some interesting questions as to the Comptroller's authority. If CBCTs are not to be regarded as branches (and the Comptroller's ruling is very clear about that), then of course the Comptroller has no approval power under section 36 (c) over their establishment. The original ruling imposed only a notification requirement, which the Comptroller has justified[45] under his statutory authority to "call for special reports from any particular association whenever in his judgment the same are necessary for his use in the performance of his supervisory duties."[46] The 50-mile limitation for exclusive CBCTs in the amended ruling, however, is a substantive restriction with no evident statutory foundation. To make a case for his authority, the Comptroller's accompanying statement cites his "broad supervisory power," his authority to issue "housekeeping" regulations and his power to issue cease and desist orders against unsafe or unsound banking practices; in the aggregate, these are asserted to constitute "statutory authority to promulgate reasonable regulations for the sound and safe development of the banking system,"[47] a view which will render unnecessary most of the detailed statutory proscriptions found in Title 12 of the United States Code. This is apparently the first occasion on which the Comptroller has discerned the existence of his plenary rulemaking power over the operations of the national banking industry, and its validity is suspect, to say the least. Thus, the Comptroller is faced with a difficult position—by ruling that CBCTs are not branches, to escape a quite inappropriate set of requirements and restrictions, he probably loses the ability to impose geographical limitations that he feels are desirable for political, rather than supervisory, reasons.[48] The present policy position, as expressed in the "interpretive" ruling, seems inherently fragile, and likely to be upset by litigation[49] or replaced by legislation.

The initial legislative effort that progressed the furthest, S. 245[50] introduced in 1975 by Senators Proxmire and McIntyre, purported to be only a temporary moratorium bill and was ultimately tabled in the Senate Banking Committee, but some of its features are nonetheless worth noting. No effort was made to overturn the Comptroller's position that EFTS terminals were not branches and, hence, were outside the capital requirements. The bill, however, would have imposed geographical limits, making federal institutions conform to any state rules or, in their absence, tying them to locations within 25 miles of a home office or 10 miles of a branch and within a single state.

The outcome of the branch issue is crucial to the future of bank development of EFTS, but it is not the only legal hurdle they must overcome. We turn next to other ways in which EFTS networks may be shaped by long standing doctrines in bank regulation.

DIRECT STATE REGULATION OF NATIONAL BANKS

Even if terminals are not branches and national banks are not therefore subjected to state locational rules by virtue of section 36 (c), there is a residual question as to whether a state law undertaking to regulate terminal networks, whether operated by a bank or by any business, will be valid as applied to national banks. For example, at this time over half of the states with special EFTS legislation have included in the law a mandatory "sharing" provision of some sort. The exact terms vary, but a common pattern is to require any bank establishing a CBCT to make it available for use by all other banks and their customers on a nondiscriminatory basis, conditioned upon payment of a "reasonable" or "fair" share of all costs. Such statutes can make the creation of competing EFTS networks much more difficult to achieve (see chapter 8). Assuming that a state statute makes quite clear its intent to regulate the operations of local national banks in this manner, can it do so validly?

National banks are federal instrumentalities, and there is no doubt that Congress may free them from state constraints to whatever degree it deems fit.[51] But where Congress has not spoken on the matter, the rule is that "national banks are subject to the laws of a State in respect of their affairs unless such laws interfere with the purposes of their creation, tend to impair or destroy their efficiency as federal agencies or conflict with the paramount law of the United States."[52] Will state restriction of national bank EFTS terminals so interfere with the attainment of the objectives of the national banking system that such restriction will be invalid? The available precedents offer little guidance as to how the courts will go about analyzing that question, and of course the exact content of the state regulation will affect the outcome. But in *First Nat'l Bank in St. Louis* v. *Missouri,* the Court has said:

Clearly, the state statute, by prohibiting branches, does not frustrate the purpose for which the bank was created or interfere with the discharge of its duties to the government or impair its efficiency as a federal agency. This conclusion would seem to be self evident, but if warrant for it be needed, it sufficiently lies in the fact that national bank associations have gone on for more than half a century without branches and upon the theory of an absence of authority to establish them. If the nonexistence of such branches or the absence of power to create them has operated or is calculated to operate to the detriment of the government, or in such manner as to interfere with the efficiency of such associations as federal agencies, or to frustrate their purposes, it is inconceivable that the fact would not long since have been discovered and steps taken by Congress to remedy the omission.[53]

It is evident that one could argue the *St. Louis Bank* analogy both ways.

National banks have gotten along without EFTS terminals for more than a century, but the technology is newly arrived and the inability of national banks to make full use of it might well impair their efficiency and frustrate the most effective discharge of their duties and attainment of their purposes.

If we narrow the focus to mandatory state sharing statutes, we can carry the argument a little further. The whole purpose of attempting to extend the coverage of such statutes to national banks would be to inhibit the competition they will otherwise afford to state banks. But on the assumption (which we are making in this part of the discussion) that EFTS networks have been held *not* to be branches within the federal definition, we are outside the area in which the McFadden Act is designed to limit competition between the state and national banking systems. The anticompetitive character of the state sharing law should, therefore, be seen as conflicting with the national banking laws, in which case state law is overridden by the federal law.

This conclusion is reinforced when the "paramount law of the United States" is thought of as referring to the antitrust laws as well as the national banking laws. The point is not that the antitrust laws operate to invalidate anticompetitive forms of state regulation; they have not been construed that broadly.[54] The process is somewhat more subtle and indirect. The antitrust laws are regarded by the Supreme Court as expressing a general and important national policy in favor of economic competition, and that in turn may color the view the Court takes of the extent to which competition, among national banks and between state and national banks, is a tenet of federal banking laws. If the Court takes the attitude that it is desirable to infuse more competition into our banking structure, as it well may,[55] the prospect is enhanced that mandatory state sharing statutes will be struck down as applied to national banks.

As we noted at the outset, however, if Congress enters the field explicitly, the matter is at an end. The degree of uncertainty that must prevail under present doctrine contributes to the likelihood of eventual federal legislation.

INTERSTATE OPERATIONS

Most obviously at stake in the outcome of the branching issue is the pattern and extent of deployment of EFTS terminals within the state in which the bank's home office is located, but there are also implications for their interstate use. If terminals are branches, then their interstate operation is forbidden to national banks by section 36 and to state banks under existing state legislation. That does not mean, however, that interstate terminal networks can not be established, but only that banks can not be the ones to establish them. On the other hand, if terminals are not branches, then the prospects that a bank can itself operate them across state lines are much improved. We will consider each of these possibilities in turn.

INDIRECT CHANNELS

Suppose, for example, that the armored car service in Plant City had not been furnished by the First National Bank but by another company. If that company were a sister subsidiary of the holding company that owned the bank, the outcome would be unchanged: the car was an unauthorized branch.[56] But what if the company were a completely independent enterprise like Brink's or Loomis, expanding its line of customer service? It would no longer be possible to dispose of the matter as a sham[57] or subterfuge to which the bank was resorting. Similarly, what if an EFTS terminal network was operated strictly as a communications service by a telephone or telegraph company or a computer systems producer?

That would transform the legal issue into whether the service firm was itself performing banking functions to the extent that it was in effect an unlicensed bank. The various states have defined the business of "banking" in differing ways; New York has referred to "receiving deposits, making discounts, receiving for transmission or transmitting money in any manner whatsoever, or issuing notes or other evidences of debt to be loaned or put into circulation as money,"[58] while California has focused on the "soliciting, receiving, or accepting of money or its equivalent on deposit as a regular business."[59] The broader definitions have run into difficulty, since there are many nonbank businesses that customarily extend credit (sometimes by means of discounting notes) or cash checks or hold clients' funds; to avoid the over-inclusive reach of literalness, the courts have been forced into constructional acrobatics[60] or the legislature into lengthening exceptions. If a generalization could be attempted against such a background, it would be that the essence of the business in which only a bank may engage has been the acceptance of deposits subject to transfer or withdrawal on demand. That activity would probably be illegal in every state except for a licensed bank,[61] and some states would extend the prohibited area still further.

It would seem reasonably clear that a firm running an EFTS network, between retailers and one or more banks, was not itself accepting deposits or making discounts and was probably not engaged in transmitting money. But what about the retailer? To cite the strongest case, if he cashed a customer's check, in part by handing over currency and for the balance by authorizing a transfer at the bank from his deposit account to that of the customer, would that mean he was accepting deposits? The answer would appear to be, no; the customer did not end up as the creditor of the retailer, and the latter held no deposit.[62]

If this kind of analysis is generally followed, then even though a bank EFTS terminal is regarded as a branch, it will still be possible for EFTS networks to come into operation beyond the branching limits—provided they are owned and operated by others.[63] Such a network can even service but a single bank, but it will have to be as an independent contractor.

On the other hand, if the foregoing analysis is not widely accepted by the courts and they rule instead that an EFTS terminal performing credit and debit card functions does constitute part of the banking business, then interstate networks will still be achievable by other means. One method will be the assemblage of geographically dispersed correspondent or franchisee banks into a single system; each terminal will be owned by and connected to a local bank. Another method will be for a bank, through its parent holding company, to acquire financial institutions which are authorized to engage in the banking business to the necessary extent in those out-of-state areas which it wants to encompass within its EFTS network. The out-of-state acquisition of additional banks by a bank holding company is, for all practical purposes at the present time, prohibited by the Douglas amendment to the Bank Holding Company Act, which requires specific authorization for such acquisition in the law of the state in which the acquired bank is located.[64] But it is still possible for a bank holding company to found or acquire nonbank financial institutions elsewhere in the nation, provided their activities are "so closely related to banking . . . as to be a proper incident thereto."[65] Lending subsidiaries, such as mortgage banking or factoring or finance companies, have been found to qualify; likewise, the Federal Reserve Board has said that industrial loan companies (and perhaps it will add savings and loan associations), which receive public funds though not technically in the form of a demand deposit, are "closely related" to banking.[66] Thus, even if terminal functions are regarded as too much a part of banking to be permissible for general businesses, it might be possible to base them on the kind of banking activities allowed those nonbank financial institutions that a bank holding company can own and operate in different states.[67]

DIRECT EXTENSION

Our premise now changes, to the assumption that terminal operations by a bank are held not to constitute branching under section 36 (f). In that event, section 36 (c) will not prevent a national bank from extending an EFTS network across state lines. Will anything else stand in the way?

Even if terminals were not branches under federal law, they might be deemed banking operations or branches under state law. In that case, state law will generally[68] prohibit their establishment by out-of-state banks; is there any question as to the law's validity?

The analysis begins with the limits, under the commerce clause,[69] on the power of the state to exclude out-of-state firms from engaging in certain local activities. If the state's purpose is avowedly, or patently, anticompetitive— that is, simply the protection of domestic enterprises from rivals—the prohibition is invalid.[70] But if other purposes are invoked, such as protecting the interests of local depositors or borrowers, the answer is less clear. The burden on interstate commerce is balanced against the weight of any such legitimate local concerns, with attention also to the possibility that "reasonable nondiscriminatory alternatives, adequate to conserve legitimate local interests, are available."[71]

The outcome of such a balancing obviously depends in part on the exact form of the state restriction and the reasons advanced to justify it. If a unit banking state bans EFTS terminals for all banks, domestic as well as out-of-state, as inconsistent with the goals of its banking system, it might be difficult to mount a commerce clause attack on the legislation; but action that drastic seems improbable. More likely and familiar is legislation limiting terminals to domestic banks and restricting them in number or in distance from an established office. A geographical limitation of this sort "plainly discriminates against interstate commerce"[72] and could only be saved by a showing of overriding local justifications. Furthermore, in the case of an out-of-state national bank, there is the "federal instrumentality" consideration previously mentioned.[73] While a restriction against terminal operation by out-of-state banks would quite possibly be sustained, by analogy to branch operation and its traditional legal treatment, the position of an out-of-state national bank would at least be markedly stronger. Apart from the case to be made for a specific state statute in terms of its particular avowed purposes, it is difficult to say more than that the Comptroller's ruling, even if upheld and reinstated, would by no means settle the matter.

CONCLUSION

The foregoing analysis is not written on stone but readily susceptible to alteration by legislation, state or federal. An act of Congress could change the picture drastically, on any of the points mentioned. What the analysis does provide is a sense of the starting point for legislative battles: the position that will prevail in the absence of a new federal statute. That in turn defines, for each contending party, whether its objectives require it to muster the political force to enact a bill into law or only the much lesser degree of political effectiveness required to stop a measure from passage.

This initial position, in summary, has the following attributes. (1) The Comptroller's basic ruling that CBCTs are not branches under federal law (and section 36) was well-founded and could conceivably be sustained in the Supreme Court despite the *Plant City* decision. *Plant City* itself is sufficiently flawed that sooner or later it may receive reconsideration. At present, however, the tide of lower court decisions is running strongly against the Comptroller's stand. (2) Even if the Comptroller's ruling were ultimately upheld, it would not mean that the states may not still restrict the use of terminals by national banks, but something of a paradox appears. The more banking functions the terminals can perform, the weaker the position of a state in regulating their use by a local national bank, but the stronger its position in keeping out banks from other states. (3) The party in the best position to mount a strong challenge to the bans on interstate CBCTs that are showing up in state legislation will probably be, not a bank at all, but an independent data communications and processing company such as TRW or NCR, selling its services to retailers on the one hand and to one or several banks on the other. At the outset, the fewer the banking functions associated with the terminal, the stronger will be the company's case.

REFERENCES

1. 12 C.F.R. sec. 7.7491 (1975); 39 Fed. Reg. 44416 (1974).

2. *Colorado ex rel. State Bank. Bd.* v. *First National Bank of Fort Collins,* 394 F. Supp. 979 (D. Colo. 1975), *rev'd and remanded,* 540 F.2d 497 (10th Cir. 1976); *Ohio* v. *Smith,* No. C-1-75-153 (S.D. Ohio, May 10, 1975; *Missouri ex rel. Kostman* v. *First National Bank in St. Louis,* 405 F. Supp. 733 (E.D. Mo. 1975), *aff'd* 538 F.2d 219 (8th Cir. 1976), *cert. applied for,* 45 U.S.L.W. 3193 (Sept. 15, 1976); *Independent Bankers Ass'n. of America* v. *Smith,* 402 F. Supp. 207 (D.D.C. 1975), *aff'd* 534 F.2d 921 (D.C. Cir. 1976), *cert. denied,* 45 U.S.L.W. 3221 (Oct. 5, 1976); *Illinois ex rel. Lignoul* v. *Continental Illinois National Bank,* 409 F. Supp. 1167 (N.D. Ill. 1975), *aff'd in part and rev'd in part,* 536 F.2d 176 (7th Cir. 1976), *cert. denied,* 45 U.S.L.W. 3221 (Oct. 5, 1976). *Contra, Oklahoma ex rel. State Bank. Bd.* v. *Bank of Oklahoma,* 409 F. Supp. 71 (N.D. Okla. 1975), *app. dismissed per stipulation.*

3. *Independent Bankers Ass'n of America* v. *Smith,* 534 F.2d 921 (D.C. Cir. 1976), *cert. denied,* 45 U.S.L.W. 3221 (Oct. 5, 1976); *Illinois ex rel. Lignoul* v. *Continental Illinois National Bank,* 536 F.2d 176 (7th Cir. 1976), *cert. denied* 45 U.S.L.W. 3221 (Oct. 5, 1976); *Missouri ex rel. Kostman* v. *First National Bank in St. Louis,* 538 F.2d 219 (8th Cir. 1976), *cert. applied for,* 45 U.S.L.W. 3193 (Sept. 15, 1976); *Colorado ex rel. State Bank. Bd.* v. *First National Bank of Fort Collins,* 540 F.2d 497 (10th Cir. 1976).

4. 41 Fed. Reg. 36198 (1976)

5. The Comptroller sought certiorari in the *IBA* case but it was denied; 45 U.S.L.W. 3221 (Oct. 5, 1976).

6. 12 U.S.C. sec. 36(d) (1970). The amount of capital required by law for a new bank ranges from $50,000 in localities with a population of no more than 6,000 to $200,000 in cities with a population of over 50,000 (12 U.S.C. section 51 [1970]).

7. 12 U.S.C. sec. 36(f) (1970).

8. See 39 Fed. Reg. 44416, 44418–19, 44421–22 (1974).

9. *First National Bank in Plant City* v. *Dickinson,* 396 U.S. 122 (1969).

10. *Ibid.* at 135.

11. *Ibid.* at 137.

12. *First National Bank of Logan* v. *Walker Bank & Trust Co.,* 385 U.S. 252 (1966).

13. 396 U.S. at 131–34.

14. Act of February 25, 1927, ch. 191; 44 Stat. 1224.

15. *Idem* sec. 7, 44 Stat. 1228.

16. Act of June 16, 1933, ch. 89; 48 Stat. 162.

17. *Idem* sec. 23, 48 Stat. 189–90.

18. Act of July 15, 1952, Pub. L. No. 82-544; 66 Stat. 633.

19. 12 U.S.C. sec. 51 (1970).

20. 12 U.S.C. sec. 36(d) (1970).

21. 12 U.S.C. sec. 36(c) (1970). See *Howell* v. *Citizens First Nat'l Bank of Ridgewood,* 385 F.2d 528 (3d Cir. 1967).

22. *Cf.* S. Rept. No. 473, 69th Cong. 1st Sess. 8–10 (1926).

23. In *Walker Bank,* relied upon by the Court in *Plant City* as authority for the "competitive equality" principle, the definition of a branch was not in issue. The premises in question clearly constituted a branch bank; the issue was whether *de novo* establishment was permissible for a national bank although state banks were limited to establishing the branch through acquisition of an existing bank.

24. See Davis R. Dewey, "State Banking Before the Civil War," vol. IV, *National Monetary Commission* 136–140, Government Printing Office, Washington, D.C. (1910).

25. John T. Holdsworth, "The First Bank of the United States," 4 *National Monetary Commission* 36–38, Government Printing Office, Washington, D.C., (1910); Davis R. Dewey, "The Second United States Bank," 4 *National Monetary Commission* 171–72, 194–98, Government Printing Office, Washington, D.C. (1910).

26. 29 *Op. Att'y Gen.* 81, 88 (1911).

27. *First National Bank in St. Louis* v. *Missouri,* 263 U.S. 640, 657 (1924).

28. Act of February 25, 1927, ch. 191, sec. 7(d); 44 Stat. 1228.

29. 12 U.S.C. sec. 36(d) (1970).

30. *See* 12 U.S.C. sec. 51 (1970). A major department store downtown in a city may have 1,000 or more cash register stations, which would translate into a capital requirement for "branch" terminals of $200 million. The statutory provision could be rendered less ridiculous, if still not appropriate, by interpreting the entire store as constituting one "branch," without regard to the number of terminals it contains; there is, of course, no particular basis in the statute for that construction.

31. *Colorado ex rel. State Bank. Bd.* v. *First National Bank of Fort Collins,* 394 F. Supp. 979 (D. Colo. 1975), *rev'd and remanded,* 540 F.2d 497 (10th Cir. 1976).

32. *Cf. Independent Bankers Ass'n of America* v. *Smith,* 534 F. 2d 921, 944 n. 88 (D.C. Cir. 1976).

33. *Colorado ex rel. State Bank. Bd.* v. *First National Bank of Fort Collins,* 394 F. Supp. 979, 985 (1975).

34. 402 F. Supp. 207 (D.D.C. 1975), *aff'd* 534 F.2d 921 (D.C. Cir. 1976) *cert. denied,* 45 U.S.L.W. 3221 (Oct. 5, 1976). The Tenth Circuit also followed this position on appeal in the *Fort Collins* case: *Colorado ex rel. State Bank. Bd.* v. *First Nat'l. Bank of Fort Collins,* 540 F.2d 497 (10th Cir. 1976).

35. 534 F.2d at 941.

36. 12 U.S.C. sec. 36(c) (2) (1970).

37. Alabama, Connecticut, Florida, Georgia,Idaho, Iowa, Kansas, Louisiana, Maine, Maryland, Massachusetts, Nebraska, New Hampshire, New Jersey, New York, North Carolina, North Dakota, Oklahoma, Oregon, Rhode Island, South Carolina, South Dakota, Virginia, Washington, Wisconsin. This analysis is based on the survey of state legislation in *State Banking Law Service* 214–17, American Bankers Association, Washington, D.C. (August 1976).

38. In addition, Utah had enacted a moratorium bill to ban EFTS installation until July 1, 1977, to permit a study of the issues, and Illinois had established a study commission on the subject.

39. Maine, New Jersey, New York, and Oregon are the four exceptions.

40. Connecticut, Florida, Idaho, Iowa, Kansas, Maine, Maryland, Nebraska, New Hampshire, New Jersey, North Dakota, Oklahoma, Oregon, South Dakota, Washington, Wisconsin.

41. Connecticut, Florida, Georgia, Iowa, Kansas, Maine, Maryland, Massachusetts, Nebraska, New Jersey, North Carolina, Oklahoma, South Carolina.

42. Alabama, Oregon, South Dakota, Wisconsin.

43. 40 Fed. Reg. 21700 (1975).

44. 40 Fed. Reg. 21700, 21704 (1975); 12 C.F.R. sec. 7.7491(b) (4) (1976).

45. 39 Fed. Reg. 44416, 44420 (1974).

46. 12 U.S.C. sec. 161(a) (1970). The statutory provision is concerned with reports of condition, but would probably be given a generous construction.

47. 40 Fed. Reg. 21700, 21702 (1975).

48. For a decision invalidating an analogous geographical limitation adopted by a state banking department, see *Livestock State Bank* v. *State Banking Commission,* 80 S.D. 491, 127 N.W. 2d 139 (1964).

49. Following the adverse decision in *Independent Bankers Ass'n* v. *Smith,* the Comptroller "suspended" his Interpretive Ruling 7.7491 pending the outcome of the appeal; following the unsuccessful appeal to the D.C. Circuit, he was ordered to "rescind" his ruling and did so in Banking Circular 76 on August 23, 1976, 41 Fed. Reg. 36198 (1976), while noting that further review was being sought from the Supreme Court. Certiorari was denied by the Supreme Court in the IBA case in October 1976; see 45 U.S.L.W. 3221 (Oct. 5, 1976).

50. See *Hearing on the Electronic Funds Transfer Moratorium Act of 1975 (S. 245)* before the Subcomm. on Financial Institutions of the Senate Comm. on Banking, Housing and Urban Affairs, 94th Cong. 1st Sess. (1975).

51. See, for example, *M'Culloch* v. *Maryland,* 17 U.S. (4 Wheat.) 316, 436 (1819); *Farmers' & Mechanics' Nat'l Bank* v. *Dearing,* 91 U.S. 29, 33–34 (1875); *Owensboro Nat'l Bank* v. *Owensboro,* 173 U.S. 664 (1899).

52. *First Nat'l Bank in St. Louis* v. *Missouri,* 263 U.S. 640, 656 (1924). See also *National Bank* v. *Commonwealth,* 76 U.S. (9 Wall.) 353, 362 (1870); *Anderson Nat'l Bank* v. *Luckett,* 321 U.S. 233, 248 (1944).

53. 263 U.S. 640, 659 (1924). The Court first found that national bank branching was unauthorized and invalid under federal law, which would seem enough to end the matter; the discussion of the force and applicability of state law was designed to support the status of the State as the party plaintiff in the proceeding.

54. See the discussion of *Parker* v. *Brown* in Chapter 8.

55. See *United States* v. *Citizens & Southern Nat'l Bank,* 422 U.S. 86, 118 n.30 (1975); *United States* v. *Marine Bancorporation, Inc.,* 418 U.S. 602, 612 n.8 (1974).

56. *Jackson* v. *First National Bank of Gainesville,* 430 F.2d 1200 (5th Cir. 1970), *cert. denied* 401 U.S. 947 (1971).

57. *Idem* at 1202.

58. N.Y. Bank. Law sec. 131.1 (McKinney 1971).

59. Calif. Fin. Code sec. 102 (West Supp. 1976).

60. See, for example, *Meserole Securities Co.* v. *Cosman,* 253 N.Y. 130, 170 N.E. 519 (1930).

61. Even this area is being invaded by S&Ls and mutual savings banks, through devices such as N.O.W. accounts and third party payment procedures, but they too are licensed financial institutions.

62. Such retailer activities have been held by the Nebraska Supreme Court not to constitute carrying on the business of banking. *State ex rel. Meyer* v. *American Community Stores Corp.,* 193 Neb. 634, 228 N.W.2d 299 (1975) (the "Hinky Dinky" case).

63. This would apply to in-state networks in unit banking states, as well as to interstate networks. That course of events apparently would be contemplated with equanimity by the Court of Appeals in the *IBA* case: *cf.* 534 F.2d 921, 946 n. 98 (D.C. Cir. 1976).

64. 12 U.S.C. sec. 1842(d) (1970). Iowa is the only state with such a statute, and it is limited to holding companies already possessing two or more local affiliates, a class with but a single member. The statute was upheld against an equal protection attack in *Iowa Independent Bankers* v. *Federal Reserve Board*, 511 F.2d 1288 (D.C. Cir.), *cert. denied* 423 U.S. 875 (1975).

65. 12 U.S.C. sec. 1843(c) (8) (1970). The Federal Reserve Board, in determining whether a particular activity is a "proper incident" to banking, is instructed to consider whether "its performance by an affiliate of a holding company can reasonably be expected to produce benefits to the public, such as greater convenience, increased competition, or gains in efficiency, that outweigh possible adverse effects, such as undue concentration of resources, decreased or unfair competition, conflicts of interests, or unsound banking practices" (*Idem*).

66. 12 C.F.R. sec. 225.4(a) (1976). The Board has not yet taken the plunge into the politically charged issue of authorizing S&L acquisitions; 12 C.F.R. sec. 225.126(h) (1976).

67. S&L ownership, however, is also limited to a single state. 12 U.S.C. sec. 1730a(e) (3) (A) (1970).

68. At this point only four states (Alabama, Oregon, South Dakota and Wisconsin) have adopted legislation permitting, on a basis of reciprocity or sharing, out-of-state financial institutions to operate domestic CBCTs.

69. A statute worded to put out-of-state banks in a disfavored class might at one time also have been subject to attack under the equal protection clause; *cf. Morey* v. *Doud*, 354 U.S. 457 (1957); *American Trust Co.* v. *South Carolina State Bd. of Bank Control*, 381 F. Supp. 313 (D. S. C. 1974). After *New Orleans* v. *Dukes*, 96 S. Ct. 2513 (1976), however, the prospects for a successful equal protection attack "in cases of exclusively economic regulation" are most uninviting.

70. *Buck* v. *Kuykendall*, 267 U.S. 307 (1925). See *United States* v. *Citizens & Southern Nat'l Bank*, 422 U.S. 86, 118 n. 30 (1975) ("Anti-branching laws . . . are now widely recognized as a simple device to protect outlying unit banks from the rigors of regional competition.").

71. *Dean Milk Co.* v. *City of Madison*, 340 U.S. 349, 354 (1951).

72. *Idem*.

73. See p. 129 *supra*.

[8]

The Sharing Statutes and Competitive Policies

A number of states, as previously mentioned, have now passed statutes which authorize the establishment of an EFTS net only on the condition that the proprietor of the net share the facility with any other bank in the state which requests access to the facility. In addition, the Comptroller's May 8, 1975, version (now rescinded) of his Interpretive Ruling imposed a similar requirement: CBCTs more than 50 miles from a bank's office must be "available to be shared at a reasonable cost by one or more local . . . financial institutions"[1] such as S & Ls or credit unions as well as banks.

Not all of these statutes are drawn clearly enough to avoid numerous problems of interpretation. If, within a state with a sharing statute, a national bank establishes a net, is it required to provide access to all request-ing state banks? To all requesting national banks? To other kinds of financial institutions as well? If there is in existence a franchised interstate net and a bank within the state becomes a franchisee-user, is either the franchisee or the franchisor then subject to the statute, with the practical result that such a system cannot be franchised to any bank within the state unless the franchisor is prepared to make access available to all banks within the state? More importantly still, if a bank is in a position to demand access to a net, what are the standards that determine the level of payments which may be required of the bank by the net operator? Many of the statutes leave some or all these question wholly unresolved. In the case of any particular statute, it may be that there exists a clear provision or explicit legislative history that would

138

shed light on these issues. But our impression is that the preponderance of the statutes were hurriedly passed under pressure from small country banks alarmed by the prospect that deployment of the technology by larger competitors who could employ it efficiently might cause erosion of the small banks' entrenched monopoly positions. Given the legislative environment, it is probably correct to say, at least in most instances, that many of the interpretive questions raised not only were left unresolved but went unconsidered.

THE INTERPRETATION OF SHARING STATUTES

What are such statutes likely to accomplish? Legally imposed sharing requirements do exist in a few other institutional contexts, primarily under the antitrust laws in certain circumstances, and we may turn to them for instruction. There are several antitrust cases that order compulsory "admission-to-membership" and discuss the terms on which it is to be granted; and there is one decision by the Civil Aeronautics Board worth attention.

Unfortunately for our present purpose of enlightenment, the great majority of the antitrust cases that require an exclusive organization to admit to membership a new applicant have involved organizations that had a well defined set of fees and charges applicable to a sizeable preexisting membership. In those cases, it was sufficient for the court to say that the newcomer had to be admitted on the same terms applicable to the preexisting members.[2] Hence, this body of cases is helpful only to the extent it suggests that judges are quite likely to resort to preexisting standards for fees and charges, at least where it appears that they will operate in a reasonable and equitable manner with respect to the newcomers. In the case of franchised EFTS systems, these cases are strongly suggestive.

Perhaps the most famous of the antitrust cases requiring sharing is *United States* v. *Terminal Railroad Association*.[3] The case involved a combination of railroads serving St. Louis that had acquired control of all available facilities for connecting railroads on the east bank with those on the west bank of the Mississippi River. The Supreme Court ruled that, as an alternative to dissolution of the association, it could adopt a plan for admission of any requesting railroad to proprietary membership in the organization and for equal treatment of all connecting railroads, whether or not the road chose to apply for membership. In setting forth standards for the open admissions policy and the equal treatment policy, the Court was exceedingly vague: it referred to admission upon "such just and reasonable terms as shall place such applying company upon a plane of equality in respect of benefits and burdens with the present proprietary companies."[4] And as to railroads that chose to use the facilities but not become members, the Court spoke of "such just and reasonable terms and regulations as will, in respect of use, character and cost of service, place every such company upon as nearly an equal plane as may be with respect to expenses and charges as that occupied by the proprietary companies."[5]

Although there were several subsequent enforcement proceedings regarding the Terminal Railway Association, the Supreme Court never defined with any greater precision the standards for admission or for access. The Court took the position that further definition of the standards constituted the making of determinations with respect to rates and charges and, hence, was appropriately a task left for the Interstate Commerce Commission. Perhaps the maximum guidance that can be drawn from the *Terminal Railroad* case, like the other antitrust cases discussed, is that the courts will be drawn reluctantly, if at all, into the formulation of pricing standards; they will turn to the relevant administrative agencies for implementation where the private parties have not provided adequate standards by their own prior behavior in the marketplace.

Another well known antitrust case, which is closely analogous, is *Associated Press* v. *United States.*[6] The behavior complained of in this case was that the association was selectively discriminating against newspapers that happened to be competitors of member newspapers. New memberships were available without the payment of any significant fees or charges to newspapers that did not stand in such a competitive relationship, perhaps because it was of value to old members to have news reports submitted by a new member from its geographic area. Upon application for membership by a competitor of an existing member, however, the existing member affected had the right to demand that substantial fees be paid. In this case, too, it was sufficient for the Court to rule in fairly general terms that one applicant could not be treated less favorably than another on the ground that the first was a competitor of an existing member. Hence, the *Associated Press* case, like the other antitrust cases, is not very helpful in the present context.

Although the Supreme Court's opinion in the *Associated Press* case was entirely confined to the very general point previously mentioned, there were portions of the district court opinion that might be thought to shed some light upon the issues at hand. The association sought to justify in economic terms the charges that were imposed on new applicants who were competitors of existing members. The district court replied:

The defendants seek to justify [the charges] upon the theory that it merely reimburses the competitors for that share in the capital assets which they must yield to [the applicant] out of their collective interest. There are two answers to this. First, no such payment is required of an applicant who does not compete . . . though he becomes equally a co-owner of the capital assets. . . . Second, the percentage was not in fact computed upon the value of the share in the capital assets to which an applicant becomes entitled on admission, even though we include in capital such questionable items as the employees' benefit fund . . . or the value of the goodwill (which, in part at any rate, must be dependent upon the power to exclude competitors).[7]

On the basis of this language, one could argue, although not very forcefully, that the district court recognized the propriety of demanding from a new applicant a pro rata contribution to past capital investment and that the failing of the Associated Press was only that it imposed the requirement in a discriminatory and anticompetitive way.

The most detailed treatment of admissions standards that we have been able to find appears in a Civil Aeronautics Board proceeding styled *Air Cargo, Inc.*[8] *Air Cargo* involved the consolidation of the ground facilities of Eastern Airlines and United Airlines. The CAB approved the consolidation on the condition that Air Cargo allow any other authorized aircraft to utilize those facilities. The two airlines objected, partly on the grounds that "the condition will result in discrimination against the original and present owners of Air Cargo."[9] The CAB responded that such discrimination would not result. While refusing to spell out the standards in any detail because it thought that such issues should be left for future case-by-case determination, the CAB did give some guidance on the standards for participation:

[The requirement of participation] will not, however, prevent the members of Air Cargo from imposing as a condition of accepting any new participation reasonable terms as to the sharing of the benefits and obligations of the enterprise, including the cost of developing the enterprise.[10]

We have been unable to find any subsequent proceeding involving the administration of admissions standards to Air Cargo. But the language of the CAB clearly supports the proposition that an entity that has asserted its legal right to mandatory sharing can be required to pay fees, which cover not only current operating expenses including depreciation, but make a payment to the proprietor to compensate him for a pro rata portion of the capital net worth of the enterprise.

Thus, when the question arises of what payment may be demanded of entities that assert their right of access under state sharing statutes, very little by way of detailed guidance will be found either in the directly applicable statutes, which have been passed to date, or in decisional law on analogous problems. The general response of state court judges to the situation is therefore a matter of speculation. First, we would expect the judges to be strongly influenced by any authorized regulations promulgated by the pertinent state banking official; probably even interpretive guidelines adopted by such officials for their own administrative purposes, although not officially promulgated as regulations, will be influential. Second, we would expect a general recognition among state judges that fees should cover general operating expenses including current depreciation expense and, in addition, either a reasonable rate of return on invested capital of the proprietor or a capital contribution corresponding to some concept of a pro rata share of the capital investment in the system. Indeed, some of the present statutes so provide in general terms.

THE ANTICOMPETITIVE EFFECTS OF SHARING PROVISIONS

Some of the problems that must be faced in implementing sharing provisions are analogous to the problem of imposing public utility type rate regulation on an established enterprise. It will probably be true in this new context, as it has historically been true in such public utility cases, that the most difficult and controversial questions will be two: how does one determine the amount of capital that should be recognized as having been invested in the enterprise and what allowance does one make for the phenomenon of risk in determining the appropriate rate of return on that capital?

There is a substantial body of decisional law in the public utility area bearing on both these questions, but it is confused and contradictory and yields few confident answers.[11] It would be inappropriate in this study to examine that body of law in any detail, but a few general observations seem appropriate in this context. The prospects for any ongoing enterprise newly subjected to public utility regulation are discouraging. Government regulatory endeavors are often harshest at their outset, and the fact that the enterprise has not previously been regulated typically will generate a number of difficult issues on which that harshness may come to bear.

One of these issues is the extent to which risk should be allowed for in determination of the appropriate rate of return. In an area such as EFTS —which is experimental, uncertain in its marketability and, like any specific system, vulnerable to technological obsolescence—the allowance for risk should certainly be a very generous one. Viewing *ex ante* the many uncertainties involved, including the grave uncertainty whether any patent protection will prove to be available on developments in the software area, the investor must see relatively high rates of return in prospect if capital is to flow into this arena.

But the view of the rate regulator will be *ex post*. The EFTS net to which access will be sought will necessarily be a relatively successful one; unlike unsuccessful projects never brought to the marketplace and unlike less successful projects marketed without encountering enthusiastic reception, the net which raises regulatory issues will be one into which banks are willing to fight their way. With perfect hindsight, the regulator will tend to conclude that *this* net has not faced extraordinary risk.

Moreover, a variety of political factors will push the regulator toward low risk premiums in the rate of return. Typically, the net operator will be a large, out-of-state enterprise. The applicants will be smaller, local and those same politically active enterprises that obtained passage of the sharing legislation in the first instance.

Under these circumstances, the rate regulator will be brought only with great difficulty to the economically correct view of the situation: capital will not flow into any development unless the rate of return on successful projects is high enough to provide an attractive rate of return on all projects, successful and unsuccessful. Only under that circumstance are new investments, viewed *ex ante,* financially sound.

Thus, mandatory sharing statutes threaten greatly to retard EFTS development, for they necessarily contemplate that some governmental entity will determine the financial terms on which sharing must be permitted. That entity, be it judicial or administrative, will turn to public utility rate regulation precedents as the relevant repository of standards. And the standards that will be found are inappropriate for application to an industry that is technologically intensive and characterized by potentially competitive structure.

Existing public utility precedents applied in conjunction with sharing statutes threaten EFTS net operators with unfavorable and economically unsound outcomes in a second context. It will often be the case that the newly regulated enterprise has, prior to onset of regulation, made substantial expenditures that ought properly to be viewed as capital expenditures and included in the rate base, for example, expenditures for research and development. But, for its own tax and accounting purposes, the firm will often have treated these items as expenses in the preregulation period, or it will have written them off on an amortization schedule that treats the item as having a useful life far shorter than its actual useful life. The question then arises whether the item in question is to be included in the rate base at a value that corresponds to its actual economic value as of the onset of regulation or whether the fact that it was previously charged against profits in the unregulated period bars its inclusion in the rate base.

It is clear from an economic standpoint that the rate base should include all capital values, including those just described, that are necessary to the production of the utility service, if the prices that result from the regulatory process are to provide appropriate signals to customers for their planning. In the future, expenditures of this type will be a component of rates. Nevertheless, at the onset of regulation, they are often excluded from the rate base.[12]

Exclusion from the rate base is usually justified by reasoning that the enterprise has already recaptured those costs from consumers in the preregulation period and that consumers should not have to pay twice. This argument has emotional appeal, but it rests on dubious use of the metaphor of "recapture." It is true, of course, that the expenditures have been written off for accounting purposes. But it is not true that prices to consumers or revenues to the enterprise would have been lower had the accounting treatment been otherwise. Nor is it true, typically, that the consumers who have paid the firm's prices in the preregulation period are those who will presently pay for the regulated service. Exclusion has the effect of giving regulation a retroactive aspect—the firm is required to provide useful capital assets out of historic, unregulated profits.

Unlike the expectation that *ex ante* risk will not be properly taken into account, about which no private measures can be taken by way of anticipation, the expectation that preregulation expenditures may be excluded from the rate base should prompt enterprises to review their current accounting practices. A shift to capitalization of items heretofore expensed and to straight-line from accelerated depreciation of such items might be warranted notwithstanding the current tax consequences.

A third predictable error, in addition to erroneous assessment of risk and improper definition of the rate base, is that rates of return will be fixed, initially, at a low level, which, while arguably adequate to sustain static existence of the enterprise, will greatly reduce incentives to engage in the dynamic process of rivalrous entry into new markets. The purpose of public utility regulation is generally thought to be the prevention of exploitation by the utility of a monopoly position—to assure that it earns only a competitive as opposed to a monopolistic rate of return.

But aggressive entry by a firm into a market already served to some degree by existing firms—entry designed to expand market share by providing a better service, for example by introducing a new technology such as EFTS —is generally attracted only by the prospect of earning, at least for some period of time, profits above the minimum competitive level. A sophisticated entrant may be fully aware that its innovative techniques will be emulated by others with the passage of time, as will generally be the case; but supracompetitive returns for some period of time motivate the undertaking. Whether these higher returns, which characterize the period from the time of entry to the time of successful emulation by others, are called monopolistic returns or competitive returns during disequilibrium is a matter of semantics: the critical fact is that the aggressive expansion of a new technology to new geographic markets is largely dependent upon them. Hence, the type of expansion that should characterize EFTS during the years ahead, if its benefits are to be brought to all potential users, will be greatly retarded if the prospective entrant foresees rate regulation and merely competitive returns. Ironically, the more "efficient" the regulator is, the more pronounced this retardation will be.

Thus, for a number of reasons, the mandatory sharing statutes represent unwise economic policy. By forcing a substitution of regulation for competition in a context in which the latter is an attainable objective, they are likely to retard innovation and deployment of EFTS. Rates of return are likely to be set too low initially, both because risk is misappraised and because rate bases are inappropriately defined. And, perhaps more importantly, public utility type regulation, because it is essentially a cost-plus method of pricing, has a strong potential for creating cost-insensitivity on the part of the regulated firm. In all these senses, the sharing statutes can be said to be anticompetitive.

But there is another and more conventional sense in which we expect that mandatory sharing will be an anticompetitive force. Although the statutes enacted at present do not explicitly limit the number of nets that may enter the market, we expect that they will lead both to limitations on those numbers and, where more than one net is permitted, to suppression of competition, or at least of price competition, between those nets. This result is inevitable unless, despite the fact that the first net will be subjected to rate regulation, free entry is afforded to subsequent nets and they are permitted to engage in both price and service rivalry, a combination of events we believe to be most unlikely.

A fully developed explanation of why this combination of events is unlikely would require presentation of a complete model of the regulatory process and its interactions with its parent legislature and its regulated industry, a task we will not undertake here. Our reasoning, in skeletal form, is as follows. For reasons already stated, a regulatory authority functionally analogous to a public utility commission will be engrafted or created to administer the mandatory sharing statutes. It will employ some number of well-paid bureaucrats and a much larger number of staff, many of whom will come to have close relationships with the parent legislature. After an initial period of showcase toughness with respect to the regulated EFTS net operator, the familiar symbiotic relationship between agency and utility will emerge. The utility will establish its own links with the legislature. Rates for most network users will be permitted to creep upward. But the network will be permitted to retain only a small portion of those monopoly revenues; some politically favored groups will be provided with services at rates below actual costs—rural areas or municipal treasurers or banks in low-income areas, for example—and these "good works" will siphon off most of the excessive revenues. The good works will also create a new political constituency supportive of the regulatory agency.

Once this set of relationships is in place, the potential emergence of open competition will represent a threat to all the interests that have come into existence. The regulated net will protest the unfairness of unregulated competition. Competition would, indeed, deprive it of those customers paying premium rates and leave it with only the unprofitable beneficiaries of good works. Those beneficiaries will protest, for their benefits would disappear if cross-subsidization were terminated. But deregulation of the initial network would also end the employment of all or many agency personnel. Indeed, the mere recognition that competition is feasible would threaten their employment. A study will be made by the agency and its legislative oversight committee, and the study will show that competition is not feasible. The sound course in the public interest, the study will conclude, is either to block entry entirely or to subject the new entrants to that regulation originally imposed to guard against the evils of "natural monopoly." Entry, thus limited, may be sufficiently unattractive so that there will be little practical difference between the two choices. Examples of this political dynamic stretch from early railroads to late communications satellites.

THE VALIDITY OF SHARING REQUIREMENTS

What is the possibility that sharing requirements, whether promulgated by the Comptroller or enacted by state legislatures, will not, in fact, bring about these undesirable consequences because they will be judicially invalidated on the ground that they conflict with the antitrust laws? In chapter 5 we attempted to describe how an antitrust court should, and probably will approach arguably anticompetitive arrangements made by private entities, in particular unnecessarily broad EFTS consortia, applying section 1 of the Sherman Act and its interpretive gloss known as the rule of reason. That discussion quite deliberately did not take into account the direction or extent to which a court, attempting to apply antitrust law, will be influenced by other bodies of statutory material bearing on the problem before it. We now turn to the problems raised when the anticompetitive arrangement has been approved, authorized or mandated by some state or federal government entity. In such a case, tension will arise between the objectives underlying antitrust law and some other body of statutory or regulatory law. In the context of EFTS, the other body of law will usually be bank regulatory laws, of which the sharing statutes are an excellent example.

In cases involving that conflict, at least one of the parties to the case will be urging upon the court the view that classical antitrust principles ought to be subordinated, or modified, to accommodate policies found in bank regulatory legislation. In any particular case, the legislation brought into question may be federal or state or both. Although the extent to which the court is likely to depart from antitrust principles in deference to regulatory legislation may not be significantly affected by whether the legislation is federal or state, the doctrinal rubric under which the analysis will proceed is quite different depending upon whether state or federal legislation is involved.

THE ANTITRUST LAWS AND FEDERAL REGULATORY STATUTES

Where it is contended that federal bank legislation or regulations issued pursuant thereto by the Federal Reserve Board, the Comptroller of the Currency or the FDIC ordain results at variance with the implications of antitrust principles, there is no doubt that the federal courts must take those legal sources into account. The antitrust laws do not constitute a part of the United States Constitution, and, where their implications diverge from those of other bodies of federal law, the usual techniques of statutory interpretation and accommodation are invoked to resolve the conflict.

It is true that the antitrust courts tend to think and to talk about antitrust principles, and the competitive milieu which they contemplate, as representing the "normal" situation; and they tend to think and to talk about statutory departures from that norm as representing "exceptions." This judicial attitude finds its clearest articulation in the often quoted dictum that "repeals [of the antitrust laws] by implication are not favored"[13] and in the now famous quotation from the *Silver* case: "[Since] [t]he Securities Exchange Act contains no express exemption from the antitrust laws . . . [r]epeal is to be regarded as implied only if necessary to make the . . . Act work, and even then only to the minimum extent necessary."[14] But the cases which contain these assertions do so as often in the breach as in the observance.

Direct and conscious conflict would present an easy case. If there were some congressional regulatory statute which, in so many words, created an exemption from the antitrust laws for EFTS consortia or if there were a congressional statute which explicitly addressed itself to the balancing of competitive considerations versus the attainment of scale economies or some other rival consideration, the position contained in this specific statute would prevail. But the federal bank regulators have no explicit substantive authorization to restrict the deployment by banks of EFTS nets or to force cooperative rather than competitive deployment. (The power of the Comptroller to disapprove new branches, which we discussed in chapter 7, is the closest approximation, although in our view it is inapplicable to EFTS terminals in any event.)

Hence, antitrust conflict with existing regulatory authority will most likely involve statutory provisions constituting broad and general supervisory powers. We take as an example a regulation, promulgated by one of the federal banking agencies, that requires banks that are under its jurisdiction and that install customer networks in any community to share the network with any other bank in the community that wishes to share it. The regulation imposes the further obligation to act cooperatively (for example, by revealing software and operating procedures) to the extent necessary to facilitate such sharing.

A case challenging the regulation because of its anticompetitive consequences could be resolved into two analytically distinct questions, even though the questions are unlikely to be treated by the court as being truly independent of one another. The first question is whether, in light of the organic statute administered by the regulatory agency, the agency has authority to promulgate the regulation; the second question is whether the regulation encroaches so fundamentally on antitrust principles that it must be subordinated to those principles. If the questions are really treated as wholly independent, then the first is controlling and the second is irrelevant; if the regulation is within the agency's authority, its anticompetitive properties will not invalidate it.

Rather than treat these as two separate questions, however, the courts are likely to cast the issue in a unitary form along the following lines: taking into account the fact that the regulation transgresses fundamental antitrust principles in conjunction with such other doubts as there may be about the authority of the agency to promulgate this regulation, do we find that the agency has the authority to require the behavior called for by the regulation? In this context of determining the scope of agency authority, the anticompetitive character of a new regulation is likely to be of significant influence on the reviewing court.

In determining whether antitrust principles will prevail and the agency be found to have exceeded its statutory authority, it must be recognized that there are other factors that are likely to bear heavily on the outcome in an individual case. In what forum does the challenge to the regulation arise and by whom is the challenge brought? If the initial trial type hearing is commenced and maintained in a federal district court, with the result that a federal district judge makes the initial findings of fact and conclusions of law, the prospect that the regulation will be held invalid is enhanced; if the initial trial type hearing must be conducted before the agency, either because the successful invocation of the doctrine of primary jurisdiction forces the court to stay its hand or because the case is initially brought before the agency, the prospect that the regulation will be held invalid is significantly diminished.

Cutting across the choice of initial forum is another important variable: is the challenger a private party or will the antitrust division of the Department of Justice have a major role? If the antitrust division takes the lead in urging the conclusion of invalidity, the prospect that the regulation will be held invalid is enhanced; if the challenge is exlusively by private parties, the prospect for invalidating the regulation is significantly lessened.

These nonsubstantive considerations can be of major significance. Suppose, for example, the Comptroller were to issue a regulation both characterizing EFTS operations by individual banks as an "unsafe or unsound practice" and purporting to authorize national bank participation in EFTS customer networks only if they are operated jointly by all the banks in the community acting as a consortium. Then, the chances for successful attack on the ground that the ruling is beyond his authority and transgresses the competitive principles of the Sherman Act would be far better if the attack were launched in a federal district court by the Justice Department against the cooperating banks, or by a noncooperating bank with the active assistance and participation of the Justice Department, than if the attack were made by one or more national banks in the context of a hearing before the Comptroller, with his decision subsequently given court review.

The factors underlying this predictive assertion are fairly obvious. First, the governmental official, whether it be a federal district judge or a regulator, who has and exercises the power to control the procedural aspects of the hearing through which the "facts" are determined will influence significantly the content of the record. That same officer will then proceed to make the initial findings of fact; and in that process he will inevitably exercise a great deal of discretion, discretion that as a practical matter is not subject to much review on appeal. He will exercise discretion as to what witnesses he chooses to believe and disbelieve. He will exercise discretion as to what interpretation to place upon atomistic bits of evidence in the process of converting them to molecular findings of fact. To the extent that the officer has a conscious or unconscious bias in favor of competitively structured markets or in favor of protecting the position of the regulatory authority, those biases will be likely to influence strongly the way in which that discretion will be exercised.

Second, quite different biases are likely to be found in a randomly selected federal district judge, on the one hand, then in a randomly selected federal regulator, on the other; the judge is likely to be more favorably disposed toward competitive markets, and the regulator is likely to be more favorably disposed toward governmentally imposed solutions. To explain with confidence why this is so would carry us far afield. Perhaps it is attributable to the tendency of the regulator to justify the regulatory institution with which he has chosen to associate himself and is therefore identified. It is our impression that regulators, far more often than judges, typically have spent a large proportion of their pre–current-appointment careers as government employees; and perhaps such persons as a class, either by acculturation or by self-selection, have atypically high estimations of the wisdom and efficacy of governmental intervention in general. But whatever the reasons may be, we believe that the relative biases are as stated. The interaction of these relative biases with the great de facto power lodged in the person who controls the hearing procedurally and makes initial findings of fact underlies the first proposition we have advanced: the probability that antitrust considerations will prevail over an anticompetive regulatory order is significantly reduced if the regulatory agency constitutes the forum where the trial record is made.

The reason why it is advantageous to have the active participation of the antitrust division of the Department of Justice seems more intuitively obvious and calls for less commentary. Whoever the fact finder may be, he will understandably view with a tinge of cynicism a private litigant who asserts or whose stance implicitly asserts that he is motivated simply by a desire to promote the public interest through intensifying competitive rivalry in his own industry or in an industry which he is desirous of entering. Such motivation on the part of the antitrust division is more likely to be accepted at face value.

Against this background, we may return to our original inquiry into the fate of a mandatory sharing regulation issued by the Comptroller or another of the federal banking agencies. The direct statutory authorization for such a rule would, under existing legislation, be inexplicit and conjectural. The damage it would do to the fundamental antitrust principle of competition between firms would be both clear and consequential. If the other circumstances of a challenge were propitious—the challenge was before a court and with the assistance of the antitrust division—we would expect such a regulation to be struck down as unauthorized and invalid. It will be recalled that our inquiry has not been wholly hypothetical; there was just such a sharing requirement, with respect to terminals established more than 50 miles from a bank's nearest office, in the Comptroller's now rescinded CBCT ruling.[15]

THE POSITION OF STATE REGULATION

A second and quite different context in which the competitive principles of the Sherman Act will come into contention for supremacy with other bodies of law is at the state level. Given that a substantial number of states have already passed statutes that create an obligation to "share" with other banks any EFTS that may be established, state imposed sharing requirements may rest squarely upon these statutory footings without need for implementing regulations; or state administrative officers may promulgate sharing regulations in an exercise of a more general statutory power. But in either event—at least by the conventional view of state law and federal court relationships, which we will question hereafter—the question whether the state action is "authorized" is not open to the federal antitrust court as it is when federal regulatory conduct is at issue. State authorities are the final authority on the question of delegation, as on other questions of the meaning of state law. The conduct of the state legislature and its administrative bodies must be viewed as a totality; and, if it is to be subordinated to federal antitrust policy, it must be subordinated on the ground that the federal law is supreme under Article VII of the Constitution and prevails in the event of conflict with state law.

The basic proposition with which we must start is that the federal antitrust laws generally have not been thought of as having the potential to preempt state regulatory statutes. The matter cannot be permitted to rest with the mere statement of that proposition, however, for the relationship of antitrust law to state activities is complex, confused and changing.

The intial proposition is usually referred to by the name of the case in which it was first discussed at length by the Supreme Court—the doctrine of *Parker* v. *Brown*.[16] That case involved a California raisin producer who, desirous of selling more product at competitive prices, was attempting to enjoin state officials from enforcing the anticompetitive provisions of a California agricultural act. The state program was challenged primarily on the ground that it constituted an undue burden on interstate commerce and only secondarily on the ground that it conflicted with the Sherman Act. The lower court granted the injunction on the "undue burden on commerce" theory. On direct appeal, the Supreme Court reversed and upheld the California program, rejecting both the commerce clause and the Sherman Act bases for challenge.

The Court dealt with the Sherman Act in sweeping terms:

We find nothing in the language of the Sherman Act or in its history which suggests that its purpose was to restrain a state or its officers . . . from activities directed by its legislature . . . That its purpose was to suppress combinations . . . by individuals and corporations abundantly appears from its legislative history. . . . The state in adopting . . . the prorate program made no contract or agreement . . . but, as a sovereign, imposed the restraint as an act of government which the Sherman Act did not undertake to prohibit.[17]

The Court gave more extended and more sympathetic consideration to the possibility that the California act constituted an undue burden on commerce or was preempted by the federal Agricultural Marketing Agreement Act of 1937. But, in the end, the Court concluded that the California act was entirely harmonious in its purposes and methods with the federal agricultural legislation; and these two potentially more promising bases for preemption were also rejected.

From the time of the *Parker* decision until the Supreme Court's recent decision in *Cantor* v. *Detroit Edison Co.*,[18] a case to which we will return, the doctrine of *Parker* v. *Brown* was generally thought to be as follows: if state authorities, acting pursuant to an otherwise valid state law, establish a regulatory scheme with respect to an industry and in that context require anticompetitive behavior of the regulated firm, the mandated behavior of those firms is immune from Sherman Act assault. But that immunity attaches only if the state intervention is direct and substantial. The state cannot provide antitrust immunity merely by authorizing anticompetitive behavior on the part of private entities; it must require the activity.

In the years since *Parker* itself was decided, the great majority of cases involving the doctrine have been antitrust suits, either by private individuals or by the United States government, against individuals or corporations who have invoked the doctrine of *Parker* v. *Brown* as a defense, arguing that their behavior is immunized from antitrust attack by the existence of some state regulatory regime. An example is afforded by the recent Supreme Court decision in *Goldfarb* v. *Virginia State Bar*,[19] in which individual homeowners commenced a class action against the Virginia Bar Association for damages and injunctive relief, contending that the action of the Bar in promulgating and adhering to minimum fee schedules for lawyers constituted price fixing in violation of section 1 of the Sherman Act. Analytically, cases such as *Goldfarb* appear to pose two distinct issues: (1) Are the private parties or defendants who are invoking the name of the state actually required to pursue their anticompetitive behavior by some duly authorized and compulsory manifestation of state power? (2) Is the manifestation of state authority so inconsistent with the federal antitrust laws as to render the state policy unconstitutional under the supremacy clause of the federal constitution?

Parker, as previously stated, has been thought to furnish a dispositive answer to the second of these questions: states are free to substitute regulation for competitive markets. Clearly *Parker* does not provide all the answers to the first question, and it has been this question with which the courts have struggled over the intervening years. In *Goldfarb*, the Court said, with reference to the first question:

Through its legislature Virginia has authorized its highest court to regulate the practice of law. That court has adopted ethical codes which deal in part with fees and far from exercising state power to authorize binding price fixing, explicitly directed lawyers not "to be controlled" by fee schedules. The . . . [Bar Association], a state agency by law, argues that in issuing fee schedule reports . . . it was merely implementing the . . . ethical codes.

The threshold inquiry in determining if an anticompetitive activity is state action of the type the Sherman Act was not meant to proscribe is whether the activity is required by the state acting as sovereign. . . . Here we need not inquire further . . . because it cannot fairly be said that the State of Virginia through its Supreme Court rules required the anticompetitive activities. . . . It is not enough that . . . anticompetitive conduct is "prompted" by state action; rather, [it] . . . must be compelled by the direction of the State acting as . . . sovereign.[20]

A careful reading of the Court's response to the question whether defendants' conduct was "required by the state" reveals a weakness in the usual analysis of *Parker*: whether the conduct was required is itself a question of state law as to which the state, conventionally, is said to be the final authority. But there is no suggestion in *Goldfarb* that, had that issue been clearly settled by Virginia courts, the Supreme Court would have accepted that resolution and ruled the conduct exempt from antitrust principles. In our judgment, the Court would not have done so. Rather, it would have gone on to inquire into the characteristics of the process through which the mandate was implemented. If it found that a broad delegation of discretion had been made to an entity only remotely supervised by the state legislature and not itself "governmental" as opposed to "private" and if it concluded that the anticompetitive conduct was mandated by that delegee rather than by the legislature, the compliant conduct would have been held vulnerable under the antitrust laws notwithstanding that, as a matter of state law, the scope of the delegation embraced the power to issue such mandates.

In short, in our view, the *Parker* doctrine has always limited antitrust immunity to private conduct which is not only *required* by state law but which is also adequately supervised by a politically responsible governmental entity. The state must substitute regulation if it removes the discipline of the marketplace. The antitrust laws do preempt anticompetitive state arrangements that do not meet these requirements.

The traditional, more permissive articulation of the *Parker* doctrine has achieved the same operational results which obviously flow from our articulation by an indirect route: in applying the lenient articulation the federal courts have assumed responsibility for interpreting the scope of state delegations of authority.

We are confident that we have not overstated the preemptive potential of the antitrust laws. But even if it is accepted that they have the potential we have described, the state sharing statutes would, in most contexts, seem to be invulnerable. The basic mandate—to afford participation to any applicant from a class of financial institutions—is a direct legislative enactment. The detailed implementation, in particular the determination of reasonable rates, would be made either by state courts or state bank regulators in the initial phases and, quite likely, by public utility commissions when the characteristics of the implementation process came to be recognized more clearly. Hence, the extended treatment we have given the *Parker* doctrine would be difficult to justify were it not for two additional considerations.

First, national banks and out-of-state network operators have grounds on which to argue the preemption of state sharing statutes other than antitrust grounds: namely, the national banking laws and the interstate commerce clause.[21] It probably constitutes good tactics, in such a preemption case, to cite the antitrust laws and to devote a section of the brief to making the almost inevitably fruitless argument that the state law is preempted by the grand competitive principles embodied in the Sherman Act. But one should realize this is primarily a tactic, designed to emphasize the socially undesirable aspects of the state's behavior, so as to increase the probability that the judge will adopt an interpretation of federal banking laws or the commerce clause conducive to the conclusion that those laws preempt the state's endeavor. In these contexts, the objectives of antitrust may cumulate with other preemption arguments to reach results neither would achieve independently.

Second, a very recent Supreme Court decision, *Cantor* v. *Detroit Edison Co.*,[22] indicates that the Court is disposed to accord the antitrust laws greater preemptive effect in the future than it has heretofore. Although the general direction of the Court's motion is clear, its precise extent and doctrinal formulation is very uncertain. Hence, we have found it desirable to summarize the doctrinal foundation from which *Detroit Edison* initiates its foray rather than attempt to describe the legal terrain at the end of that recent excursion.

Detroit Edison was a private suit for damages and injunctive relief by a retail seller of light bulbs against a regulated electrical utility, asserting that the utility violated the antitrust laws by imposing a tie-in sale of light bulbs and electricity. Residential purchasers of electricity were provided, without separate charge, with "free" light bulbs. Since homeowners paid the costs of the bulbs in their electrical rates whether they accepted bulbs or not and since no alternative source of cheaper electricity-sans-bulbs was available given Detroit Edison's regulated monopoly status, homeowners had little incentive to purchase bulbs from plaintiff.

But Detroit Edison was required by its then existent tariff on file with the Michigan Public Service Commission so to distribute bulbs, and it was undisputed that it had a legal duty to do so while the tariff remained effective; and for that reason the District Court, citing *Parker* v. *Brown*, granted summary judgment for the utility.[23]

The Supreme Court reversed. However, the three dissenters thought it irrelevant that (1) the utility had engaged in the same course of action prior to the commencement of regulation; (2) the utility had voluntarily submitted to the PSC the tariff, which, once filed, required the bulb distribution; (3) other Michigan electrical utilities regulated by the PSC had no such tariff or program; and (4) the state regulatory statute made no reference to light bulb distribution. The dissent, in short, regarded the existence of Detroit Edison's duty as simply a question of Michigan law; so viewed, the duty was not in doubt.

A plurality of four Justices, joined in part by a fifth, emphasizing the considerations recited above, ruled that the mere existence of a state law duty did not create antitrust immunity, apparently because (1) the defendant had played such a major role in bringing the duty into existence, (2) they found no evidence that the duty reflected a policy being pursued by the State of Michigan and (3) they believed the utility could cause its duty to be terminated merely by filing a new tariff.

The concurring opinion of the last Justice tracked the plurality opinion closely but went even further in some respects. Whereas the plurality opinion left open the possibility that merely formal recitals by a state legislature, or perhaps even by the state PSC, would satisfy the requirement that the defendant's duty be a manifestation of "sovereign policy," Justice Blackmun explicitly contemplated a "weighing of interests" approach: "I would assess the [state] justifications . . . in the same way as is done in equal protection review . . . ."[24]

The plurality opinion was far less explicit as to whether substantive balancing of interests was to be utilized. It gave *Parker* a bizarre interpretation, implying that it held only that the state officers had antitrust immunity and that it left open the antitrust liability of the cooperating raisin growers. The plurality placed heavy emphasis on the utility's role in bringing its "duty" into being and used this fact to support the conclusion that the State of Michigan had no policy regarding light bulbs which would be thwarted by applying antitrust proscriptions to Edison's conduct. By implication, the plurality was necessarily asserting either that (1) the PSC, too, had no "real" policy regarding light bulbs or (2) that the PSC policy regarding light bulbs did not need to be accepted as Michigan policy. Thus, for the most part, the opinion suggested that the issue was one of clarity in state legislative articulation of policy or in explicitness in delegation of power to make policy. To this extent the opinion was consistent with the thrust of earlier cases such as *Goldfarb*, although it extended the federal inquiry into state delegation much farther; the Michigan PSC might have been thought more clearly a governmental organ than the Virginia Bar Association.

In other portions, however, the plurality opinion seemed to suggest that even an unambiguously articulated state interest may not be sufficient to shelter compliant private conduct from antitrust attack and hence that the state policy will, for all operational purposes, be nullified by the antitrust laws. Thus, it argued that no congressional intent to immunize state regulated industries can be inferred from the mere fact that federal antitrust and state regulatory policies often differ. Although they may differ, the opinion asserted, often there is no conflict. The opinion continued:

[E]ven assuming inconsistency, we could not accept the view that the federal interest must inevitably be subordinated to the State's . . . .

Congress could hardly have intended state regulatory agencies to have broader power than federal agencies to exempt private conduct . . . .

The Court has consistently refused to find that (federal) regulation gave rise to an implied exemption without first determining that exemption was necessary in order to make the . . . act work "and even then only to the minimum extent necessary."[25]

The significance of these cryptic passages is uncertain. In the federal agency context, two expressions of congressional policy, neither unambiguous, are compared; from them the courts divine a "true" congressional intent; no invalidation of either is, in theory, involved. Hence, the reference to federal agencies is inapposite unless the federal courts are now to become authoritative interpreters of state legislative instructions and delegations to state agencies, a process akin to but more far reaching than that involved in *Goldfarb* and other *Parker* v. *Brown* progeny. In theory, though not necessarily in result, this process is quite different from the approach of Justice Blackmun who, we infer, would accept state law as authoritative as to where policy could be made and what that policy was. Accepting that as datum, he would "weigh" it against federal antitrust policy and, upon finding it insufficiently weighty, would invalidate it.

With the passage of time and fact situations, the Court may be pushed closer to Justice Blackmun's position. The plurality position, assuming it is now different, rests very heavily on the complicity of the private defendant (or the industry to which it belongs) in begetting the sheltering state law. This approach seems doomed to encounter serious first amendment difficulties; for it causes a statute, valid and capable of sheltering an antitrust defendant if enacted on the legislature's initiative, to be invalid if openly advocated by the subject industry. Treble-damage penalties are thus brought about by political activity. The Court was quite conscious of these difficulties when it recognized antitrust immunity for lobbying activities in the *Noerr* decision.[26]

Our hesitant expectation is that the Court will draw back from its emphasis on lobbying activity for first amendment reasons. It may also eschew Justice Blackmun's path because it portends a momentous return to a variant of economic substantive due process. The focus of inquiry will then continue to be on the clarity of state legal compulsion, with increased emphasis on whether the state has provided a regulatory alternative to the marketplace.

It seems clear that, at a minimum, the Court's dissatisfaction with anticompetitive state schemes is likely to manifest itself in readier resort to more traditional sources for finding a preempting federal law, sources less potentially far reaching in their scope than the antitrust laws—for example, the first amendment via the 14th,[27] the commerce clause[28] and substantive federal statutes such as the National Bank Act. But even more extensive judicial intervention may be in the wings.

Thus, although its full implications are unknown, *Detroit Edison* improves the prospects that state banks might successfully challenge state mandatory sharing statutes and thus achieve the status of competitive EFTS network operators. Even thus enhanced, those prospects probably are not very good.

The prospect that national banks, on the other hand, will be able to fight their way free of those statutes appear far better; for they will be able to combine the augmented preemptive effect of antitrust law with preemptive arguments based on the national banking laws and the commerce clause. The state officials, in their reliance on *Parker*, will be forced to advance some reason why national bank compliance is necessary to the achievement of a valid state regulatory scheme. And since states, for the most part, do not regulate national banks as such, they must argue that compliance is necessary to effectuate state regulation of state banks.

The argument is likely to involve some variation on the following theme. Because of the high capital requirements of an EFTS customer network and because of significant scale economies in such nets, adoption of a mandatory sharing statute would be necessary to assure that the smaller state banks would be included in whatever consortium emerged for the purposes of creating such a net and hence would remain competitively viable. Furthermore, the statewide consortium of state banks, large as it would be, nevertheless would not attain full scale economies. As a result (1) rivalry between the state consortium and a net operated by one or more national banks would be unstable by reason of the traditional natural monopoly arguments or (2) the proposed national bank net would be able to realize scale economies to a greater degree and its proprietors would enjoy competitive advantages with respect to state banks.

Our investigations suggest that there may be somewhere between seven and 35 states in which sufficient business activity occurs within the state to support two EFT systems with sufficient transaction volume to enable each to realize the preponderance of attainable scale economies. Hence, in many states the argument could plausibly be made that competitive rivalry between two or more nets would not be stable. This argument, of course, presupposes that the nets which would be functioning within the state would necessarily function as an intrastate unit; and clearly there is no technical reason why EFTS should not extend across state boundaries. Unfortunately, our long history of confining within the boundaries of a single state the offices of any one bank makes that assumption superficially plausible. Its plausibility, in our view, is no more than superficial, even disregarding the distinctions between offices and terminals, because it ignores the fact that the net itself might have its hubs and essential processing unit in one state and service franchisee banks in a number of states without necessarily involving any single bank in what are currently impermissible interstate banking activities. Nevertheless, given that history, if the bank regulators of a particular state, with the explicit or perhaps merely the implicit support of the state legislature, were to take the position that an EFTS customer network must be a wholly intrastate activity, one cannot be sure the courts would reject that position; nor can one confidently predict that the courts would, in response to such a position, deny the state officials the benefits of the natural monopoly argument, notwithstanding that they themselves had created the monopoly condition by artificially circumscribing the geographic market.

In at least the largest states, commercial activity is sufficient to support at least two EFTS customer networks, even if they operate on solely an intrastate basis. It might nevertheless be possible to argue, in the case of some fraction of these states, that a net that serviced a consortium made up only of state banks would not be able to realize the preponderance of attainable scale economies. And in these cases, too, state officials would be able to advance a plausible justification for applying the state mandatory sharing statute to national banks.

Finally, state bank officials in any state might argue that limitations on entry and competition are employed by the state as a device to reduce the number of state bank failures and that curbing competitive EFTS nets is a needed adjunct to that valid purpose. This overtly anticompetitive argument runs head on against the hostility to such state banking restrictions exhibited by the Supreme Court in *Citizens & Southern*;[29] yet there is no basis for confident assertion that it would fail.

Hence, the position of state officials would appear to be weakest in those states in which the level of commercial activity is not only sufficient to support two or more nets, but in which the fraction of that commercial activity corresponding to the market share of state banks is fully sufficient to support a single net. Even in these states, some other arguments would be available to them.

Although in the preceding paragraphs we have been able to classify the 50 states into subcategories on the basis of relatively weaker or relatively stronger postures from which state bank regulators can assert the *Parker* defense, we do not mean to suggest that the defense will lose in the weaker cases and prevail in the stronger ones. Unfortunately, there are no judicial precedents that shed a clear light on the question whether the *Parker* defense will prove successful in all of these cases, in none of them or only in those enjoying what we have characterized as the stronger posture. The outcomes of the cases will depend critically on the attitude of the courts, particularly the attitude of the Supreme Court, toward the importance of competition in banking. The outcome in some of the cases may depend, as well, on the attitude of the federal courts toward the proposition that a state is entitled simultaneously to restrict the geographic market in which an EFTS customer network can operate and then suppress competition in that area because the state's circumscription of the market has given rise to a natural monopoly phenomenon.

Notwithstanding the differences among the circumstances from one state to another, resolution of the preemption issue in the first case to reach the Supreme Court is likely to control the result in all states. If the first case to reach the Court is from a state in which the stronger antipreemption arguments are available, we hesitantly predict that the state officials will probably prevail. If the first case to reach the Court is one in which only the weaker antipreemption arguments are available, the application of state sharing statutes to national banks will probably be struck down.

REFERENCES

1. 12 C.F.R. sec. 7.7491, 40 Fed. Reg. 21700 (1976), *rescinded at* 41 Fed. Reg. 36198 (1976).
2. See, for example, *Gamco Inc.* v. *Providence Fruit & Produce Bldg.*, 194 F.2d 484, 489 (1st Cir. 1952).
3. *United States* v. *Terminal Railroad Association*, 224 U.S. 383 (1912).
4. *Idem* at 411.
5. *Idem.*
6. *Associated Press* v. *United States*, 326 U.S. 1 (1945).
7. 52 F. Supp. 362, 371 (S.D.N.Y. 1943).

8. *Air Cargo.Inc.*, 9 CAB 468 (1948).
9. *Idem.*
10. *Idem* at 471.
11. See, for example, *FPC* v. *Hope Natural Gas Co.*, 320 U.S. 591 (1944).
12. *Idem.*
13. *U.S.* v. *Borden Co.*, 308 U.S. 188, 198 (1939).
14. *Silver* v. *New York Stock Exchange*, 373 U.S. 341, 357 (1963).
15. 12 C.F.R. sec. 7.7491 (1976); 40 Fed. Reg. 21700 (1976).
16. *Parker* v. *Brown*, 317 U.S. 341 (1943).
17. *Idem* at 350–352.
18. *Cantor* v. *Detroit Edison Co.*, 96 S. Ct. 3110 (1976).
19. 421 U.S. 773 (1975).
20. *Idem* at 788–91.
21. See chapter 7 *supra.*
22. *Cantor* v. *Detroit Edison Co.*, 96 S. Ct. 3110 (1976).
23. 392 F. Supp. 110 (E.D. Mich. 1974), *aff'd without opinion*, 513 F.2d 630, (6th Cir. 1975).
24. 96 S. Ct. 3110, 3127 (1976).
25. *Idem* at 3119–20.
26. *Eastern R.R. Presidents Conference* v. *Noerr Motor Freight, Inc.*, 365 U.S. 127 (1961).
27. See, for example, *Virginia State Board of Pharmacy* v. *Virginia Citizens Consumer Council*, 96 S. Ct. 1817 (1976).
28. See, for example, *Southern Pacific Co.* v. *Arizona*, 325 U.S. 761 (1945).
29. *United States* v. *Citizens & Southern National Bank*, 422 U.S. 86 (1975).

[9]

The Problem of Privacy

A set of issues rather different from those previously discussed relates to the concerns sometimes expressed about the possible impact of EFTS developments upon individual privacy. A recent, quasi-official report on this subject was rendered to the Office of Telecommunications Policy by Professor James B. Rule: *Value Choices in Electronic Funds Transfer Policy.*[1] Rule poses the concern in the following way:

There is nothing about EFT which constrains the social purposes which it, like other new forms of bureaucratic monitoring of persons' activities, will serve. As presently envisaged, Electronic Funds Transfer systems would work only to monitor persons' financial affairs. But EFT mechanisms could equally well serve other social ends. In its most unpleasant manifestation, such a system could serve to store data on persons' political reliability, and to monitor their activities and movements to that same purpose. . . .

[A] really thoroughgoing state-oriented system of EFT . . . would be a system where the state would know the EFT account number of each user, and could use that number to gain immediate access to the account data. It would be a system, again, where all financial transactions had to go through EFT. Preferably fingerprints or voiceprints could serve to identify users, rather than plastic cards, so that no one could conceal his or her identity while using the system. And in such a system, agents of the state would constantly monitor the use of the EFT network, ready to swoop down upon any user who might be wanted for the settlement of obligations with any arm of the government. Under such a relentless system of state surveillance, the only way of avoiding state action would be to avoid contact with the EFT system altogether. And if all wage payments and other financial transactions worked electronically, this would be no easy matter.[2]

Seen in these terms, EFTS becomes an integral part of the concern over surveillance, data banks and privacy, a concern that in recent years has come increasingly to public[3] and congressional[4] attention. Practically everyone reacts strongly and negatively to a prospect of achieving the "Big Brother is watching you" world of George Orwell's *1984*. Thus, some EFTS critics conjure up a vision of society in which each person is identified by number in a central data bank, which maintains a record on all of his or her activities and is consulted for on-line authorizations of his or her every move.

Given the emotions such a picture arouses, it becomes possible to see every accumulation of data about individuals, by anyone and for any purpose, as a step in that direction. But when the emotions subside, it becomes apparent that so extreme a view is absurd and indefensible. It would lead to the conclusion that all record keeping is too dangerous to permit. No one could have a checking account or a college transcript or an employment record; telephone books, biographical dictionaries and professional rosters would be forbidden, though perhaps obituaries would be allowed. Carried out fully, this attitude would tend to make everyone an unknown in his dealings with others, thereby rendering all sorts of transactions more risky and, hence, more costly.

A more balanced view would regard privacy as a value or "good," which is prized highly by many persons and desired to some extent by almost all. Like any other good, it costs something to produce, and the amount of that cost varies in different circumstances. It is not a homogeneous good; both the demand and the cost will depend on the exact type of information in question, precisely who is being given access to it and for what purpose. Conversely, one must also recognize the value of information, to the person being described as well as to others. A person with a poor record of meeting credit obligations may see privacy (or lack of information) on the subject as most desirable, while a person with a good record of prompt payment of debts may see the availability of reliable information (or lack of privacy) on the matter as most beneficial.

In short, in this area, as in most others, it is necessary to make distinctions; the broad generalizations are of very little help. The analysis of privacy has to depend on the context; it will not do glibly to lump together subjects as diverse as military domestic surveillance, police criminal history files, census surveys, company personnel records, hospital billing services and consumer credit bureaus. The kinds of information involved, the extent of privacy different people desire and the costs of achieving it—all will vary greatly.

There is one underlying factor in the present wave of concern, however, that is common to all these contexts, and that is the capacity of the computer to lower search and analysis costs for a large volume of records. The degree of privacy to which we have been accustomed in the recent past has been in part a function of the cost of compiling and accessing data files; as the computer reduces that cost, a lowered level of privacy across a variety of contexts results. It is no accident that so much of the contemporary privacy literature focuses on the role of the computer and the data bank.[5]

But it is not the purpose of this chapter to discuss the entire range of privacy considerations, nor would it be appropriate to do so. EFTS forms only a very small part of this larger picture.[6] Essentially, it involves the use of terminals and a communications network to achieve cheaper and more rapid billing and payment transfer. Surveillance of political activities, maintenance of criminal history dossiers, sensitive medical or psychiatric information and the like are all only distantly related to EFTS—unless one defines EFTS to cover everything, as does Rule. Indeed, even the process of credit *rating* and the information utilized for this purpose is a subject separate and distinct from EFTS as such; a yes/no authorization signal or at most some conclusory evaluation number may be accessible on-line, but the underlying personal data will remain in off-line storage files just as they have for all of commercial history. In the analysis which follows, we will focus on those privacy issues that are inherent in EFTS and not on questions that are important to a general treatment of privacy but tangential at best to electronic funds transfer.

We start by describing the types of information that EFTS will make accessible. Then, we will examine the categories of privacy concerns to which that information may properly give rise. Finally, we will turn to suggestions for private and public measures that could usefully be adopted in anticipation of those concerns.

EFTS INFORMATION

To begin any privacy analysis, one must specify the kind of information involved and how it is gathered and stored. What sorts of data will an operational EFT system itself generate or require? First, there will be records of *account* activity—of payments made and (under descriptive billing systems) of goods or services purchased. This information is already contained, of course, in the present system of checking account payments and credit card billing or transmission of invoices. It is possible that EFTS will add somewhat greater detail to the purchase description, in part to serve retailer needs in connection with POS operations. Thus, there will also be records of retail *store* activity—of sales made in different departments (and remaining inventory), of accounts billed and of payments received. Again, most of this information is presently produced by or available from accounting departments of major retailers; some EFT systems may be designed to integrate with such needs and produce the data much more promptly.

A second category of information will be that derived from the foregoing primary records. Customer files can be analyzed for a variety of purposes, such as determining whether a particular way of assigning costs is appropriate. A customer file can also provide limited inputs into a credit extension decision, if the customer has applied for a loan or line of credit. The file will reveal some information about sources and stability of income, expenditure levels and the average account balance in relation to transactions volume, the payment record on prior bills (to the extent that they are submitted through the system) and similar matters. Such information will be of some value, but for the most part line of credit determinations and authorizations will continue to rely on non-EFTS information, much of it furnished by the customer in his application and verified to a limited extent from other sources.

Likewise, it is probable that retailers will generate a wide range of management information from their side of EFTS operations. This may be a major potential benefit of some types of EFT systems, aiding retailers in their purchasing and marketing decisions, but it does not seem worth exploring from a privacy standpoint. However, there is a related possible use of customer file information that is worth mention. If a POS system affords sufficient purchase detail, a bank or a retailer will be able to determine who among its customers has bought a given product or type of product and what some of his or her socioeconomic characteristics are. Analyzing large groups of customers by employing the sorting capacity of computers can be an efficient aid to market research. Another possible output of such a study will be a customer list of those interested in certain activities or types of products, which can then be used for direct mail advertising. Of course, retailers have been using their credit-customer address lists for direct mail advertising for many years.

THE EXTENT OF PRIVACY CONCERNS

Having identified the kinds of information that are involved in the operation of an EFT system (as opposed to all the possible uses of a computer by a government agency or intelligence service), we can focus on the privacy elements they contain. It will again be helpful to make distinctions.

Privacy concerns should not be confused with questions relating to the reliability and security of an EFT system. By reliability, we refer to the functional dependability of the system. How vulnerable is it to breakdowns and operating errors, from natural or human causes? When they do occur, how well does it detect them? How rapidly can they be corrected? By security, on the other hand, we refer to the capacity of the system to resist unwanted outside intrusion. For example, in a credit card or debit card system, how difficult is the card to counterfeit? How safe against impersonation is the method of card holder identification? How vulnerable is the transmission net to outside monitoring or to the insertion of false commands or signals? How secure is the central computer from theft of information or from manipulation of files?

These issues overlap with privacy to the extent that a security breach might also result in dissemination of information about which there is a privacy concern. But whether or not a privacy element is involved, security breaches pose a threat to the viability of the entire system, in terms of theft and fraud. Any EFT system that hopes to survive and win acceptance will have to devote substantial effort and expense in design and operation to obtaining adequate reliability and security and thereby, among other things, prevent *unauthorized* access to its computer files. We will return to this subject subsequently.

The more substantial privacy concerns relate to *authorized* access to the kinds of EFTS information previously identified: account activity records and purchase list data. There are two kinds of authority for access to be considered—that derived from personal consent and that derived from statutory enactments without regard to personal permission.

Where there is explicit disclosure of possible access and knowing consent to it, it is obvious that there is no real issue of privacy. Indeed, the dissemination of account balance and payment information from his file is often of great value to an individual in other transactions, which is why he gives credit references. As already noted, it is very much to the advantage of a borrower with a substantial income or a history of prompt payment of debts to have that information available to new lenders or creditors in a form that is accurate,[7] comprehensive, up-to-date and, at the same time, inexpensive.

Problems that arise in this area flow from lack of clarity or from misunderstanding. When a customer establishes a credit card or DDA relationship with a bank, what is the understanding as to who will be given access to account information and for what purpose? Suppose, for example, purchase data were sufficiently precise to enable a bank to prepare a list of customers with a revealed interest in a specific category of products and make it available for direct mail advertising. (It should be noted that private possessors of highly selective lists usually do not furnish copies to others, which would quickly destroy their value; instead, they more often retain the list and charge others for making mailings on their behalf.) The information conveyed in such mailings, which could in general be attuned to demonstrated interests much more accurately than at present, would no doubt be of genuine value to some recipients and an annoyance to others. How would bank account holders react to such a limited form of invasion of privacy? Some might be grateful, others very hostile and still others would care very little, but in many cases both bank and customer would find it difficult to define their existing contractual agreements with much precision.[8]

By far the most serious privacy issues, however, stem from access authorized by statute to some government agency or investigator without the consent or even the knowledge of the account holder. To make people aware of what kind of information has been obtained and compiled about them, the Privacy Act of 1974[9] requires federal agencies to publish an annual list of the records systems they maintain and permit individuals to find out if they are included and to inspect their own file.[10] The Privacy Act does not, however, attempt to define or constrain file contents, beyond a general admonition to maintain only "relevant and necessary" information.[11]

It is true that bank account data would hardly rank at the very top of anyone's list of sensitive areas; they all involve transactions by the depositor with other parties, transactions that the accountholder knows are, at the very least, also going to pass through the hands of bank personnel. For better or worse, highly confidential transactions are never put into such a documented and semipublic form. Nonetheless, there is concern as expressed by Justice Douglas in his dissenting opinion in *California Bankers Association* v. *Shultz*:

In a sense a person is defined by the checks he writes. By examining them the agents get to know his doctors, lawyers, creditors, political allies, social connections, religious affiliation, educational interests, the papers and magazines he reads, and so on ad infinitum. These are all tied to one's social security number; and now that we have the data banks, these other items will enrich that storehouse and make it possible for a bureaucrat—by pushing one button—to get in an instant the names of the 190 million Americans who are subversives or potential and likely candidates.[12]

The issue of compulsory and unrestricted government access to records is at the core of the privacy issue, and we shall return to it.

There is another dimension to the anxiety over future privacy that runs through the forebodings of Justice Douglas and many others, however, and that is the fear of omniscience and universality. Only the government could create the monolithic control machine of Justice Douglas' dissent or of Orwell's *1984*, and whether or not it does so will hardly depend on whether EFTS is used for bill paying. But even at the privately operated EFTS level, the Rule Report asks us to "imagine a system in which all pay checks and other income had to be credited to electronic accounts, and where credit grantors had the prerogative of charging bad debts to the EFT account of the indebted person without the latter's consent."[13] No doubt one can imagine such a system, and all sorts of other chimera. If we put aside government compulsion for the moment, however, it may be more useful to consider the inherent limits of a private EFT system.

First and foremost, its adoption and use will be a matter of individual choice, not fiat. To the extent that people find EFTS advantageous and preferable to alternative methods of handling purchases and payments, they will use it; to the extent they don't, they will avoid it.[14] Our earlier economic analysis has led to the conclusion that the larger stores and the larger account holders will comprise the bulk of the EFTS market. Although they will account for the largest share of transactions, measured in dollar terms, numerically they are in the minority. Hundreds of thousands of stores and millions of individuals will make limited or no use of EFTS, just as millions of households do not now have demand deposits. In particular, almost all interpersonal transactions, not involving any retailer or firm, will not go through any EFTS terminal. The spectre of complete EFTS control over all transactions is indeed an exercise in pure imagination, unsullied by reality. The person who is especially concerned about the greater privacy vulnerability of EFTS, if that turns out to exist at all, will simply handle a particular transaction or transactions in general as at present, with a check or cash or even a laundered Mexican account.

Second, our prior analysis of scale economies has suggested that a natural and competitive course of EFTS development will lead to an overlapping series of rival networks and not to a single grid centrally run. So, the instantaneous monitoring of all citizens, or even of that fraction which actually makes use of EFTS for payments purposes, is also an unreal prospect. Indeed, from a policy standpoint, one of the significant advantages of rivalrous private systems is that they will compete in offering degrees of privacy at prices corresponding roughly to their cost.

Third, the more fevered forebodings are always completely divorced from cost considerations. Electronic communications networks and computers lower a variety of costs, but they do not abolish them. For EFTS operations, most account data presumably will be transferred, at daily or other short intervals, from computer memory core to stored tapes or discs (which are much less expensive). For some purposes, such as preparing account holders' monthly statements, the system will be designed to permit cheap and speedy access to the stored information. But for purposes of the type contemplated in the "universal social control" scenarios, finding a single transaction might require running tapes with literally millions upon millions of stored events, and compiling a transaction history on an individual would require mounting and running hundreds of such tapes or discs. Search costs will remain an operative and often prohibitive constraint.

The combined effect of these natural limits on private EFTS should put privacy concerns into a more realistic perspective; the adoption of such systems will not deliver us to the doorstep of *1984*. That is by no means to say that privacy considerations are completely unjustified or warrant no attention, and we turn next to some of the steps that should be seriously examined.

RESPONSES TO PRIVACY ISSUES

PROBLEMS OF UNAUTHORIZED ACCESS

As previously noted, unauthorized access is primarily a problem of system security design and operation. There are a number of well-recognized ways of increasing system security, by measures such as (1) controlling physical access to terminals, computer centers and data libraries, (2) controlling operational access through sign-on procedures, operator identity verification and message restrictions and (3) countering unauthorized line monitoring or intrusion by scrambling and encryption devices.[15]

Complete reliability and security, however, are unobtainable, as in all forms of human endeavor. Efforts in this direction are carried to elaborate and sophisticated extremes in connection with military and diplomatic communications, at enormous expense and still without total success. The question is what level of security is suitable for a given type of system, and an extensive cost–benefit analysis is required to provide an answer. The level deemed necessary for protection against fraud and theft is likely, on the whole, to provide more than adequate protection for privacy invasion as well.

How is that level to be determined? This is a context in which the interests and objectives of the system operator correspond closely with those of the file subject: both have a stake in preventing unauthorized access to the information and procedures of the system. The corresponding economic incentives are most efficiently established if legal responsibility for damages from security breaches is assigned to the party best able to adopt the most cost-effective countermeasures. System users should have a legal remedy for actual damages from security breaches resulting in theft or fraud loss or privacy invasion; liability should probably be assigned to the system operator for breaches of computer and line security and to the terminal operator for breaches of terminal security (possibly with a defense of establishing cardholder negligence). These parties are all linked together in contractual relationships, so the shifting of responsibility among them by agreement, if not blocked by ill-advised legal provisions, should assist in arriving at efficient solutions.

The normal working of contract rules and negligence doctrine is likely to produce such a set of arrangements, though the process might be expedited by the adoption of uniform liability legislation.[16] The main pitfall to be avoided, however, is legislation attempting to prescribe a level of security or mandating the security measures to be adopted or the technology to be used. The legislature has no way of knowing what level of security is "proper" for each set of customers, information and uses; standards and technology written into law today are obsolete tomorrow. In a competitive EFTS environment, system operators will have continuing incentives to search out security levels and improved technology that correspond to the security needs and values of their customers.[17]

PROBLEMS OF AUTHORIZED ACCESS—CUSTOMER CONSENT

Most of the apparent difficulty in this area derives from uncertainties on the part of both bank and customer as to what access to or uses of account data are to be expected. To some critics, among the foremost dangers presented by EFTS is that it will enable the financial profiles of account holders to be opened up to commercial exploitation by the bank or affiliated enterprises.[18] The extent to which that will be so depends on the terms of the agreement between customer and bank. At present, much of that agreement is left to custom and implication, about which there can be dispute.[19]

The answer would seem to lie in a clearer, explicit specification in the customer-bank agreement regarding access to and use of data pertaining to the customer.[20] If substantial numbers of people do in fact strongly object to the presence of their names on bank-derived mailing lists, or the receipt of the resulting communications, banks in competing for their patronage should find it worthwhile to offer to exclude them from such surveys.[21] Once such matters are expressly covered in the customer agreement, the bank would unquestionably be liable for any damages from its violation, but the mere fact that the agreement had become more precise would make disputes over differing expectations much less likely.

If legislatures are unable to resist the temptation to intervene in this area, their efforts would best be directed at assuring that customers are afforded a set of options regarding data use among which they can make explicit choices. Different options would, of course, impose different costs on the network, and the operator should be permitted to charge appropriate cost differentials.

PROBLEMS OF AUTHORIZED ACCESS—GOVERNMENT ENTITLEMENT

Nonconsensual governmental access, in our judgment, is the really important and sensitive area of privacy concerns, for the ultimate fear is of
authoritarian government control. Government access to information initially gathered by private parties for their own independent purposes is
certainly not the most acute aspect of authoritarian control; restraints on the
use of military and police forces are far more significant and so are restraints
on the acquisition of information about citizen behavior by the government
itself through various means of surveillance.

But government access to outside information is nonetheless an issue of
major import. Can the government obtain whatever it wants? What, if any,
showing of need must it make, and to whom? Is the subject of the information entitled to notice and an opportunity to challenge the inquiry in court?

Those questions pertain to record searches of all sorts by government
agents, and the answers are not and should not be uniform. The type of data
involved, the location where they are kept and the occasion for the inquiry
should all enter into the final balance that is struck between the needs of law
enforcement and the demand for privacy.

EFTS records form one rather small part of this larger picture, and much
of the information they will contain is already being recorded on microfilm
and in paper files at the account holder's bank. At present, the balance that
has been arrived at permits government agents relatively easy informal
access to bank records, though it usually takes a subpoena to obtain their
production for submission into grand jury proceedings or court trials as
evidence.[22] In *United States* v. *Miller*,[23] the Supreme Court in 1976 held that
a depositor's account records were not private papers but part of the business
records of the bank, in which the depositor had no legitimate expectation of
privacy insofar as the Fourth Amendment protection against unreasonable
search and seizure was concerned; the depositor could not therefore object to
the validity of the subpoena whereby his bank records were obtained and
introduced into evidence against him in a criminal prosecution. Partly in
response to this and similar holdings, Congress included in the Tax Reform
Act of 1976[24] a provision[25] requiring that the depositor be given notice of an
IRS summons to a bank for his records and a period in which to object and
contest enforcement of the summons. That by no means resolves all the
issues in this area, but it is a significant move in the direction of providing the
individual with greater procedural safeguards in connection with access by
goverment agents to his transaction records.

Whether the present balance between privacy and law enforcement should
be maintained or further modified is a question likely to be affected only
slightly by the presence or absence of operational EFT systems. Limiting the

ability of government to intrude into the lives and activities of its citizens is the most important of all the privacy concerns; access to bank records in general is a rather minor subpart of that issue; and the advent of EFTS will itself enlarge an individual's bank records to only a minor degree. If electronic transfer of funds is to be viewed with alarm, it should be on some other ground.

REFERENCES

1. James B. Rule, *Value Choices in Electronic Funds Transfer Policy*. Report to the Office of Telecommunications Policy, Washington, D.C. (October 1975). (Hereafter cited as Rule.)

2. *Idem* at pp. 32, 57–58.

3. See, for example, Arthur N. Miller, *The Assault on Privacy*, University of Michigan Press, Ann Arbor (1971); Alan F. Westin, *Privacy and Freedom*, Atheneum, New York (1967); Alan F. Westin and Michael H. Baker, *Databanks in a Free Society*, Quadrangle Books, New York (1972).

4. See, for example, the extensive series of hearings and studies by Senator Ervin's Subcommittee on Constitutional Rights of the Senate Committee on the Judiciary: *Hearings on Federal Data Banks, Computers and the Bill of Rights*, 92d Cong. 1st Sess., Part I (1971), Part II (1971); 93d Cong., 2d Sess., Part III (6 v., 1974); *Hearings on Criminal Justice Data Banks (S. 2542 et al.)*, 93d Cong., 2d Sess. (2 v., 1974); *Hearings on Military Surveillance (S. 2318)*, 93d Cong., 2d Sess. (1974); *Hearings on Privacy—The Collection, Use, and Computerization of Personal Data (S. 3419 et al.,)* joint hearing with the Ad Hoc Subcommittee on Privacy and Information Systems of the Senate Committee on Government Operations, 93d Cong., 2d Sess. (1974); see also *Hearings on Electronic Surveillance for National Security Purposes (S. 2820 et al.)*, before the Subcommittee on Criminal Laws and Procedures and Constitutional Rights of the Senate Committee on the Judiciary, 93d Cong., 2d Sess. (1975).

5. See, for example, HEW, *Records, Computers, and the Rights of Citizens* (1973); Countryman, "The Diminishing Right of Privacy: The Personal Dossier and the Computer," 49 *Texas L. Rev.* 837; Miller, "The Dossier Society," (1971); *U. Ill. L. Forum* 154 (1971); see also notes 3 and 4 *supra*.

6. The Privacy Protection Study Commission is to examine the field and render a report by 1977. See Public Law 93–579, sec. 5; 88 Stat. 1905–09. The Domestic Council Committee on the Right of Privacy, chaired by the Vice President, is also at work in this area.

7. Under the Fair Credit Reporting Act (Pub. L. 91–508, 84 Stat. 1127 [1970]), a person is entitled to know the information a consumer reporting agency has in his credit file and to correct errors. 15 U.S.C. secs. 1681g–i, (1970).

8. For government agency practices, see *Hearings on Sale or Distribution of Mailing Lists by Federal Agencies (H.R. 8903 et al.)* before a Subcommittee of the House Commmittee on Government Operations, 92d Cong., 2d Sess. (1972). Federal agencies are now forbidden to sell mailing lists; 5 U.S.C. sec. 552a(n) (Supp. IV, 1974).

9. 5. U.S.C. sec. 552a (Supp. IV, 1974) (enacted as Pub. L. 93–579, 88 Stat. 1896).

10. 5 U.S.C. secs. 552a(e) (4), (d) (1) (Supp. IV, 1974).

11. 5 U.S.C. sec. 552a(e) (1) (Supp. IV, 1974).

12. *California Bankers Association* v. *Schultz*, 416 U.S. 21, 85 (1974).

13. Rule, *op. cit.* p. 51.

14. This central fact is one that consumer advocates seem prone to disregard, in worrying about consumers losing check "float" or the power to stop payment or the like. Cf. P. Schuck, "Electronic Funds Transfer: A Technology in Search of a Market," 35 *Md. L. Rev.* 74 (1975). If such losses are not either eliminated or more than offset by other gains, people will stay with existing payments systems.

15. For more detailed examination, see Bank for International Settlements, *Security and Reliability in Electronic Systems for Payments* (1975).

16. However, credit card interchange systems, with analogous problems, have handled them satisfactorily without specialized legislation. See Comment, "Bank Credit Cards—Contemporary Problems," 41 *Ford. L. Rev.* 373 (1972)

17. If EFTS is forced into a regulated utility mode, these incentives will be significantly blunted. More governmental involvement in security procedures will be justifiable; but on the other hand, the smaller number of EFT enterprises and the resultant reduction in diversity of security approaches will reduce the amount of information available as a basis for such involvement.

18. See *Hearing on Electronic Funds Transfer Moratorium Act of 1975 (S. 245)* before the Subcommittee on Financial Institutions of the Senate Committee on Banking, Housing and Urban Affairs, 94th Cong., 1st Sess. at 90 (1975).

19. Cf. *Peterson* v. *Idaho First Nat'l Bank,* 83 Idaho 578, 367 P.2d 284 (1961), and *Milohnich* v. *First Nat'l Bank,* 224 So. 2d 759 (Dist. Ct. App. Fla. 1969), finding an implied term of nondisclosure of confidential information.

20. For one proposal along such lines, see *Hearings to Amend the Bank Secrecy Act (S. 3814 et al.)* before the Subcommittee on Financial Institutions of the Senate Committee on Banking, Housing and Urban Affairs, 92d Cong., 2d Sess. at 200–03 (1972).

21. This might, of course, affect the cost of serving such customers. An analogy would be the telephone company's charge for unlisted numbers.

22. See *Hearings to Amend the Bank Secrecy Act (S. 3814 et al.)* before the Subcommittee on Financial Institutions of the Senate Committee on Banking, Housing and Urban Affairs, 92d Cong., 2d Sess., at 114–16 (1972).

23. *United States* v. *Miller,* 96 S. Ct. 1619 (1976).

24. Pub. L. 94–455 (1976).

25. Section 1205, enacting a new section 7609 of the Internal Revenue Code.

[10]

The Critical Policy Decisions

In the preceding chapters we have sought to describe and understand the prevailing legal and economic settings in which electronic funds transfer technology is developing and the forces that will be interacting in determining the future of EFTS in the banking system. But the legal forces which will shape that future are for the most part a matter of deliberate choices, some of them yet to be made, as legislatures enact statutes and agencies and courts construe them. In this final chapter we wish to focus on the more pivotal of those choices that we as a society will be making through our governmental institutions in the years immediately ahead. Some of these issues have been touched upon in our prior discussion, and we will draw on but not repeat that analysis; at this point we wish to direct attention to those policy decisions as a group, beginning with the least difficult. The way these questions are resolved will determine how much of the enormous potential of EFTS is realized.

PRIVACY

The privacy problem is a multifaceted one, and hence distinctions are extremely important. In its rather minor EFTS dimension, it is one of the simpler issues, in terms of analysis if not necessarily of emotion. The problem can assume alarming proportions only when it is wrapped up with much broader issues of government surveillance and intrusion or when the EFT "system" is described in ways that imply it is exclusive and all-encompassing.

But when EFTS is seen as a set of alternative payment mechanisms that will never be exclusive and that will have to compete for consumer acceptance and patronage, most of the privacy concerns we have discussed may be reduced to quite manageable and unthreatening dimensions.

The critical element in policy choices regarding privacy concerns is likely to be whether that sense of perspective is kept in mind and legislative over-reactions are avoided. A case can be made for the proposition that legislation clarifying responsibility for damage resulting from invasions of privacy would be useful in some areas. In the absence of such legislation, courts would in due course assign liability among system operators and users by extensions of familiar tort rules, but that process does take time and entails periods of uncertainty. The main danger is that legislation might go much farther and prescribe uniform standards of protection or require the use of specified devices and procedures. The level of protection (with its accom-panying level of cost) desired by users is *not* uniform across customers or types of data, and the selection of technology to be used is *not* something the legislature should freeze into law or regulation.

That is not to say that there are no real or vital privacy issues with which the legislature should be concerned; there are, but they center on questions of governmental access and intrusion without consent. Private EFT systems are voluntary and nonexclusive systems, so consumer preference will play a powerful role in forming their practices as to information gathering and access. But to the extent that the content or use of data becomes a matter of government edict, there will be little leeway for catering to individual pref-erence. The most substantial question before the various study commissions now underway should be the extent to which *governmental* needs for access to different sorts of private information should be allowed to override an individual's refusal to authorize access and his desire for privacy, in a variety of contexts.

BRANCHING

In one sense, the question of whether EFTS terminals are bank branches is also simple, indeed trivial. We do not believe Congress made that choice in 1927, and the nature of branching requirements and restrictions is such that it would be inane to make it today. There is no conceivable reason to impose a capital requirement of tens of thousands of dollars on each POS terminal sitting on a counter or integrated into a cash register, and territorial pro-tectionism is carried to an extreme by rules that decree no bank may connect to a terminal beyond its city limits or in a locality in which any other bank has its home office. It would be helpful, but perhaps asking too much, for the courts to see what is at stake and avoid the pitfalls of mechanically "effectuating the legislative intent" by sweeping under the branching statute everything at all related to what was in fact included. If they do not, however, the legislature will ultimately have to retrieve the situation and afford EFTS terminals a status and treatment different from branches.

One unsympathetic to the legal profession might observe that only a lawyer would think of framing an inquiry into the proper use of remote computer terminals in terms of whether or not they are branch banks. But underlying the narrow point of statutory interpretation is a policy choice of considerable consequence and more general applicability, to which we now turn.

GEOGRAPHIC SCOPE OF OPERATION

Although our estimates were concerned more with establishing proper orders of magnitude than with making precise predictions, they make it evident that to operate most efficiently EFTS networks will have to attain substantial size—tens of thousands of terminals. To be cost-justified, each terminal will probably have to handle several hundred thousand dollars of transactions annually, ruling out most of the smallest stores, service establishments and restaurants. In short, outside of concentrated metropolitan centers, the cost advantages of EFTS can be fully realized only by networks able to reach out geographically for the necessary volume.

Hence it is of central importance that terminal deployment not be artificially constricted by one legal device or another. One such device is to characterize terminals as branches, as noted above, and thereby to bring into play the panoply of geographical limitations that apply to branch banks. A recent tabulation listed 13 states as prohibiting all bank branches and another 15 as permitting branches only in severely limited numbers or areas.[1] If applied to POS terminals, such laws would mean that no bank, and in most cases no plausible assemblage of banks, could establish an EFTS network at anything approaching its most efficient scale of operations. That, of course, is why most state laws dealing with EFTS terminals proceed to accord them treatment quite different from branches. But a majority of states and the entire national bank system do not have any specific EFTS legislation, and for them the issue is in the hands of the courts. So far, courts (and at a prior stage, state attorneys general) have on the whole not been very perceptive about the issue they are deciding, and the outcome has been characterization of terminals as branches.

If that result were allowed to stand, one possible consequence would be, not to prevent the formation of EFTS nets, but to shift their establishment from banks to nonbank financial intermediaries or to companies completely outside the financial field. Federal savings and loan associations, for example, and most state S & L's as well, do not labor under an equivalent of the McFadden Act and unit banking rules. Savings and loan associations historically have not offered demand deposits and checking accounts, but that situation is currently being eroded at a rapid pace by state legislation, NOW accounts and third-party payment arrangements.[2] Thus, if banking became sufficiently ensnarled in the branching controversy, it is not inconceivable that the consequence would be a transfer of retail banking, or at least the payments mechanism side of it, to other institutional hands. Another possibility is that bank holding companies or even nonfinancial firms, presumably those already deeply involved in the computer and electronic data processing and communications fields, might fill the gap by providing terminals to retailers and communications access to banks.

In response, local banks might mount a legal assault on such developments, claiming that they amounted to outsiders attempting to engage in the "banking business," which is by statute the exclusive domain of institutions licensed as banks. As we have noted, the ultimate legal prospects of such an attack are not especially promising.[3] More importantly, from the standpoint of public policy, such exclusionary efforts are undesirable. It would be far more beneficial to let all such entrants compete in establishing EFTS networks and offering their services—provided that banks are not themselves artificially hobbled by a totally inappropriate set of branching rules.

COMPETING NETWORKS

As the foregoing discussion implies, EFTS networks are not a natural monopoly and competition between them is much to be desired. The basis for our conclusion on the natural monopoly question has been set forth at considerable length in chapter 6 and need not be reiterated here, but the advantages of rivalry between different networks may be worth repeated emphasis. The pressure of network competition should, as compared to the operations of a single network regulated in the public utility mode, lead to a more rapid pace of innovation, a greater proliferation of services and extensions of coverage, a range of individual choice regarding levels of privacy protection (and associated costs), and more effective discipline over prices and costs and operating efficiency. These are major advantages, and the history of public utility regulation gives no reason for believing it can duplicate them.

These advantages can all be lost, however, if EFTS operations are converted into "unnatural" monopolies. Private efforts to form a consortium among all the banks in some locale would run into considerable difficulties under the antitrust laws, so long as there were other ways of approaching the point of minimum cost operation. In most instances there would be such other ways if networks were not cut off from geographical extensions to attain the size required. Thus we are brought back again to the heavy costs imposed by legal barriers, whether in the form of tight constraints on "branching" or sweeping prohibitions on "interstate banking," to efforts to serve customers in more distant markets.

A still more direct way to thwart EFTS competition is to force, by law, such operations into one central system. The Federal Reserve Board has shown some predelictions for such an approach, with the Board itself as the body presiding over the system, but so far it has met with effective resistance from the Department of Justice and others. Less clearly perceived has been the likelihood that mandatory sharing statutes will have the same effect, on a state by state basis; the resulting shared net will be a private one in form, but almost inevitably it will come to be regulated as a new species of public utility, and the prospects of competitive rivalry will become poor or non-existent.

The common thread through a number of these critical policy issues is whether EFTS is going to be jammed into the conceptual category of branch banking, in which case a whole array of restrictive attitudes will be applied almost routinely and without any further thought, or whether it is going to be treated as a new dimension in the evolution of banking and outside the existing regulatory apparatus, in which case the phenomenon will have to be examined in its own terms and the question of the costs and benefits of territorial limitations will have to be freshly appraised.

OFFICE REDUCTION

To banks, one of the costs of unfettered EFTS deployment will be the investment sunk in office premises that will become redundant or obsolete. As terminals afford customers quicker and more convenient access to bank services over an increasing range of transactions, the need for large manned office centers to which customers can resort in person will diminish. There will be a reduction in investment in conventional bank offices in absolute terms, and there will be short-run costs imposed by the process.

In statewide branching states, the reduction in branch capacity will occur mainly through closing some branches and cutting back on the size of others; in profitability terms, the process may be painful for some individual banks, but will not be dramatic. In limited branching and particularly in unit banking states, however, reduction in office capacity will of necessity mean a reduction in number of banks; it is a counterpart of the way in which the law in those states has forced bank expansion to take place.

One way to reduce the number of banks is through bank failure. These words still convey a rather special sense of catastrophe and disaster, derived from the Great Depression and the Bank Holiday of 1933. Since that time, of course, federal deposit insurance has been instituted and over 500 banks, including several in the billion dollar category, have failed without notable disruption of the economy or even the local community. If bank office reduction took this form, the overwhelming preponderance of failures would be of small banks in unit banking states, and there can be no question of the adequacy of the deposit insurance fund to deal with that type of situation.[4] Despite the fact that the subject is still somewhat emotionally charged, exit by failure of the firm is not really an unthinkable way of reducing excess capacity in banking.

But outright failure is not the only, and certainly not the preferable, way of reducing the number of banks and bank offices. An individual bank need not go the full route to insolvency; while still a going concern, it has numerous elements of value, including customer relationships that may contribute to the foundation for a branch or a terminal network. Merger is another means of exit, and one preferred by both the supervisory agencies and the stock-holders; it should be so preferred, for it is usually less costly for the whole community. But again one runs up against legal barriers to the economically desirable course. The tighter forms of branching restriction prevent a pro-spective acquiring bank from opening a branch, or even a set of terminals if those are to be treated as branches, to service and thus keep the customers of the disappearing bank. In some states the branching limitations can be skirted through the device of holding company acquisition of a series of individual banks, but that affords little help when the problem is one of reducing the number of individual banks and offices. Thus we encounter yet another reason why the maintenance of narrow geographical constraints upon bank operations, whether through branch offices or EFTS terminals, is socially counterproductive. The cost of reducing excess office capacity will be significantly less if statutes and supervisory policies do not prevent the exit of firms through merger.

NATURAL MONOPOLY

The main argument for geographical restrictions is offered by "protected" banks. Recognizing that their own objectives of private monopoly gain and market protection may not be generally persuasive, they contend that banking is itself a natural monopoly with constantly declining marginal and average cost curves. If state boundary limits did not stand in the way, the argument runs, one or a handful of giant banks would sweep all competition aside, and then their vast power would enable them to rule the nation. Thus, state line barriers, or even the much smaller areas relevant under limited branching or unit bank rules, are a means of "preserving competition." In essence, a host of limited and petty monopolies is the price we must pay to avoid one giant monopoly.

A full exploration of this argument would take us too far afield from our main concerns, but there are a number of weaknesses in it that should be pointed out. The whole foundation for the argument is the proposition that banking is in fact a natural monopoly, and the supporting evidence for that is inadequate, to say the least. There are a number of studies that show bank average cost curves decreasing as size increases, though they also indicate that the bulk of scale economies are obtained well below the hundred million dollar size category, with cost curves becoming relatively flat thereafter.[5]

Putting aside all the technical difficulties that beset bank cost studies and taking at face value the curves that show, for any size category, that a larger scale of operations would be still more efficient, we note that those results are exactly what would be predicted by the theory of retail banking outlined in chapter 2. A study of costs *to the bank* will always show it operating on a portion of its cost curve that is still declining, even though there exists a minimum point beyond which average costs increase with size; it is only when costs to the customer are taken into account that the operation can be seen to be taking place at what is actually a minimum point on the *combined* average cost curve of the bank and its customer.[6] In other words, the data that may seem to suggest an endlessly decreasing average cost curve for banks are quite consistent with the sharply contrasting proposition that many banks have already attained the size corresponding to the most efficient scale of operations for their location and would prove quite impervious to competitive assault by still larger banks.

For those who prefer the test of experience to the light of theory, we suggest consideration of the banking structure in those states that have long had full statewide branching. The natural monopoly argument implies that the largest bank in each such state would have become, not merely the largest, but virtually the *only* bank in the state. The advantages supposed to accrue, without limit, to sheer size should have turned statewide banking states into one bank states, with the process due to continue to an ultimate winner if the state line barriers ever drop. That is not, of course, what we find in any such state. California, for example, has had statewide branching for many decades, and it has the giant Bank of America headquartered in San

Francisco with over a thousand branches throughout the state; unfortunately for the natural monopoly theory, it also has about 200 other banks, ranging in size from under $1 million (13 of them, at the beginning of 1975) to over $1 billion (seven besides the Bank of America).[7]

And for those unwilling to trust fully either theory or experience, lest they prove somehow misleading and the error uncorrectable, we offer a pragmatic compromise. Let banks branch, not only in their home state, but in those states immediately contiguous to it. Or more modestly, let banks extend EFTS terminals into those states that are contiguous. No bank could thereby dominate the entire nation, and it would be quickly seen whether any one bank could drive out all significant competitors in even its own region; the evidence of California and New York City is strongly to the contrary. But such an expanded scope of banking markets would achieve many of the benefits pointed out in this study, and would be an enormous improvement over our present Balkanized approach to bank competition. If Congress authorized, or in the case of EFTS if the courts simply did not block, such an extension of market areas for national banks, state legislatures would follow suit for state banks in very short order.

MORATORIUM LEGISLATION AND THE COSTS OF DELAY

The dominant theme of our economic analysis of EFTS has been that the aggregate savings it offers to consumers in payments and banking transactions are of a very high order of magnitude. The cost reductions in time and processing for individual transactions are reasonably to be measured, on the average, in the tens of cents, but those reductions are applicable to many billions of transactions. We would conservatively estimate the expected cost savings, attainable on the basis of existing technology, to be over a billion dollars per year, and with improvements in technology and more widespread utilization, the number could run much higher.

It is against that background that proposals for a "moratorium" in EFTS deployment, while one or another study is being conducted, should be evaluated. It is a common instinct for legislators to wish that a changing world could be stopped in its tracks long enough to permit a problem to be considered at leisure or—more realistically—to permit contending interest groups to bargain out a compromise which it is safer for a legislator to support. That instinct often takes the form of study and moratorium legislation, designed to freeze the status quo; bills to that effect received serious consideration in Congress in 1975 and have been enacted in several states.

The call for more study always has appeal in an imperfectly understood world; future developments in any area, when one stops to worry about it, are fraught with possible peril. But at the same time it should be clear that a moratorium is not really a neutral act; it is a decision, purportedly limited in duration, in favor of blocking a trend already underway. And each year that the realization of the full potential of EFTS is halted carries a price tag to consumers, unfortunately not fully visible, of over a billion dollars.

Our conclusion, as is evident, is that such a price for more study is wholly unwarranted. The benefits to consumers from unfettered development of EFTS in banking far outweigh associated risks and should not be thwarted by legislation designed, though not avowedly, to protect some existing banking interests in their positions of special legal privilege. That is the core of the policy decisions that as a society we will be making, actively or by default, over the coming decade.

REFERENCES

1. *State Banking Law Service 85,* American Bankers Association, Washington, D.C. (1976).

2. See, for example, T. A. Pfeiler, "NOW Accounts: A Legal Prognosis," 42 *Legal Bulletin* 149 (U.S. League of Savings Associations, July 1976). The Federal Home Loan Bank Board has been particularly aggressive in devising new regulations to permit S&Ls to offer check substitutes; see, for example, 12 C.F.R. secs. 545.4-1, 2 (1976).

3. See chapter 7 *supra* at pages 131–32.

4. See K. Scott and T. Mayer, "Risk and Regulation in Banking: Some Proposals for Federal Deposit Insurance Reform," 23 *Stan. L. Rev.* 857 (1971).

5. See, for example, Frederick W. Bell and Neil B. Murphy, *Costs in Commercial Banking: A Quantitative Analysis of Bank Behavior and Its Relation to Bank Regulation,* Research Report to the Federal Reserve Bank of Boston, No. 41 (April, 1968). The literature is reviewed in Jack M. Guttentag and Edward S. Herman, "Banking Structure and Performance," N.Y.U. Inst. of Fin. *Bulletin* (February 1967).

6. *Cf.* Figure 4, page 20 *supra.*

7. FDIC, *Annual Report–1974,* p. 200, Table 105 (1975).

Index

183

About the Authors

William F. Baxter, Professor of Law at the Stanford Law School, has acted as consultant to the Federal Reserve Board and other organizations in both public and private sectors. He is the author of *People or Penguins: An Optimum Level of Pollution,* published in 1974, and co-author of President Johnson's Task Force Report on Antitrust Policy ("The Neal Report").

Paul H. Cootner is C. O. G. Miller Distinguished Professor of Finance at the Graduate School of Business, Stanford; he has published articles and chapters on commercial banking, securities speculation, and related subjects.

Professor Kenneth E. Scott of the Stanford Law School has contributed articles to major legal journals. From 1973 to 1975, he served as Chairman of the Banking Committee of Administrative Law Section of the American Bar Association, and as General Council of Federal Home Loan Bank Board, 1963–1968.